SEXUAL MYTHS
AND FALLACIES

D0912692

SEXUAL MYTHS
AND FALLACIES

James Leslie McCary, PH.D.

SCHOCKEN BOOKS • NEW YORK

Dedicated to Mary S. Calderone and the other pioneer workers of SIECUS (Sex Information and Education Council of the U.S.) whose diligent and untiring efforts have contributed so significantly to the improvement of the mental health of Americans.

PREFACE

Recently I was privileged to address a group of obstetricians and gynecologists at the annual clinical meeting of the American Medical Association. My subject was sexual mythology. The response to the lecture was exceptionally gratifying, as these physicians expressed genuine concern that they set their own thinking straight in the particular areas of human sexuality of which they were uncertain. Ancillary to this concern was their wish to possess sex information broad enough to dispel the myriad of misconceptions possessed by their patients, which are based, classically, on old wives' tales.

The most unexpected result of the lecture and, I think, the most significant one — was the response I received from the general public following a release of my talk by the national news services. In the weeks following, I received letters from people living in many parts of the country — people of all ages and from all walks of life — asking for further information. They were concerned not only about expansion of the specific myths and fallacies touched on in my lecture, but also about a variety of other sexual problems, much of which revealed an almost tragic ignorance in this most vital area of their lives.

The response of the physicians attending the Denver meeting and the inquiries made afterwards by the public intrigued me. They also crystallized my conviction that, to help those in great need of a better understanding of sex, one has to begin by shooting down sacred cows of sex to whom homage has been paid all these years. For these reasons this book has been written.

The material in this volume is primarily an elaboration of Chapter 16 of my book, *Human Sexuality.** In the parent book, only twenty myths were examined in detail; a further fifty were listed, but without explanation other than that each one of them was false. I have now undertaken to enlarge upon all seventy of those myths; particular attention has been given to the most recent research findings touching on any of them that have become available since the parent book was written. I have also included several additional myths that seemed worthy of attention, since questions on those particular subjects have appeared frequently in my recent correspondence.

Research findings in the fields of psychology, medicine, biology, and sociology have consistently demonstrated that accurate sex information is directly related to a stable and fulfilling sex life. A happy sex life is a

* Published by Van Nostrand Reinhold Company, New York.

possibility only when the scientifically unsound, corrosive, and guilt-ridden notions concerning human sexuality are replaced by the truth. I hope that the information presented in this book will serve the reader well.

No book ever becomes launched through the single-handed efforts of its author. First of all, I must say a word of sincerest gratitude to Betty Stewart, who undertook the task of typing — and retyping and retyping once again — the manuscript, always with good humor, grace, and efficiency. I wish also to thank Ellen Brochstein and Suzanne Hoover, who, with patience and good nature, stepped into the breach to help in countless ways in the preparation of the manuscript.

As has been the case in much of the writing of the author, this book would not be a reality without the extraordinary ability and energy of Elizabeth Miremont Smith. This unusually talented lady has contributed a tremendous amount of time and effort in compiling facts and in writing and editing much of the material; she has, as well, involved herself in most of the other tasks going into the production of this book. I hope she is close by when I undertake any future literary ventures.

JAMES LESLIE McCARY

University of Houston

April, 1971

INTRODUCTION

MYTHS AND FALLACIES

When any facet of the human condition becomes as shrouded in misinformation and downright superstition as human sexuality has, it is almost inevitable that a welter of myths and fallacies should mushroom. The tragedy is that such misinformation becomes perpetuated not only by word of mouth (typically whispered) from one young person to another, but also by those legitimately in a position to educate the young. Scientists have made noteworthy advances in sex research in recent years. Yet educators — parents, physicians, teachers, clergyman — ignore these contributions to a greater understanding of sex because of their own equivocal sex education, or because they are fearful of speaking freely on sex, still a hypersensitive subject in many people's minds. Just as contradictory maternal attitudes regarding sex are transmitted to successive generations of daughters, so also do sexual illogicality and bigotry become the bequest of one generation to the next.

Beliefs for which there is no conceivable foundation in truth are by no means limited to the uneducated and the unsophisticated. Highly educated professional people can harbor a harrowing collection of sexual misconceptions that, if not corrected, will continue to haunt their own sex lives. What is worse, this misinformation will almost certainly be handed down as indisputable truth to those whom they influence and instruct.

It is my feeling that the ignorance currently dominating the subject of human sexuality will never be obliterated, and the sexual stability essential to good mental health never achieved, until an adequate sex education is made available to everyone. Unfortunately, recent efforts along these lines have been seriously obstructed by a small band of raucously militant men and women. Most of them, of course, have taken neither time nor trouble to investigate objectively the issue of sex education in the school systems. The vociferousness of those opposing sex education is particularly discouraging when it frightens into silence those more timorous souls who do not understand the issues clearly, yet who have the right to know and to make their own decisions. Too often the extremists succeed in scrubbing out the honest efforts of the schools to teach sex, despite the fact that polls across the nation reveal the large majority of the public favor sex education in the schools. The allegation that sex instruction poses a dire threat to morality and, by some form of extension, to the very future of America, is but one of the myths that I have attempted to explode in the following pages.

The selection of myths and fallacies contained in this volume represents some of the more sophisticated questions put to me in letters, by students, and by lecture audiences. If these represent the sophisticated questions, one can imagine the level of the less sophisticated ones.

I hope that my efforts to dissipate some of the clouds of misinformation enveloping the subject of human sexuality will bring an additional measure of well-being to your lives.

CONTENTS

SEX DRIVE

REPRODUCTION AND BIRTH CONTROL

HOMOSEXUALITY

SEXUAL DISORDERS AND SEXUAL ABNORMALITIES, REAL AND IMAGINED

SEX OFFENSE

Sexual Physiology and Functioning

Much mythology has grown up concerning the internal and external sexual organs and their various functions. The human male and female sexual systems are complicated; and most adults, lacking a sound sex education, arrive at physical maturity with only a scanty knowledge of the human reproductive systems and with a surprising amount of downright misinformation. Most of us know that our reproductive systems are complex, and that there are both differences and similarities between the male and female systems; otherwise we remember little of any worth or accuracy from our previous instruction in this subject.

Not until Masters and Johnson wrote their two volumes on sexual functioning has anyone known for certain precisely how the male and female body structures respond during sexual excitement and climax. If behaviorists and physiologists could only guess at the physiology of sex, the ignorance of the lay person becomes understandable. For this reason, such subjects as the size of the penis and the presence or absence of the hymen can assume inordinate importance in some people's thinking and questions about them typically are settled in such authoritative atmospheres as locker rooms and schoolyards.

There are, of course, other examples of faulty understanding of sexual structures and functions. Until this century, for example, "nice" women (at least in the Western world) were not assumed to experience any sort of sexual response in their marital relations. Indeed, they never spoke about sex; and even their primary physiological function, child-bearing, was mentioned only in the most euphemistic terminology. Small wonder, then, that these women and their husbands had only a distorted concept of female sexuality; certainly female orgasm was an unknown dimension, except possibly as evidence of

[1]

depravity or promiscuity in the woman who experienced orgasm. Such ignorance and secrecy provided the rich soil in which a field of folklore might and did flourish, much of which survives to this day.

Many men have been mystified and frightened by nocturnal orgasms. Assuming, from childhood, that the occurrence is something shameful, they have carried such attitudes into their adult lives. Similarly, girls are frequently beleaguered with dark warnings concerning menstruation, as a result of which their daily activities as well as their sex lives are senselessly curtailed during their menstrual cycles.

All these subjects are discussed in this section. In addition, I have included several other beliefs that, in their error, enjoy wide popular acceptance, despite their particularly broad variance from the truth. Among them is the debilitating effect on a man's athletic performance that sexual activity is alleged to have. Another, which in my opinion badly needs to be set right, concerns the notion that if one wishes to live a long and healthy life he must avoid sexual activity.

————

FALLACY:

NOCTURNAL EMISSIONS ("WET DREAMS") ARE INDICA-TIONS OF SEXUAL DISORDERS.

FACT:

Almost all men have erotic dreams, and about 85% of them have had dreams that culminated in orgasm. They are primarily a phenomenon of single males in their teens (particularly) and twenties, although it was shown by the Kinsey sampling to occur in men as old as eighty-six. These emissions characteristically begin when a boy is about fourteen or fifteen and occur at that time about once every ten to thirty-five days.

One would expect that nocturnal emissions would largely cease after marriage, and indeed they do for many men, but Kinsey found that approximately 50% of all men have experienced them after marriage. They make up a very small proportion of total sexual outlet, however, at any age level.

That such a large percentage of men have nocturnal orgasms during the course of their lives obviously dispels the suggestion that any pathological factor or moral defect produces them. Even among the most strict moralists, condemnation of nocturnal emission has never been severe, as even these moralists recognize that it is a phenomenon beyond the conscious control of the sleeping male.

In the belief that it is better for boys not to have even this harmless sexual release, some have suggested that "thinking pure thoughts" before retiring will cut down the incidence of nocturnal orgasm. Others have attributed the phenomenon to clothes that are too tight, the position in which the boy sleeps, some irritation of the penis itself, or an overwarm bed. These conditions may possibly have some precipitating effect, but the most logical explanation appears to be that the male, having insufficient sexual outlets otherwise, responds to his heightened sexual tensions by having an orgasm in his sleep when conscious controls are absent. In the Kinsey sampling, however, men with both high and low frequencies of other sexual outlets have equally infrequent nocturnal orgasm; and men with both high and low rates have frequent nocturnal orgasm, leaving Kinsey to conclude that the biologic, psychic, and mechanical factors involved in "wet dreams" cannot be stated with authority, and that further study is needed.

It is understandable that the adolescent with an inadequate sex education who wakes up to find that he has had a "wet dream" may be upset and feel guilty about it. It is important to help him to understand what has happened, and why. If the dream itself was disturbing (e.g., a sexual experience with his mother), it is also essential that the boy be made to understand that all dreams just happen, and that distorted erotic dreams are as much beyond his control as nonsexual ones are. It is foolish to moralize about them, and it is erroneous to regard them as evidence of sexual or physical disorder. Incidence and frequency of nocturnal emissions, incidentally, are found to be almost identical among active and inactive members of each religious group, and among males from urban and rural areas.

The relationship between the incidence of nocturnal emission and a man's level of education is worth attention. Those men who had no more than eight years of school had the lowest incidence — 75% — while among those whose formal education lasted twelve years or less, the incidence was 85%, and among those with thirteen years of school or more, over 99%. Kinsey's conclusion was that the less educated, in keeping with their unresponsiveness to the sexual arousal offered by pornographic material, have fewer dreams of any sort, including dreams of sexual content, than do better educated males.

The capacity for dreaming does appear to be related to the capacity for imaginativeness, as does response to nudity, pornography, or erotic art. The sex life of the man with little education, then, depends upon physical, rather than psychic, stimulation and upon direct, unadorned sexual expression. The man of higher educational achievement may have less sexual intercourse than his more poorly educated brother, yet his total sexual outlet may be the same because his range of sexual outlets is wider. For example, he may do more petting not followed by orgasm than the less well-educated man does. As a consequence, heightened sexual tensions at bedtime, in combination with his capacity for imagination and dreaming, result in the tensions being drained off through a nocturnal emission.

―――――――

FALLACY:

WOMEN DO NOT EXPERIENCE NOCTURNAL ORGASMS.

FACT:

Wrong! Of the women canvassed in Kinsey's *Sexual Behavior of the Human Female,* 70% reported having patently sexual dreams, and about half of this group have had dreams that culminated in orgasm. Age, education, religion, occupation, urban or rural origins, and single or married status appear to bear little correlation with the *frequency* of nocturnal orgasm, in contrast to the experience of men. But the *number* of women having sexual dreams increases with advancing years, in contrast to the number of men having them, the incidence reaching a peak among women in their forties. This is, no doubt, only further evidence of the waning of men's sexual interest after about twenty years of age, while women's sexual needs do not peak until they are in their thirties.

When women's total sexual outlet is considered, nocturnal orgasm plays a minor role (about 2% to 3% of their total sexual release), a state of affairs also applicable to men. In all age groups the incidence among women, married or single, averages three to four times a year.

About the only detectable difference between men and women in the effect of their personal histories on the occurrence of nocturnal orgasm is that devoutly religious female virgins have the experience rather less often than all other groups. A possible explanation is that they have had less overt, conscious sexual experience upon which to draw during sleep.

Many persons hold the view that involuntary orgasm is the only permissible form of sexual expression, other than sexual intercourse between married partners. However, the small percentage of total sexual outlet that nocturnal orgasm provides both men and women might come as something of a surprise to holders of this view, especially to those who regard nocturnal orgasm as the ultimate protector of premarital sexual virtue. Involuntary orgasm also suggests to many persons a form of compensation for sexual abstinence. However, little scientific evidence exists indicating to what degree total abstinence is possible, with or without the compensatory assistance of nocturnal orgasms.

Perhaps the mistaken belief that only men have orgasms while they sleep arises from the fact that women's sex dreams ending in orgasm leave no unmistakable evidence as men's do — namely, an ejaculate. Nevertheless, a close vulval examination following an erotic dream would quite likely reveal an excess of vaginal secretion, such as would be present in any other instance of intense sexual excitation.

FALLACY:

> WOMEN EJACULATE, AS MEN DO.

FACT:

Ejaculation in the male comes about through contractions of the internal sex organs and glands — the terminal portion of the vas deferens, the seminal vesicles, and the prostate gland — which drive sperm and the seminal fluids into the urethra and out the penis with considerable force. Since the female does not possess these accessory sex glands or organs, or any similar to them, and indeed secretes no fluids similar to the male's seminal fluids, it is not possible for her to ejaculate.

The Kinsey researchers observed that the myth of female ejaculation is to be found primarily in literature purposefully designed to be erotically stimulating. But, as they pointed out, ejaculation is, in fact, "the only phenomenom in the physiology of sexual response which is not identically matched in the male and the female, or represented by closely homologous functions."

Ordinarily, erection sets the stage for ejaculation. The stimulation of the glands of the penis, the presence of sex hormones in the blood, impulses from taut seminal vesicles and ejaculatory ducts, nerve responses from erotic odors, sexual thoughts: all these messages stimulate the brain to bring about and maintain an erection of the penis, as well as to build up impulses in the ejaculatory center of the lower spinal cord. Nerve impulses from the male genitals are carried by the dorsal nerves of the penis to the pudendal nerves and enter the ejaculatory center via posterior penile roots (involving sacral spinal nerves 3-4). These impulses then travel to the appropriate section of the lower spine (lumbar spinal nerves 1-2) where they, along with stimulation from the other areas mentioned, build up to such a threshold that there is a sudden triggering of the process called ejaculation.

There is, first, a peristalsis (flowing contraction) of the ampulla of the vas deferens, the seminal vesicles, and the ejaculatory ducts, which moves the ejaculatory fluid (semen) containing the sperm to the membranaceous part of the urethral tract; second, there is an accompanying clonic (alternation of contraction and relaxation) spasm in the urogenital floor muscles, which discharges the semen by spurting it through and out the penis. This physical reaction is accompanied by a distinct and highly pleasurable sensation known as *orgasm.* The strength of the ejaculatory force varies from man to man. Some ejaculate with such force that the discharged semen may go three feet or more beyond the penile meatus, while in other males the semen may go only a few inches or simply ooze out the urethra. The strength of the force usually depends upon such factors as general health, age, degree of sexual stimulation, and the condition of the prostate. Most men report that semen is ejaculated with little force, although men sometimes tend to correlate the subjective pleasures of orgasm with the force of ejaculation.

The mucous lining of a woman's vagina contains no glands. The vagina itself, however, in a manner not completely understood, secretes a mucous-like fluid that is similar in appearance and manner of production to beads of perspiration that break out on the brow. These beads eventually flow together to form a glistening coating over the entire vaginal vault. The "sweating" process begins shortly after a woman becomes sexually aroused in any manner — within ten to thirty seconds, as a matter of fact — thus providing the lubrication necessary for ease of penile intromission. (Vaginal "sweating" is the first indication that a woman is responding to sexual stimulation.) As her sexual excitement heightens, the lubrication becomes more abundant — in fact, it is an excellent indicator to a man that his partner is, at least physiologically, ready to proceed with intercourse.

The secretions of the Bartholin's glands also contribute to vaginal lubrication, but not to nearly so significant a degree as was once thought. These two glands are located just within the vaginal opening, and they secrete their fluids primarily in response to the stimulation of intercourse itself, or just prior to the orgasmic phase of sexual response — the phase at which both the male and female reach orgasm and the male also ejaculates. The lubrication supplied by the Bartholin's glands therefore appears too late to aid in penile penetration, and in too small a quantity, in any event, to lubricate the whole vaginal vault. During masturbation, as a matter of fact, Masters and Johnson have demonstrated that the Bartholin's glands frequently secrete nothing.

Other than the "literary" efforts of those authors whose primary aim is to sexually titillate their readers, and who are consequently unconcerned with physiological exactness, there is perhaps another reason for the belief that women ejaculate. During orgasm, the muscles circling the outer one-third of the vagina contract from three to as many as fifteen times, sometimes strongly enough to expel from the vagina some of the secretions collected on its walls. The fluid thus ejected from the vagina may well give the superficial appearance of an ejaculation.

FALLACY:

> SIMULTANEOUS ORGASMS ARE MORE SATISFACTORY THAN THOSE EXPERIENCED SEPARATELY AND ARE, MOREOVER, NECESSARY FOR SEXUAL COMPATIBILITY IN MARRIAGE.

FACT:

The desirability of simultaneous orgasms for husband and wife has long been the subject of speculation. Naturally, if both husband and wife prefer orgasms at the same time — and many couples do, claiming that it affords them the ultimate in sexual enjoyment and satisfaction — then they should strive for this goal. However, some aspects of sexual response should be considered before a couple embark upon the uneven struggle toward simultaneous orgasm, or before they accept the premise that it offers the ultimate in amatory achievement.

Essential to rewarding sexual activity is the effort to give one's partner the fullest measure of consideration and satisfaction. If either person is primarily concerned with gratifying himself or is caught up in his own impending orgasm, he cannot give full attention to his partner. Similarly, if overmuch attention is being devoted to the partner's sexual gratification, appropriate concentration on one's own response and pleasure is impossible.

Furthermore, men and women react quite differently in their respective bodily movements at the time of orgasm. The man's tendency is to plunge into the vagina as deeply as possible at the moment of his orgasm, to hold this position for a length of time, and to follow, perhaps, with one or two deep, deliberate thrusts. The woman's tendency, on the other hand, is to have the same stroking, plunging movements of the earlier stages of intercourse continued during the orgasmic reaction, with perhaps an acceleration of the thrusts and an increase of pressure in the vulval area. These two highly pleasurable patterns of movement are obviously incompatible. Since they cannot both be executed at the same time, whichever pattern is carried out during simultaneous orgasm must perforce detract from the full pleasure of one of the partners.

Therefore, the arguments would appear stronger against than for simultaneous orgasm. It is easier for a man to achieve orgasm, but he is usually capable of only one. The sensible conduct of coition, consequently, would seem to be that the husband delay his own pleasure until his wife is fully satisfied. Both partners can devote full attention to giving the wife as many orgasmic responses as she wishes, and then both can concentrate wholly on providing the husband with as satisfying an orgasm as possible. If the wife is not able to reach an orgasm, even after protracted intercourse, an alternate course is for the husband to reach his orgasm, then to bring his wife to climax orally, manually, or mechanically.

Marital happiness and sexual adjustment (the latter being a healthy attitude toward sexual activity, even in the absence of responsiveness) bear a high degree of relationship to one another, although marital happiness shows little correlation with overall sexual responsiveness (the latter meaning pleasure and satisfaction in sexual activity). If most other aspects of a woman's marriage are satisfactory — e.g., if the relationship with her husband involves shared interests, spontaneity, naturalness, lack of defensiveness, mutual respect, the desire to please, and open lines of communication — she may be happy in the marriage even though she is sexually unresponsive.

———————

FALLACY:

WOMEN ARE INCAPABLE OF MULTIPLE ORGASMS.

FACT:

When the Kinsey group first published its report on female sexual behavior, their statement that women are capable of several orgasms during one sexual encounter was met with cries of disbelief. Fifteen years later the results of the Masters and Johnson research clinically established that, if the stimulation producing a woman's first orgasm is continued, a second, third, or even tenth orgasm may be induced.

Many people, both men and women, refuse to believe that women possess this capability, and, furthermore, they cannot accept the fact that women may have a need for more than one orgasm. Some women, not possessing a particularly strong sex drive themselves, may fail to understand such a need in their sisters. For other women, the suggestion of multiple orgasm clashes with their concept of what is acceptable behavior in bed; these women fear that their husbands would be offended by such "unladylike" sexual abandon as repeated orgasmic response.

Men, especially, have difficulty in understanding a woman's capacity or need for multiple orgasm, because the sex drive of the average male is well satisfied, at least during one sexual encounter, with one climax. (As one of my female patients said recently about her husband, "After he's had one orgasm, you might as well knock him in the head, because he's through for the night.") Despite the fact that men generally consider themselves to be sexually superior to women, the truth of the matter is that only about 7% of men — almost all of this small percentage being in their teens or early twenties — are capable of more than one orgasm during a single sexual experience. Yet almost all women are capable of multiple orgasms. If properly stimulated, about 50% of them are capable of going from orgasm to orgasm within the space of a very few minutes, and regularly do so.

Finally, the difference in the time required for a man and a woman to reach orgasm beclouds the issue. The man's penis is obviously directly stimulated during sexual intercourse, but stimulation of the woman's clitoris is indirect in most, if not all, positions of sexual intercourse. Consequently, a woman usually requires from ten to twenty minutes to reach climax through coital means, whereas a man achieves it within a minute or two after penetration. It is therefore understandable that even those well-intentioned couples who are deeply concerned about the woman's sexual satisfaction might be misled into thinking that something so difficult to achieve is hardly likely to repeat itself quickly.

All the foregoing arguments against women's capacity and possible need for multiple orgasm are invalid. They are typical, unfortunately, of the fear, misinformation, and superstition surrounding much of our society's thinking on sexual matters. Nevertheless, even the couple who possess a positive, adventuresome attitude toward sex may be puzzled over how to go about arriving at such a peak of sexual satisfaction without reducing what began as an act of love to an athletic event worthy of the Olympics. The quest, however, is not an impossible one. If the same movement, pressure, and type of sexual stimulation that led to the woman's first orgasm is continued, a second, third, or even more will often quickly follow. And, incidentally, women who experience multiple climaxes report that the second and third orgasms are more intense and pleasurable than the first one was, while those few men who are lucky enough to be able to have more than one orgasm in a single sexual experience inevitably report that the first is more pleasurable than the ones following.

The ideal, of course, is for the husband to put off his own orgasm in coitus long enough to allow his wife to enjoy as many climaxes as she wishes. Many men cannot prolong the sex act sufficiently to bring their wives even to a first orgasm, let alone a second and a third. And many wives cannot reach orgasm at all through sexual intercourse, because this method of sexual activity frequently does not permit direct or sufficient stimulation of the clitoris and vulval region, thanks to the perversity of nature in its positioning of the male and female genitalia.

So what is to be done? A conference on sexual matters between a man and woman is never out of order. They should discuss their sexual desires freely with one another and feel comfortable enough to say frankly in what way their sexual approaches might be altered to bring them greater pleasure. If the woman feels the need for greater sexual release, experimentation is the next step. If the husband can manage to put off his own orgasm in coitus long enough to bring his wife as many climaxes as she wishes, excellent. If not, they might consider changing to a coital position less stimulating to the man — e.g., the woman-above. They might also consider other techniques leading to orgasm, to be used before, during, or after intercourse — manual or oral stimulation of the clitoris, or the use of an electric vibrator.

Some couples may reject a "staggering" of the husband's and wife's orgasms with the argument that greatest sexual fulfillment is accomplished through simultaneous orgasm. Perhaps for some couples this is so. But it is a difficult goal to achieve, an impossible one for many couples, and an undesirable one for most.

Those who are ready to reject the thought of orgasm achieved by methods other than vaginal penetration should give some thought to several matters. A man's sexual capability is not discredited by the fact that he cannot quickly bring a woman to climax during intercourse. Nature has stacked the cards against his doing so. More important, sex is most rewarding when it is a shared experience, and how better to share than for each of the couple to concentrate on bringing maximum satisfaction to the other, one at a time. Beyond one's own sexual gratification, there is a great personal satisfaction in realizing that one has been the source of so much pleasure to the person one loves. Most men who are mature and experienced in sexual matters will readily agree that for them the most pleasurable aspect of their sexual relationships is bringing their partners to satisfying and fulfilling orgasms.

FALLACY:

THERE IS A DIFFERENCE BETWEEN VAGINAL AND CLITORAL ORGASMS.

FACT:

Since the time of Sigmund Freud (and perhaps earlier), there has been considerable controversy over the difference between vaginal and clitoral orgasms — that is, orgasm produced by penile penetration of the vagina, as opposed to orgasm produced by some form of manipulation of the clitoris. Indeed, in the early days of the controversy it was believed — especially by the psychoanalysts — that only mature women had vaginal orgasms, while clitoral orgasms were sure signs of narcissism and sexual inadequacy. Freud maintained that even an emotionally immature girl can achieve orgasm by clitoral stimulation; but that as she matures into a "real" woman, the primary focus of her sexual response will shift from the clitoris to the vagina.

For years physiologists have recognized that the vaginal walls contain few erogenous nerve endings and that only stimulation, direct or indirect, of the clitoris causes an orgasmic response in women. It has taken the recent Masters and Johnson research in human sexual response, however, to convince many medical men and scientists that "from an anatomic point of view, there is absolutely no difference in the response of the pelvic viscera to effective sexual stimulation, regardless of whether stimulation occurs as a result of clitoral area manipulation, natural or artificial coition, or, for that matter, from breast stimulation alone."

Many women have been concerned over their sexual adequacy because they are unable to achieve orgasm through coition. The research findings of Masters and Johnson should once and for all dispel the myth that women have two kinds of orgasm — one clitoral and the other vaginal. From a purely physiological viewpoint, direct clitoral stimulation usually generates a somewhat stronger orgasmic response than does the indirect stimulation of the clitoris in vaginal penetration. Many women find, however, that orgasm achieved by penile penetration, although the stimulation may be less intense, is a more fulfilling experience because it places them in a more traditional female role and allows more "togetherness" with their husbands during the sex act. Other women receive more gratification from clitoral stimulation alone; in fact, many women are unable to achieve an orgasm in any manner other than direct stimulation of the clitoral area.

———

FALLACY:

IT IS DANGEROUS TO HAVE SEXUAL INTERCOURSE DURING MENSTRUATION.

FACT:

This erroneous idea, along with other myths about menstruation, has been with mankind for centuries. As early as 60 A.D., the Roman historian Pliny declared that the mere presence of a menstruating woman will cause "new wine to become sour, seeds to become sterile, fruit to fall from trees, and garden plants to become parched." Furthermore, according to Pliny, menstrual fluid can blunt the edge of steel, kill a swarm of bees, instantly rust iron and brass (causing an offensive odor); and if, by chance, dogs were to taste the menstrual flow, they would become mad, and their bite venomous and incurable. Ancient men (as well as modern ones, of course) needed scapegoats upon whom to place blame for famine, pestilence, and other catastrophes. A menstruating woman, therefore, was adjudged to have the power to cause flowers to wilt by her touch and crops to fail just by passing the fields. The Old Testament called her "unclean," and in many societies she was compelled to leave the house, if not the community, during her menstrual period. This negativism was, and is, further strengthened by the universal fear of blood, since blood is associated with violence, injury, and death. These age-old attitudes toward menstruation and the menstruating woman, although much diluted and altered, have filtered down through the centuries. Small wonder, then, that couples shy away from sexual intercourse during menses. Furthermore, the taboo against "wasting sperm" by having intercourse during the allegedly "safe period" of menstruation undoubtedly has added to the cluster of misinformation surrounding coition during this time.

The influence of such folklore — evident, perhaps, in such terms for menstruation as "the curse," "doom's days," or "being unwell" — helps to reinforce a negative attitude toward menstruation. Such negativism encourages a girl, even in this enlightened age, to regard her period as a necessarily unpleasant event. Once these unwholesome attitudes are established, it is easy enough for her to develop menstrual problems that are psychological in origin. This is not to say that menstruation is not in some cases accompanied by some genuine physical discomforts, especially in a girl who is just beginning to have menstrual periods or who has a retroverted uterus; in such cases, a physician should be consulted. But in most instances the difficulties have a psychological basis.

Menstrual blood is perfectly harmless In content to both man and woman; the source of the flow is uterine, rather than vaginal, and no tissue damage occurs from penile penetration; and a woman's sex drive ordinarily does not diminish during the menstrual period. These facts point up the irrationality of any arguments against coition during menses, if the couple desire it at that time. Life is short enough as it is, so why shoot down three or four days out of each twenty-eight?

FALLACY:

MENSTRUATION BEGINS EARLIER IN GIRLS LIVING IN THE TROPICS THAN IN GIRLS LIVING IN COOLER CLIMATES.

FACT:

I suppose nearly everyone has heard this theory, and most accept it uncritically as fact. The belief has no doubt come about because girls of primitive or peasant societies living in hot climates often are married and become mothers at very early ages. One therefore assumes that their other biological processes, such as menstruation, have likewise been set in motion at an earlier age than those, say, of a Scandinavian or North American girl.

The truth of the matter is, however, that menarche — the beginning of menstrual cycles — is controlled by the individual girl's heredity, although its occurrence can be altered by circumstances of health and environment. A girl will usually start menstruating at about the same age that her mother did. Identical twin girls will typically begin menstruation within the same month. Such debilitating physical conditions as anemia, malnutrition, and severe illness during late childhood may cause a delay in all maturational processes, including menstruation.

Of interest is the fact that the average American girl begins menstruating at about thirteen years of age. Menstruation begins earlier for American girls than for girls of other countries, including those living in very hot and very cold climates. Furthermore, if hot weather precipitates the menarche, one would expect that the majority of girls would begin menstruation in the summer months. Yet, in the United States, only 25% of girls start their menstrual cycles during the summer.

The age at which girls begin to menstruate has dropped rather sharply in the past few centuries, the average decrease in age of onset of first flow being about one month per five years over the last two hundred years. For example, in Germany the average age in 1795 was 16.6 years, but by 1920 it was 14.5 years. In the United States in the late 1930s the average age was 13.5 years, but in the mid-1960s it had dropped to 13 years.

One can only guess why American girls start menstruating at an earlier age than their sisters in other parts of the world. Girls living in nations of high living standards — e.g., England and Scandinavia — also begin menstruating at an age comparable to that of American girls. One must conclude, therefore, that poor nutrition and ill health, having a detrimental effect on all growth and development, slow down the sexual maturation of girls living in underdeveloped countries. The superior nutritional and medical advantages that are the heritage of girls growing up in such countries as America no doubt hasten all maturational processes, including the sexual.

FALLACY:

LOWER ANIMALS MENSTRUATE JUST AS HUMANS DO.

FACT:

Nearly all vertebrates (animals with backbones) go through some sort of sexual cycle in which they alternate between being infertile and capable of reproduction. And nearly all of them have a period of "bleeding" associated with the rhythm of their reproductive cycles. In the human it is called *menstruation;* in subhuman mammals it is called *estrus.* The only similarity between humans and animals with respect to this "bleeding" (which is actually not a true bleeding at all) is its association with the reproductive *cycle;* the function of the "bleeding" in the two groups is entirely different.

In lower animals, the appearance of estrus indicates the start of the breeding season. Estrus means that the female is "in heat," that she has ovulated, or is about to do so. It is only at this time that she is capable of becoming impregnated by the male. Estrus also means that the female is most particularly receptive to the sexual advances of the male at this time; and that the male is stimulated into sexual activity by the special odor of the female's discharge. (Almost everyone has witnessed the almost magnetic effect that a female dog in heat has on virtually every male dog in the vicinity.)

The estrous cycles of lower animals vary incredibly. For instance, that of the mole occurs once a year, while that of the mouse occurs every five days, the delivery of the next litter of mice being postponed only by the number of the present litter being suckled. Other mammals have the capacity to breed only at the time of year most advantageous to the survival of their young when born (although probably the very different lengths of gestation mean that in the process of evolution other animals have coped with the same problem in a different way). The mare, for instance, breeds in the spring and carries its young eleven months, whereas sheep are autumn breeders, but carry their young only five months. Both species thereby assure the arrival of their offspring in the springtime, when food supplies are optimal. Breeding seasons, or estrus, together with the adaptations made by gestation periods, act together to warrant the best preservation of the young and of the species.

Menstruation in the human female (and in certain of the primates) is quite a different event from estrus. Instead of occurring at the time of ovulation and prime fertility, as estrus does, it occurs midway between two ovulations and at a time when the female is usually (although not always) the least fertile. Menstruation is a result of the degeneration and sloughing off of the uterine lining that had been prepared for implantation of a newly fertilized egg, a fertilization that did not take place. Estrus signifies that the animal is imminently capable of conceiving, and that its reproductive organs are ready for implantation of a fertilized egg. It is the case of the disappointed uterus vs. the expectant uterus.

Therefore, copulation is somewhat different in humans from what it is in animals. In the human male and female, sexual interest is not dictated by seasons and has become divorced from the procreative instinct that prompts lower animals to mate. Humans can mate at any time. For them the sexual act has evolved the extra dimension of emotional fulfillment or, at least, "fun and frolic." In lower animals sexual behavior — especially for the female — still has as its basic purpose procreation. Many lower-animal males can copulate all year round, but they usually need the stimulation of a female who is in estrus and who is, therefore, receptive to their advances. They will not pursue the matter with a female who is uncooperative, as her attitude typically is when she is not in estrus; what benefit would there be to the species, in any case, of an unfertile mating? And what lower-animal female gives a hang about the sexual urges of her ever-ready male? This state of affairs has led to the observation that man and the white mouse are the only animals that will perpetrate rape on an unwilling female.

FALLACY:

DURING MENSTRUATION, WOMEN SHOULD NOT ENGAGE IN
SPORTS; NOR SHOULD THEY TAKE A BATH, SHOWER, OR
SHAMPOO THEIR HAIR.

FACT:

The superstitions and folklore enveloping the perfectly normal
phenomenon called menstruation are legion. Taking a bath during the
menstrual period is said to be dangerous; it might even cause tuberculosis. If a
girl gets her feet wet or cold, or washes her hair, menstruation may be halted,
thus causing untold miseries. Other theories would have it that consuming
cold food and drinks, or even eating such sour foods as lemons, is harmful to
the menstruating woman. These superstitions are clearly untrue, as young
women fortunately learn through their own experience as time goes by.

Each month the uterus prepares for the possible implantation and
nourishment of a fertilized ovum by building up a spongy mass of tissue in its
lining. If no fertilization occurs, the thickened lining sloughs off and is
discharged from the body in the form of menstrual fluid — which,
incidentally, is only partially composed of blood, the rest being mucus and
tissue debris from the uterine lining. Menstruation, then, is as natural a bodily
function as breathing and the circulation of blood. Since it is in no way a
sickness, there is no medical or physiological reason why a menstruating
woman should curtail or eliminate any of her normal activities.

General good health is important to an uneventful, comfortable menstruation, and exercise is essential to good health at any age. For example, a
comparative study of members of a girls' aquatic team and of nonswimmers
at a Des Moines high school demonstrated that the swimmers suffered less
frequently and less severely from dysmenorrhea (painful menstruation) than
the girls whose swimming activity was minimal. The general opinion of
physicians is that a girl should not coddle herself during menstruation; that,
to the contrary, it is far healthier for her, mentally and physically, to go
about her work and play as usual.

One wonders why the linking of water and menstruation causes such a
panic in so many girls' minds. Bathing, shampooing, and showering cannot
possibly do any harm — it has been demonstrated through tests, for example,
that water cannot enter the vagina during a bath or shower, and cannot
therefore "stop the flow." In addition, a girl is neither more nor less subject
to chills during menstruation than she is at other times of the month. It is
true that a sharp change in temperature during bathing (an unlikely event in
any case) may temporarily stop the flow; but a girl need only be cautious

against sharp temperature changes. Rather than being harmful, a warm bath has a marvelously relaxing effect and may, therefore, help the girl who is experiencing some menstrual cramping. Furthermore, since personal cleanliness is more of a problem during menstruation than at other times of the month, bathing or showering takes on additional importance. A girl feels altogether better when she is fresh and clean of body and when her hair is shiny from a recent shampoo. There is no reason, in fact, for a girl to give up swimming during menstruation, if she enjoys it. In the latter case, of course, she should use a sanitary tampon, rather than an external pad.

Dr. F. M. Paulsen of George Peabody College, an expert in the field of folklore, has collected a long list of myths concerning menstruation, some of the most interesting of which are presented below. Of course, none of them is true.

1. If a soiled menstrual pad is picked up or handled by a man, from that time onward the woman who wore the pad will be an easy victim of sexual advances.

2. If an impotent man performs cunnilingus on a menstruating woman, his potency will be restored.

3. A frigid woman can be brought to numerous orgasms if she has sexual intercourse during her period.

4. Well-trained domestic animals will not respond to directions from a woman who is menstruating.

5. Dogs fed by a menstruating woman will develop worms.

6. Plucking pubic hair at night will assure the woman a painless menstrual period.

7. Shaving armpits or legs during menstruation will cause the woman to become weak and listless and will result in a difficult menstruation.

8. A menstruating woman's hair will not "take" a permanent wave, and kinky hair cannot be straightened during the menstrual period.

9. A soiled menstrual pad placed under a woman's pillow each time she has intercourse will prevent her becoming pregnant; an unused pad under the pillow will assist a woman in becoming pregnant.

10. If menstrual cramps disappear while a woman is petting, the pain is likely to be transmitted to her lover.

Incredible as it may seem to some, these myths were not gathered primarily from illiterate, backwoods people, but from present-day college students living in various parts of the nation!

FALLACY:

>THE ABSENCE OF THE HYMEN (MAIDENHEAD) PROVES THAT A GIRL IS NOT A VIRGIN.

FACT:

The entrance to the vagina of most virginal girls is closed off (although not entirely) by a fold of tissue called the hymen, or maidenhead. It is a tissue serving no recognized physiological purpose. Yet its absence can cause much anguish and suspicion if a prospective bridegroom places a high value on his bride's being a virgin; or if a girl, for one reason or another, no longer has an intact hymen, but nevertheless accepts society's expectation of a virgin bride.

Just how much proof, then, does the presence or absence of the hymen offer in the question of virginity? Not much, really, one way or the other. It is true that the hymenal tissue, if present, is usually ruptured in the first act of sexual intercourse. But it is equally true that some girls are born with little or no hymenal tissue, and that the tissue may have become ruptured in some other, nonsexual way. For example, most girls today engage in a far greater variety of sports, and far more vigorously so, than their grandmothers did; the chances are thereby enhanced that they may unwittingly tear the hymen in the course of strenuous exercise.

Furthermore, an occasional girl has a hymen with no opening, or one that is unusually tough and fibrous. In the first instance, a doctor must rupture the hymen; otherwise the menstrual flow cannot escape, nor will the girl be able at a future time to engage in sexual intercourse. Many girls before marriage, as a matter of fact, choose to have their doctors cut the hymen, or to provide them with dilators with which to systematically stretch the tissue so that they can engage in the first act of sexual intercourse with their new husbands without fear of pain or difficulty. (These courses of action by the virginal woman, I might add, seem most sensible to me.) Therefore, the absence of the hymen is not necessarily *prima facie* evidence that a girl is not a virgin.

On the subject of the hymen's being proof of virginity, another point needs to be made. There are a few girls whose hymenal tissue is so flexible or pliable that they can have sexual intercourse repeatedly without its rupturing. So, surprisingly enough, the converse of the above conclusion is also true: the presence of a hymen is not necessarily proof that a girl is a virgin.

Since the presence or absence of the hymen really proves nothing, one wonders why questions about its association with virginity continue. The answer must lie in the persistence of the double standard — which seems particularly unfair when one considers that there is no physiological evidence to prove or disprove to a girl that a man is a virgin, if it happens to be important to her. Having had intercourse with fifty different women, a man could still stand up and vow that he is a virgin without the slightest fear of being disproved — unless she caught sight of the fingers crossed behind his back. Yet this same man might well question the virginity of his new wife if she happens to have no hymen. All in all, there is too much issue made of a tissue!

Mothers, anxious that their daughters enter marriage as virgins and with hymens intact, sometimes question the use of tampons as menstrual protection. They are fearful, first, that use of tampons would mean that the girl has now been "penetrated," and hence can no longer be considered a virgin; and, second, that wearing a tampon might be sexually so stimulating to the vagina that the girl could not control her sexual urges. Once having tasted the fruit, she would thereafter be the potential victim of any predatory male.

Regarding the first of these concerns, only when the vagina is penetrated by a penis — and by nothing else — is a girl no longer a virgin. Therefore, using tampons as menstrual hygiene in no way destroys or "tarnishes" a girl's virginity. In any case a tampon is so slender in diameter that it can be inserted into most virginal vaginas without breaking or stretching the hymen.

With respect to the fear that tampons will sexually stimulate the vagina, one need only remember that the vaginal barrel contains very few erogenous nerve endings. The insertion of tampons or any other object can cause little or no sexual stimulation. On the other hand, the concentration of nerve endings in the external region around the vagina (the vulva) is very large. The area is considered the primary erogenous (sexually excitable) zone of a woman's body. Therefore, it would appear that an external sanitary pad would be far more likely to cause sexual arousal than using tampons — although I hasten to emphasize that such a likelihood is extremely remote. I mention it only to point out how totally unfounded are the fears that one form of menstrual sanitary protection or another is likely to cause sexual stimulation.

FALLACY:

THE BEST HEALTH IS ENJOYED BY THOSE WHO ABSTAIN
FROM SEX.

FACT:

One widespread belief, chiefly among men, is that sexual intercourse
and other forms of sexual outlet (especially masturbation) are exhausting and
therefore physically debilitating. The conclusion typically drawn is that the
man wishing to preserve his physical energy and, thereby, his physical health,
must avoid sex altogether or, at the very least, keep rigid control over his
sexual activity.

Several misconceptions about the physiology of sex have generated this
myth. The loss of a single drop of semen, so one story goes, equals the loss of
forty drops of blood; according to another tale, to recover from a single
ejaculation, the body must replace the equivalent of a pint of blood (or a
quart; I cannot remember). Another misconception is that a man has only so
many orgasms allotted to him in his lifetime, and that once the quota is
depleted, sex life becomes only a fond, lamented memory.

In most people's minds the aging process is associated with a loss in
physical vigor and stamina. Orgasm, so many men think, exacts an awesome
toll in fatigue and exhaustion. These men are consequently led to the rueful
conclusion that, to conserve their physical capabilities and, hence, their good
health, they must avoid having orgasms. It is true that many people feel a
distinct need for sleep immediately following intercourse. But, rather than
orgasm exacting its toll in exhaustion, the time of day dictates the need for
sleep. Coitus usually takes place in bed at night, when the person is already tired
and in need of sleep. Additionally, orgasm brings relief of sexual tension; and for
the couple who love one another, a significant degree of anxiety is also drained
off as a result of the emotional fulfillment that they experience in coitus. In
either instance the couple are quite likely to drop off quickly into a deep sleep
after their lovemaking. They have not exhausted themselves physically because
of intercourse and orgasm; they have merely reached a soothing state of relaxation.

The difference between genuine fatigue and the relaxed feeling following
orgasm can be distinguished in the behavior of a man in two particular sets of
circumstances. He has, say, worn himself out with playing eighteen holes of
golf in $98°$ temperature. As soon as he arrives home and climbs into bed,
exhausted, a neighbor knocks on the door. He may get up to sit and chat with
the neighbor; but his feelings of fatigue linger, no matter how interesting the
conversation. By contrast, if the same man is relaxing in bed after pleasurable

sexual intercourse, and the same neighbor arrives on the doorstep, his feelings of relaxation and inertia – coming from tension reduction and not from physical exhaustion — are quickly overcome as he enters into a lively conversation with his neighbor. He neither feels nor shows any signs of exhaustion.

Young people, especially, are prone to suspect that the fatigue experienced the day after a wild party is the result of the sexual activity in which they may have been involved. They tend to ignore — quite wrongly, of course — the heavy drinking, loss of sleep, improper eating, and other physical punishment that they may have subjected themselves to, and blame their sexual behavior for the feelings of weariness.

Not to be overlooked in a discussion of exhaustion and fatigue is the impact that our attitudes can have on our bodies. As an example, if a man *thinks* that he is going to be fatigued after ejaculation, he will quite likely convert his expectation into the physiological response of exhaustion. By the same token, if a person *thinks* that giving a lecture to his Rotary Club will exhaust him, or if the lecture elicits a negative response from the audience, causing him some emotional upset, his anxiety is similarly liable to be converted into the physiological response of fatigue. Neither the orgasm in the one instance, nor the lecture in the other, had the physiological capacity to cause the man's feelings of exhaustion; the feelings were controlled solely by his attitudes.

Another component in some men's evaluation of sex and its effects on health concerns their attitude toward "sexual excess." If a man views his sexual behavior as excessive and feels guilty about it, he is liable also to feel that his excesses merit punishment. By way of self-punishment, therefore, he may develop some sort of psychological problem or psychosomatic disorder. But what is sexual excess? The answer is that there is no such thing; it is virtually impossible to overdo sex, except in the exceedingly rare instances of certain psychotic patients. With respect to sex, one should remember that the body has excellent built-in controls. Long before the point is reached at which health might be threatened in some way, sexual activity becomes unpleasant, and the body rejects further erotic stimulation.

I suspect also that the dark warning that "sexual excesses" are the cause of deterioration of mind and body stems from the lingering attitude in many minds that sex is essentially evil. What is the Devil's handiwork can only merit the wrath of God, who will punish the Doers with bodily afflictions and abbreviated lives and reward the Abstainers with long and golden years. Which leads one to wonder at the advantages of so long a life: as Sportin' Life, speaking of Methuselah, says in "Porgy and Bess": "Who calls dat livin' when no gal will give in to no man what's 900 years?"

A relationship between good health and sexual abstinence does indeed exist — but it is a negative relationship. That is, those people who appear to have better physical health and to be less fettered with worry and fatigue also have a higher degree of sexual potency than those whose health is poor. Turned another way, it appears that men who are out of shape physically are not as likely as men of better health and physical condition to be interested in any type of physical exertion, including sexual activity.

It is reasonable to assume (if, indeed, the statement is not axiomatic) that married people have more sexual intercourse than single people of the same age. It is also true that married people in every age group have a lower death rate than single people do, whether the single persons have never been married or are left single because of divorce or the partner's death. Divorced people have, as a matter of fact, the highest death rate of all. The death rate of married men between the ages of twenty and forty-four is about half that of single men of the same age. Contrary to the widely held belief, then, it would appear that the best health does not belong to those who restrict their sexual activity.

———

FALLACY:

ATHLETIC PERFORMANCE IS DIMINISHED BY SEXUAL INTERCOURSE THE NIGHT BEFORE.

FACT:

This pronouncement is one of the most classic in the encyclopedia of sexual mythology. One suspects that it had its beginnings in the old-time notion that sports epitomize good clean living (sex, of course, being neither good nor clean). Trainers were interested in preserving their athletes' energies, to be sure, and toward this end they quite likely perpetuated another bit of sexual apocrypha — that losing a drop of semen is the same as being drained of untold quantities of blood and protein, an argument traditionally used to deter a boy from masturbating. But these early-day trainers were particularly interested in preserving the image of the athlete as a clean-minded, clean-living, all-American lad: degenerate boys indulge in sex; wholesome boys play baseball. The thesis that sex and athletics stand in opposition appears, then, to be embedded more in reasons of morality than of physiology.

Certainly the history of sports contains nothing that offers scientific support for the theory that ejaculation physically exhausts the athlete.

Indeed, Roman gladiators were provided with female companionship the night before the games — although one can speculate that it was a gesture of kindness toward those who might well not be among the living on the morrow. In recent times some knowledgeable people of the sports world have recognized the importance of regular sexual intercourse or other methods of sexual outlet as an essential part of athletic training programs.

Although most present-day coaches concede that the members of their squads are not sexless (with Joe Namath sitting in the Amen Corner), many trainers and college coaches still prefer not to have married men on their teams and, furthermore, warn their bachelor players to refrain from intercourse or masturbation the day before and the day of a big game. (One trainer said recently that sex was bad for a boxer; that it drains his strength, "particularly in the legs.") The thinking of some of these men is obviously still steeped in the puritanism of America's past. Other trainers are simply compulsive enough that they want to direct every activity in the lives of their team.

Still others oppose intercourse the night before a game because, they contend, it will render the athlete too relaxed to do his best — the greater his tension, the better will be his performance. In its application to most athletic events, the argument has no physiological basis in fact. The athlete who is tense usually will not perform as well as the one who is relaxed, because he will not have as good control over his body.

Most coaches feel that a player's behavior the night before an important game is significant only insofar as he does nothing that might interfere with a good night's rest. They realize that, to their predominantly bachelor team, sexual intercourse is rarely that alone and is typically accompanied by injudicious wining and dining and late hours. An athlete would obviously do much better to spend these valuable hours at home in bed with *Sports Illustrated.* As a case in point, a Houston university's football coach moves his entire team away from the festive atmosphere of the dormitories and into a motel the night before a home game. Several coaches of professional football teams separate their team members from their wives the night before a game as insurance that they will sleep, not play, the night hours away. The temptation is particularly strong for the young athlete away from home to feel that he is on a vacation, and to act accordingly.

To test the effect of intercourse on peak athletic efficiency, an interesting experiment was conducted recently at the University of Maryland. A professor of physical education, Dr. Warren Johnson, tested the hand grip of fourteen former athletes the morning after they had had sexual intercourse and again not less than six days after their last coitus. (The men were not informed of the purpose of the testing.) The results revealed no difference between the two time spans in the strength of the subjects' hand grip, and Dr. Johnson concluded that coitus probably makes no difference to a man's general physical ability. No less an authority on human sexuality than Dr. William Masters, himself a former athlete, said in a recent interview that after a sexual experience athletes should be able to perform at maximum ability if they are allowed a sufficiently long recuperation period — one to five minutes!

And there is another side to the question of athletics and sex. When the football coach at Weber State College was asked why he had so many children (eight), he reportedly said that he never could sleep the night before a game!

———————

FALLACY:

DIMINISHING FUNCTION OF THE SEX GLANDS SIGNALS THE END OF THE SEX LIFE OF BOTH MEN AND WOMEN.

FACT:

It is generally agreed that the failure of the sex glands — the woman's ovaries and the man's testicles — is the only endocrinal change that comes with old age. For men, however, the diminished functioning of the testicles does not mean that sperm production ceases. Fertility may be reduced, but men still become fathers at eighty. It is true that, in older men, erections occur less frequently and less vigorously than they do in younger men, and that the ejaculate is thinner. But a parallel can be drawn between reduced sexual functioning and the ability to run a 100-yard dash: one can still do both at sixty as well as one did at twenty-five; it just takes longer. A slowing down of sexual performance, therefore, should present no more of a problem to the older person than the wrinkling of the skin or the greying of the hair.

On the physical level, the sexual difficulty most frequently encountered by men in the aging process has to do with the prostate. Even when surgery is required, however, the vast majority of men who were potent before surgery retain their potency afterwards. On the subject of prostate surgery, a study was recently reported in the *Journal of the American Medical Association.* The conclusion, and it is a very important one, was that the *existence of a willing sexual partner* is the most important factor in a man's retaining his sexual ability after prostatic surgery. A willing partner, furthermore, is of prime importance to a man's maintaining potency in older age in general, according to this and other studies.

If after prostate surgery a man ceases sexual functioning, the reason may well be that he was looking for an excuse to end his sexual life. He may want to be free of the marital obligation of intercourse; or he may fear that intercourse will aggravate cardiac or other physical disabilities, even minor ones; or past attempts to find a sexual outlet have met with disapproval from his wife — or even from his children and neighbors. (The subject of prostatic surgery is discussed fully in the section entitled "Sexual Disorders.")

During menopause, women abruptly cease being able to bear children; but they remain as capable as ever of sexual intercourse. Certain conditions do develop, however, in the postmenopausal years that can make intercourse objectionable if nothing is done to counteract them. In the first place, the production of the female hormone estrogen by the ovaries is greatly reduced. The walls of the vagina consequently become extremely thin and its mucous secretions quite scanty. The movements of intercourse, therefore, can become irritating or painful, not only to the vagina itself, but also to the bladder and the urethra. Furthermore, the hormonal imbalance of the body can cause painful contractions of the uterus to occur during orgasm. Under these circumstances, a woman quite understandably might want to avoid orgasm or even intercourse itself.

With present-day hormonal therapy, however, these imbalances can be corrected with simple lubricants, estrogen creams or suppositories, or general hormone-replacement therapy. As Masters and Johnson have reported, many women actually develop renewed sexual interest in their husbands once the menopause is over. The fear of pregnancy is now gone, and the job of rearing children is usually over, and many of the financial and career worries typically associated with early marriage have been settled.

A well-rounded diet is essential in maintaining optimal sexual capability, just as it is in the preservation of other bodily functioning during the process of growing old. Food intake that is low in calories but high in protein, vitamin E, and calcium will provide the physical support necessary for continued sexual activity in later years.

Physiologically, then, there is little reason — short of actual disease — for an older man or woman not to enjoy an active sex life, even if it must be a relatively modified one.

FALLACY:

ALL COUPLES CONSUMMATE THEIR MARRIAGE ON THE
WEDDING NIGHT, AND SEXUAL INTERCOURSE IS ALWAYS A
PART OF MARRIAGE.

FACT:

It is certainly true that, for most couples, the wedding night is a time
for sexual intercourse and other sexual experiences, and that the incidence of
consummation of marriage on the first night has steadily risen in recent
decades. However, not all peoples believe in immediate sexual consummation
following the ceremony of marriage. Indeed, in some primitive cultures there
may be lengthy delays — even weeks — before a couple engage in their first
sexual intercourse, to allow for certain rituals to be carried out or, in some
cases, for the bride to become used to her groom. Even in modern America,
there is more abstinence on the wedding night than many realize, and the
reasons for it vary considerably.

In a study of one hundred men and one hundred women some years ago, a
leading sex researcher of the time found that about 40% had not completed
sexual intercourse on their wedding night. In five cases, the hymen was too
thick or tough to rupture; in five cases, the bride was menstruating, and sex
during this time was offensive to either the bride, or the groom, or both; four
couples stated that they "lacked the opportunity"; three couples "tried
intercourse but were unsuccessful"; in three cases, fear or aversion on the part
of the bride prevented it; three couples believed that they should have
intercourse only to produce children; two couples were so happy just to be
together that intercourse seemed unnecessary; in two cases, the husbands had
a premature ejaculation; two couples failed to bring along contraceptives; one
couple believed that intercourse was not something to rush into; one couple
considered their marriage to be on a plane above the physical; one couple had
a quarrel; one couple was too tired; one couple "just didn't get around to it";
and in one case the bride was "much too pregnant."

Perhaps much more surprising than wedding-night abstinence is the fact
that many women remain virginal even after years of marriage. Several
scientific investigations have been made into the causes and nature of
unconsummated marriages. One of the most extensive and revealing studies
concerned 1000 American Caucasian females ranging in age from seventeen to
forty-seven years (average age, twenty-nine years). The length of marriage —
and period of nonconsummation — ranged from one to twenty-one years
(average length of marriage, eight years), with 98% of the women having been
married for more than three years. Of the sample, 76% had married between

the ages of twenty and twenty-nine. All of the 1000 were deemed physically capable of sexual intercourse. A gynecologist examined each of the subjects, and if there was any doubt about a woman's being virginal, she was excluded from the sample. Although none of the women had engaged in coitus, about 25% of them did participate in mutual masturbation with their husbands.

The reasons given by these 1000 wives for their sexual abstinence were subsumed under the following fifteen categories:

1. Fear of pain in the initial intercourse — 203 (20.3%).
2. Opinion that the sex act is nasty or wicked — 178 (17.8%).
3. Impotent husband — 117 (11.7%).
4. Fear of pregnancy or childbirth — 102 (10.2%).
5. Small size of the vagina — 82 (8.2%). (Physical examinations revealed that neither husbands' nor wives' genitals were beyond the range of normalcy.)
6. The couple's ignorance regarding the exact location of the wife's sex organs — 52 (5.2%).
7. Preference for a female partner — 52 (5.2%).
8. Extreme dislike of the penis — 46 (4.6%).
9. Deep objection to intercourse unless impregnation is intended — 39 (3.9%).
10. Dislike of contraceptives — 33 (3.3%).
11. Belief that submission of woman to man implies inferiority — 31 (3.1%). Reasons given by these women for entering marriage included "the thing to do," "fear of being an 'old maid,'" and "security."
12. General dislike of men — 30 (3.0%).
13. Desire only to "mother" their husbands — 14 (1.4%).
14. Fear of damaging husband's penis — 12 (1.2%).
15. Fear of semen — 9 (.9%).

The conclusion drawn by the researchers in this study was that, if these psychosexually disturbed women had been given appropriate sex education at an early age, the sexual problems of at least 80% to 85% of them very likely would not have existed — or persisted. Even in the absence of proper sex education, psychotherapeutic treatment of married virgins is reported to be about 70% successful.

FALLACY:

A LARGE PENIS IS IMPORTANT TO A WOMAN'S SEXUAL GRATIFICATION, AND THE MAN WITH A LARGE PENIS IS MORE SEXUALLY POTENT THAN THE MAN WITH A SMALL PENIS.

FACT:

The size of the penis has practically no relationship to a man's ability to satisfy a woman sexually. The only exceptions would be these: the instances in which there is the psychological influence of a woman's *thinking* that penile size makes a difference; or when sexual pleasure is diminished because the penis is too large and causes the woman pain; or when the penis is so pathologically small that penetration and pelvic contact cannot be maintained.

The vaginal walls themselves have few nerve endings. But it is true that, in penetration, the penis that is larger in circumference will be more likely to make contact with the labia minora and vestibular tissue, pulling them in and out during coital movements. This contact causes a tugging of the clitoris, which stimulates it and produces erotic pleasure. A very long penis, on the other hand, may put pressure on the cervix, producing pain and detracting from some women's enjoyment. Yet other women will report that such pressure gives added pleasure, apparently because of psychological reasons, or because the pressure pushes the uterus in such a way that the erogenous nerve endings of the inner abdominal wall are stimulated. With the exceptions stated, however, the size of the penis is not related to the sexual gratification experienced by the woman.

There is little correlation between body and penile size — far less correlation, in fact, than there is between the dimensions of other organs and body size. Penile size is dictated by heredity, and in no way affects, either adversely or favorably, sexual potency. The mystique surrounding the large penis no doubt has its beginnings in the preadolescent boy's awe at an older boy's larger penis — an awe augmented, quite likely, by the braggadocio of adolescent youths in their accounts (usually fantasied) of herculean sexual achievements. The younger boys thereby come to associate larger genitals with extraordinary sexual ability, and the attitude is carried into adulthood.

FALLACY:

SEXUAL INTERCOURSE SHOULD BE AVOIDED DURING
PREGNANCY.

FACT:

Considerable investigation has been made into the pregnant woman's
physiological and psychologic patterns of response to sexual stimulation. In
general, there is little change from the nonpregnant state in sexual interest or
capacity for satisfying coition during the first three months (first trimester)
of pregnancy; and during the second trimester, there is usually an increase in
erotic feelings, even beyond those of the nonpregnant state. During the third
trimester, most women show a loss in sexual interest. There is no evidence to
indicate that the pregnant woman with no unusual complications should not
regularly engage in sexual intercourse or masturbatory activity to orgasm
until late in the third trimester. Naturally, sensible precautions should be
taken against excessive pressure on the abdomen, deep penile penetration,
and infection.

It is now known that there are strong contractions of the uterus during a
woman's orgasmic response that are not unlike those experienced during
labor. Couples should be warned, therefore, that the uterine contractions of
orgasm may cause labor contractions to begin if the woman is within three
weeks of term.

On the whole, sexual intercourse during pregnancy is valuable for both the
wife and husband. The nature of a man's sex drive and the psychological
stresses he experiences during the pregnancy and immediate postpartum
period cause him to be more likely to seek out extramarital sexual activity in
the last six weeks of his wife's pregnancy and during the first six weeks after
delivery than at any other time. Continuing sexual activity as long as possible
during pregnancy is, therefore, likely to be a hedge against future marital
discord and unhappiness if the husband would otherwise feel driven to seek
sexual release elsewhere during these weeks.

Sexual intercourse may continue up to the time of labor if three
conditions are met: (1) if there is no pain during the act; (2) if the fetal
membrane is intact; and (3) if there is no spotting or bleeding. It now appears
that, unless these adverse conditions exist, coital abstinence during pregnancy
and after delivery (that is, after the time postpartum vaginal bleeding has
stopped and any vaginal incisions have healed) is not called for. To the
contrary, sexual intercourse during this period probably should be encouraged, if the woman is psychologically disposed toward it. However, whether or
not sexual intercourse should take place during the third trimester and the

early postpartum period is an *individual* matter that should be decided by the woman and her physician, without the latter's arbitrarily following a set of rules that are not equally applicable to all women. If, for some reason, coition is contraindicated, most couples would benefit from an understanding of the value of masturbation and of mutual sexual stimulation to relieve both the husband's and the wife's sexual tensions during this time.

FALLACY:

THE OLDER MAN HAS NO ADVANTAGES OVER A YOUNGER ONE INSOFAR AS SEXUAL ACTIVITY IS CONCERNED.

FACT:

A primary requisite in successful sexual intercourse is prolonging the act sufficiently to allow each partner time to attain sexual gratification. The fault is usually the man's when coitus is too brief an experience, and the reason typically lies in his inability to control his ejaculatory processes. The fact that men between the ages of fifty and seventy have much better control of ejaculation than younger men do gives the silver-haired lover a unique advantage.

It is true, of course, that certain changes occur in all physiological processes, including the sexual one, after a man has passed fifty summers. If a man is wise enough to acquaint himself with these changes and philosophical enough to accept them, there is little reason why he cannot continue to have a thoroughly satisfactory sexual life. And because of his increased ejaculatory control, he holds an important key to being a highly satisfactory lover.

Most older men attain an erection more slowly than younger men do. The older man may require several minutes of sexual stimulation, whereas only a few seconds are typically needed for a young man to achieve a strong erection. Older men do not experience the same degree of elevation of the testicles during sexual excitement that they did during their younger years, nor is the secretion of precoital fluid nearly so copious; in fact, the latter may be absent altogether. The older man may be able to prolong, and satisfactorily so, the plateau phase of sexual response (the period of sexual excitement and pleasure preceding orgasm) for a considerably longer time than a young man can. But the pattern of his orgasmic phase alters slightly with advancing years, and orgasm itself may not last quite as long as it did in the past. The prostate of the older man does not contract with the same frequency and vigor during orgasm as that of the younger man. Furthermore, the expulsive force in the older man's ejaculation is reduced considerably, and the seminal fluid that his body produces gradually diminishes (by almost 50%). These indications of reduced physiological functioning are what frighten the aging man into the false belief that he is losing his ability to perform in a sexually satisfactory manner; but leisurely erections, less vigorous prostatic contractions, and diminished ejaculate or ejaculatory force do not affect the ultimate aim of fulfilling sexual activity: intercourse that brings orgasmic gratification to the man and his partner.

The aging man may lose his erection rather rapidly after ejaculation and may not be able to function again sexually for several hours, or perhaps even for a few days. If he or his partner desires coitus more frequently than the man's erectile ability would ordinarily permit, there is a way to get around the problem. The man should discontinue intercourse before he reaches orgasm, whereupon he can easily attain another erection within a short time with minimal sexual stimulation, and can once more begin the act of sexual intercourse. The main thing that the older man should remember is that, although his ejaculatory ability does not keep pace with his ability to attain and maintain an erection, he should not become anxious about it. By way of compensation, he now has the ability to prolong intercourse with considerable pleasure for an indefinite period of time. Many an aging man may still feel that he "can go twice"; but that thought always occurs to him before "the first time," after which he realizes that the ability existed in his mind and not in his body.

Masters and Johnson emphasize the importance of the older man's accepting two physiological facts: that he does not lose his capability for erection at any time (except perhaps in those rare instances of injury or pathology in erectile centers), and that the loss of erectile ability is not to be expected as a natural part of the aging process. "Therefore my age is as a lusty winter . . . ," said Shakespeare.

FALLACY:

>THE UTERUS "SUCKS UP" SEMINAL FLUID EJACULATED
>INTO THE VAGINA.

FACT:

The premise is an old one that the uterus during orgasm acts in such a manner as to suck up the seminal fluid from the vagina through the cervix and into its cavity, thus aiding in the migration of sperm. This theory was given credence by the Kinsey researchers in 1953, who, in addition to their own observations, listed a sizable bibliography of other researchers who also supported the theory. The theory is apparently based on the knowledge that the cervical opening (the passage, the size of a drinking straw, connecting the vagina and the uterus) widens slightly in the orgasmic phase of sexual response, and that the uterus reacts in some way at the time of orgasm.

Masters and Johnson (*Human Sexual Response*) have cast serious doubt on the theory because of the reactions of the uterus, clinically recorded by them, during orgasm. They established that the uterus does indeed contract several times in orgasm (the number of contractions depending upon the intensity of the response). They observed, however, that the flow of the contractions is from the top of the uterus, called the "fundus," toward the cervix, the lower segment of the uterus. The contractions, which are quite similar in action to those of the first stage of labor, would therefore tend to expel, rather than to draw up, any matter at the uterine opening.

Masters and Johnson demonstrated that, in sexual excitement and ultimate orgasm, there is a "tenting" effect of the vagina, meaning that its inner portion balloons to two or three times its normal dimensions. This vaginal ballooning is the result, in part, of the elevation of the uterus into the lower abdomen as fully as its supporting tissue and ligaments will allow. In the course of elevation, the uterus pulls the cervix with it away from its usual resting position against the lower back of the vaginal wall. Some investigators have perhaps erroneously concluded that, in the process of elevation, the uterus produces a vacuum or sucking effect.

In a demonstration using six subjects, Masters and Johnson filled a cap with a radiopaque fluid that matched as nearly as possible the characteristics of seminal fluid immediatley after ejaculation. The cap was fitted over the cervix of each subject, who then underwent an orgasmic experience during which X-rays were made; X-rays were also made ten minutes after orgasm had occurred. There was not the slightest evidence that the uterus exerted any sort of sucking effect on the fluid; nor did the X-rays reveal the presence of the fluid in either the cervical canal or the uterine cavity. Therefore, it must be assumed that the motility of sperm after ejaculation receives no external assistance, at least until after they have made their way into the uterus.

The migration of sperm after ejaculation is dependent upon the whipping motion of their tails. It is true that, in women who achieve orgasm, the cervical opening often dilates slightly. But this phenomenon occurs *after* orgasm, and persists for twenty or thirty minutes. While dilation could help, in an inactive way, the sperm on their journey to the uterus, the positions of the inserted penis and of the cervical opening during coitus are such that the seminal fluid is not deposited at the cervical opening at all. In fact, the penis itself may block the entrance to the uterus, the ejaculate thereby collecting underneath the penis on the vaginal floor.

There is evidence to support the belief that sperm are aided in their migration through the uterus once they enter it, and through the Fallopian tubes, by some chemical, enzyme, or other action. But these effects have not been identified, and they do not cause the uterus to suck up seminal fluid into its cavity.

————

FALLACY:

A WOMAN'S REPEATED SEXUAL EXPERIENCES WITH ONE MAN WILL LEAVE A MARK ON A CHILD LATER FATHERED BY ANOTHER MAN.

FACT:

The influence of a "previous sire" on a later conception is a theory known as *telegony*. Despite its rather widespread acceptance among breeders of animals, and regardless of the writings of such scientists as Charles Darwin, there is no scientific basis for the theory, whether one is discussing humans or animals. Inadequate knowledge of the laws of heredity and unscientific methods of observation and control in animal breeding have led some people to the conclusion that, on the human level, the offspring of a second husband might be affected by the wife's having had sexual intercourse with her first husband or having been impregnated by him. There are cases wherein a woman, who had previously borne the children of a Negro man and then had later married a white man, subsequently bore children with "Negro traits." However, these latter children were either fathered by a man with "Negro traits," or the woman had some Negro blood in her own heritage. It is genetically impossible for a causal relationship to exist between her having had a Negro as her first husband and her giving birth, after marriage to a white man, to children with negroid features.

A common occurrence appearing to give credence to the telegony theory concerns female dogs. Bitches remain in heat for several days, during which time they may mate with several males. Since female dogs have the maddening capacity for escaping the watchful eyes of their owners and mating with almost any male that happens along, it is quite possible for them to give birth to a litter of puppies of which none resembles the intended sire.

There is in this instance no "carry-over" from the bitch's previous matings; it is simply that the puppies of the same litter have been sired by different dogs.

———

FALLACY:

HUMANS CAN GET "HUNG UP" (I.E., EXPERIENCE *PENIS CAPTIVUS*) DURING SEXUAL INTERCOURSE.

FACT:

This is another faulty notion that results from man's observing the behavior of animals and attributing the same possibility to himself. Dogs do get "hung up" because of the peculiar anatomical structure of the male dog's sexual organs. There is a bone in the animal's penis (*os penis*) that enables him to penetrate the bitch's vagina before full erection. With ensuing tumescence, the penis fills the vaginal barrel, and a knot-like swelling appears on each side of it. At the same time, the walls of the bitch's vagina swell. All of these changes serve to "trap" the penis and prevent its withdrawal before ejaculation and detumescence, at which time the knotty swellings disappear, allowing the penis to be withdrawn with ease.

Most people have heard stories of couples who became locked together while copulating, the services of a physician being required before the penis could be released. The story is characteristically told as the truth and as having happened to a friend (or to a friend of a friend), although no one has ever witnessed the phenomenon or experienced it. It is true that several years ago a physician wrote an article for a medical journal reporting a case of a man's penis having been trapped in his partner's vagina; he later admitted that it was a hoax.

It is, of course, possible for a woman to experience sudden strong muscle spasms of the vagina (*vaginismus*) during sexual intercourse, and for the vagina momentarily to tighten around her partner's penis. But even in these circumstances, the pain or fear that the man would experience would cause loss of erection, permitting easy withdrawal of the penis. There are *no* scientifically verified cases of *penis captivus* among humans in modern medical literature.

======

Sex Drive

In this section I shall discuss several mistakes people commonly make in their thinking with respect to the human sex drive. The most unfortunate of these concerns older men and women, who are too often assumed to have laid aside their sexuality at some arbitrarily set middle age (usually about fifty); sex is commonly viewed as an inappropriate pastime at their age and station in life. Yet the human sex drive typically does not fold its tent and steal away, even though its intensity and pattern of expression may alter. The older person, thinking that it is unseemly to have sexual yearnings after the heyday of youth, tends to suppress and thereby destroy his own sex drive. It is extremely important for an older person to understand what to expect of himself (and what not to expect) after he has reached middle age. Otherwise he may be cheating himself of an essential means of warmth and comfort in his declining years.

The belief in aphrodisiacs, like the wistful hope that there is, after all, a fountain of youth, is perhaps universal and apparently deathless. Yet has there ever existed a substance — drink, food, or drug — that can truly stimulate the sex drive to great (or greater) heights?

There are other beliefs about the sex drive that need clarification. One is that the sex drive will dwindle and disappear altogether as a result of "using up" one's preordained endowment of sexual experiences. Another concerns sterilization as a means of birth control — a simple procedure in the male, hence a valuable means of birth prevention. Many men, however, resist sterilization, as they fear it will be followed inevitably by an ever-diminishing interest in sex. Much more serious is the anguish of the man or woman who, for medical reasons, must undergo surgical castration, or whose sex-hormone-producing organs otherwise have ceased to function. Yet there is usually no *reason for despair even in these cases. And of course there is the old saw about the sex drive of the black man being more powerful than that of the white man — a matter of envy rather than anxiety, to be sure.*

All these fears, doubts, and curiosities can be satisfied if the physiological factors governing the sex drive are understood. I have undertaken to explain those factors in this section.

———

FALLACY:

EACH INDIVIDUAL IS ALLOTTED JUST SO MANY SEXUAL EXPERIENCES, AND WHEN THEY ARE USED UP, SEXUAL ACTIVITY IS FINISHED FOR THAT PERSON.

FACT:

This notion has troubled mankind for centuries, yet it is totally false. In fact, the degree of sexual activity that humans are capable of maintaining throughout the years seems to be correlated in quite the opposite way. The earlier men or women mature physically, the longer their sexual reproductive ability continues; and the more sexually active a person is, and the earlier the age at which he begins that activity, the longer it continues into old age. These observations do not mean necessarily that if a person starts his sex life early he is guaranteed a longer and consistently vigorous sex life. They mean, rather, that the person with a stronger sex drive than average will, ordinarily, commence sexual activity earlier in life and continue it longer.

A similar fallacious assumption is that men have only a certain amount of semen or a certain number of sperm cells in their bodies; and that once the supply has been used up, no further reservoirs remain and no further manufacture is possible. Certainly this argument has been used, often with detrimental results, by adults in an attempt to discourage boys from masturbating. Most boys have heard that each ejaculation takes from his body some fantastic amount of protein, blood, strength, and the like, most of which, they are warned, will be difficult to replace — if replacement is possible at all. Experts in hormonal functioning have shown that the chemical constituents of semen are constantly being replenished by a normal intake of food, and that the production of sperm is also a continuing process. Ejaculated sperm are, therefore, easily and quickly replaced in the healthy body.

It is a physical near-impossibility for a person to experience orgasm or ejaculation too often. When one has functioned to his or her physiological limit, the sexual act becomes repellent; and, for the man, it becomes impossible to perform. After a normal rest or recovery period, however, both the desire and the ability to engage in sexual activity return to normal.

FALLACY:

OLDER MEN SHOULD NOT EXPECT TO REMAIN SEXUALLY ACTIVE; BUT IF THEY ARE STILL POTENT, THEY LIMIT SUCH ACTIVITY TO MARITAL COITUS.

FACT:

In considering the decline in older men's sexual activity, I think it is only fair to say that, on the basis of present-day research, it is not really possible to separate the emotional elements involved from the purely physiological ones in the decline of older men's sexual activity. Perhaps the decrease is due primarily to a general physiological degeneration. The reduced physiological capacity, however, is no doubt affected by psychological fatigue. The older man may simply have lost interest in the constant repetition of the same sexual experience, having exhausted the possibilities of exploring new techniques, making new contacts, or having intercourse in new situations.

The question, I think, quite naturally arises — of two men aged seventy, just why, from a physical standpoint, does one function sexually with satisfaction, while the other does not? Masters and Johnson maintain that *regularity* of sexual expression throughout the years of adult life is the crucial factor. And this regularity, they say, is essential for both men and women if they wish to maintain satisfactory sexual functioning beyond their youth and middle years. Their conclusions are borne out by Kinsey, who also found a close correlation between sexual-activity levels in the earlier years and those in the later years.

There may not be a cause-and-effect relationship here, since what is demonstrated might simply be that those with the strongest sex drive in their youth maintain it in old age. But the conclusions of such researchers as Masters and Johnson and the Kinsey group do demolish the ancient myth that one can "use oneself up sexually." It is strange and wondrous to know that some people still persist in the belief that the loss of one drop of semen in ejaculation is equivalent to the loss of forty drops (or a pint or a quart!) of blood. (Actually, the supply of semen is replenished by the body in much the same way that saliva is.) As a Polish physician observed recently, "The most effective way to secure the longest possible functioning of organs is by letting them work continuously and systematically." The point of this observation has significance for all of us: We should try to maintain our intellectual, physical, and sexual capabilities as long as possible through consistent use of them all.

If an older man is married, what are the *psychological* reasons that cause him to lose interest in sex? Masters and Johnson had some observations on this subject, and they listed as being of major importance such factors as monotony of the sexual relationship (taken to mean boredom with the wife); preoccupation with career or other economic pursuits; and fear of sexual failure. Probably the single most important factor in the older man's loss of sexual interest in his wife is monotony. The wife may have grown slovenly — often a matter that could be corrected through diet or more careful dressing habits — and thereby has become physically repulsive to the husband. Or the couple through the years have allowed sex to become a mechanical activity, totally lacking in imagination. A study made by Dr. A. L. Wolbarst of one hundred consecutive cases of older patients who had come to him for treatment of impotency revealed that many of them were impotent only with their wives.

It is unfair, of course, to place all the blame on the ladies for the sexual decline of a marriage in later years. As a man grows older, he often becomes much too caught up in his career and outside interests to maintain appropriate concern for the home and its occupants, leading to a growing detachment of the partners and a general breakdown in communication between them. Or he may overdo unaccustomed sports activities on the weekends, or eat and drink too much, or be suffering from the mental exhaustion of a "bad day at the office," all of which sap his sexual energies.

It might be pointed out that, even with a new partner and the exciting new stimulus that she frequently provides to heighten a man's virility, men almost always revert to their old level of sexual functioning within a comparatively short time. Some research done with aging rats is of interest, I think. The animals' sexual adequacy increased when they were given a chance for copulation with a number of female partners. However, as soon as the males reached a certain age, the stimulating effect of variety became less and less, and eventually copulation ceased altogether.

Quite obviously, sexual activity at any age must be suspended when one of the couple is ill. But, unfortunately, physicians themselves are ill-informed about physiological responses during sexual stimulation, and often unnecessarily caution their patients to abstain from sex during and after an illness. This is particularly true of people who have had heart attacks. Fortunately, specialists are coming to realize that their heart patients may safely engage in coitus under carefully regulated conditions; and that the tension generated by sexual frustration frequently is more harmful than the tension generated by sedate and relaxed intercourse.

Heterosexual contacts are not, of course, the only source of sexual outlet available to the older person. There is, first of all, homosexuality. From a study done of some 1700 men whose average age was sixty-four, it emerged that over 6% had engaged in homosexual acts after they had reached the age of sixty. Surprisingly, homosexual behavior had not been an important source of sexual expression to them since they were teen-agers — in fact, the vast majority were married or were widowed. For most of their adult lives, then, they had lived an entirely heterosexual married life.

Although this group included men from diverse backgrounds, from agricultural workers to professional men, the researchers did not consider them strictly typical. Even so, that the homosexual pattern emerged after the age of sixty is most interesting. Why did these men turn to homosexuality? The men themselves, all in good physical and mental health, placed great emphasis on the empathy they felt for their male sexual companions. In fact, they felt that the sexual activity was perhaps of less importance than the warmth and sensitivity they found in their partners. They considered themselves quite masculine (and so did the researchers), and they likewise considered their partners to be very virile; in fact, they expressed a certain revulsion for effeminate men. Some stated that they had become practically impotent with women by this time of their lives, but found themselves fully potent with some of their homosexual partners. The overriding need, then, was for affection, something the subjects felt they were not getting in sufficient degree (for whatever reason) from their families. As people grow older, sometimes their need for affection also grows, and the need for sexual satisfaction may increase accordingly.

It is true that some of these men felt guilty about their homosexual behavior because of religious and social disapproval. But they confessed that, guilty or not, they did not have inner resources strong enough to renounce the relationships. However, if the percentage revealed by this research is reasonably accurate, one can see that homosexuality among elderly men constitutes a relatively small source of sexual outlet.

After coitus, the most important source of sexual outlet for both sexes in later life is masturbation. About 59% of unmarried women between fifty and seventy years of age admit to masturbating. Approximately 30% of older women supplement marital coitus with masturbation; as a matter of fact, masturbation is the only mode of sexual behavior for women that does not decrease after marriage. And about 25% of men above the age of sixty-five masturbate regularly. Masturbation, then, is certainly not a practice limited to the immature, despite public opinion to the contrary. It is a valid source of sexual release for those of maturity and advanced years. Since many older people are quite troubled by the fact that they masturbate, it seems to me that those in a position to advise the elderly — clergy, physicians, and psychologists — should try to help them to accept masturbation as a legitimate way of releasing sexual tensions. This advice is valid for women, as well as for men.

FALLACY:

NEGROES HAVE GREATER SEX DRIVE THAN WHITES; THE PENIS OF THE NEGRO MALE IS LARGER THAN THAT OF THE WHITE MALE

FACT:

There is no scientific evidence to support the contention that one race is more sexually active than another. The basis for the prevalent notion that Negroes are sexually more immoderate than whites lies, to a great extent, in certain general conclusions of research groups. Their findings reveal a greater amount of sexual activity among poorly educated Americans of low socioeconomic status than among those who are more fortunate. Since a greater number of black citizens — sadly, a majority — fall into the first group than whites do, many people erroneously conclude that racial, rather than environmental or class, factors account for the differences in sexual activity. A Duke University investigation into sexual behavior during the human aging process demonstrated that black subjects between the ages of sixty and ninety-three were more active sexually than whites, but the researchers also pointed out that the black subjects were of the lower economic classes.

We have also been taught — mistakenly — that people from culturally and economically deprived classes are more primitive and aggressive (and thus, presumably, more sexually potent) than are people from higher classes. This prejudicial belief exaggerates in many people's minds the sexual powers of the Negro. Generally, studies show that when economic and educational levels are carefully matched between blacks and whites, there is little, if any, difference in the sexual attitudes and behavior of the two groups.

Many people have the idea that the Negro's penis is larger than the white man's, and that the larger the penis, the greater the man's sexual powers. Many studies have proven that the size of the penis has absolutely nothing to do with the sexual ability of a man, except in those cases in which hormonal deficiency has stunted both penile growth and sexual drive. It is believed by some that because body configurations of black and white males are somewhat different, the flaccid penis of the Negro is accordingly slightly larger than that of the white man. Scientific investigations that involved careful measurement of the sex organs have shown that, indeed, the flaccid penis of the average black male is slightly longer than that of the white man. However, there appears to be little or no relationship between the size of any penis when flaccid and its size when erect.

FALLACY:

ALCOHOL IS A SEXUAL STIMULANT.

FACT:

"Lechery [drink], sir, provokes, and unprovokes; it provokes the desire, but it takes away the performance...." These words, spoken in Shakespeare's *Macbeth*, are an accurate summary of the effect of alcohol on a man's sexual capacity.

From a physiological standpoint, alcohol acts as a depressant on the neurological system and, as such, can inhibit a person's sexual functioning as much as it impairs speech and motor coordination. The more intoxicated a person is, the more hindering and anesthetizing the effect of alcohol becomes. Grossly intoxicated persons, for instance, have been known to suffer severe injuries, and yet not to be aware of them at the time.

The anesthetic effects of alcohol are felt equally by both men and women; but the alcohol-induced sexual failure is more pronounced in a man, of course. Taken in large enough quantities, alcohol blocks the neural pathways that govern erection, causing temporary impotence that cannot be overcome, even with a very strong sexual desire and hard determination, until the alcohol loses its anesthetizing effect on the body. Few things are more incongruous or, alas for the male, distressing than the mating of a firm determination with a soft penis. Old Crow, then, may well be one of virtue's greatest protectors!

A woman, of course, is capable of sexual intercourse when she is drunk (or asleep, or dead, for that matter). But her chances of achieving a satisfactory orgasm, or any orgasm at all, are greatly diminished because of alcohol's deadening effect on all nerve centers, including those in the vulval area, the lower spinal cord, and the brain, all of which work together to produce the orgasmic response.

But alcohol works two ways. If it is taken in too great quantities, it chokes off sexual responsiveness in both men and women. In moderate quantities, however, it may serve to reduce fears and guilt feelings that would otherwise interfere with sexual performance and sexual enjoyment. Herein, no doubt, lies the explanation for drink's undeserved reputation as an aphrodisiac, a sexual stimulant.

Herein also lies its real danger. Since alcohol intake generally makes one more reckless than one would be cold sober, all too often it removes inhibitions and self-control that are essentially self-protective. How often has one heard, "He got me drunk, or I never would have . . . ." Or, ruefully, from the boy, "How could I ever have gone to bed with *her*?" Just as driving and alcohol do not mix, neither do drinking and certain sexual behavior, except to create a potentially disillusioning or dangerous situation, unless the couple know beforehand what they might do under the influence of drink and are willing to accept the consequences.

It is true that some couples whose sexual adjustment is being hampered by anxieties, fears, or tension may find it advisable to have a light drink before joining one another in bed. Furthermore, there are other tensions unrelated to sex that nevertheless act as inhibitors to sexual impulses. As examples: the man's stress from an upsetting day at the office, the boss having outdone himself as the King of the S.O.B.s; or the woman's tension following a harrowing day in which the washing machine broke down and the triplets had diarrhea. In these cases, the physically deterrent effect of alcohol is outweighed by its emotional effect in reducing the anxiety that is interfering with sexual responsiveness.

The use of alcohol in certain instances, then, may be quite sensible and helpful. But if alcohol remains a necessary ingredient in a couple's sex life, it would seem much wiser to get rid of the sexual inhibitions through some form of psychotherapy, rather than continue to mask them with 90 proof.

FALLACY:

CERTAIN SUBSTANCES ARE VALUABLE AS APHRODISIACS.

FACT:

Since the dawn of mankind, I suspect, men (especially, but women, too) have been intensely interested in bolstering their flagging sexual desire and capacity. Through the ages, an incredible variety of unrelated foods, drinks, herbs, drugs, and wondrous mechanical devices have enjoyed the reputation of being sexual stimulants, although the popularity of most as such has been brief. Of this collection, foods more than the rest have historically dominated the field for their alleged sexually arousing properties. (There are today, in fact, a number of "aphrodisiac cookbooks" on the market.) The aphrodisiac reputation of certain foods probably came about because either (1) they were new and were therefore assumed to have mystical powers of sexual rejuvenation; or (2) they bear a superficial resemblance to sexual organs, and the ancient "doctrine of signatures" could therefore be applied: the cure for an ill lies in something resembling it. For example, extracts from yellow flowers were used in the treatment of jaundice, a red cloth to counteract the effect of scarlet fever, and the application of a bloodstone in the treatment of hemorrhage. The skull lichen, shaped like its name, was used to treat epilepsy; it was considered particularly effective if found on a skull in a cemetery rather than on its usual host, a rock or tree!

When potatoes, for instance, were first introduced to Europe, they were thought to be sexual stimulants. One finds reference to them in Shakespeare. "Let the sky rain potatoes . . . ; let a tempest of provocation come"; and in Beaumont and Fletcher: "Will your ladyship have a potatoe-pie? 'Tis a stirring good dish for an old lady after a long lent. . . ."

For centuries, many civilizations have celebrated religious occasions by feasting on foods shaped like sexual organs, especially breads and pastries. Possibly the two foods most celebrated in the history of aphrodisiacs are truffles and oysters, which bear a superficial likeness to testicles. (I saw a bumper sticker on the freeway recently which read: "Eat Louisiana oysters — and love longer.") Other such foods are the banana, of obvious similarity to the penis, and the vanilla root, shaped like a vagina. In fact, the word *vanilla* is a composite of Spanish and Latin words meaning "sheath" and "vagina." In one of the most obvious applications of the "doctrine of signatures," many Chinese place unshakable belief in the potency of the horn of the rhinoceros (powdered, to be sure). It is not difficult to see how the succinct word *"horny"* came to have the meaning of "strong sexual desire" in the vernacular.

However, chemical analysis of these and countless other foodstuffs alleged to be sexually arousing reveals nothing that could have any significant physical effect on the complicated genital structure of either man or woman. Why, then, do people continue to place such unwarranted value on these foods as aphrodisiacs? First of all, it is often difficult to distinguish between fact and folklore; few of us are experts on the properties of various foods, and fewer still on the physiology of sexual desire. The psychological impact, therefore, of *believing* that raw bull's testicles ("prairie oysters," as they are sometimes called), or clams, or celery, or tomatoes are aphrodisiac is sometimes strong enough to produce, at least for a while, an elevation in sexual desire and performance. What was only a temporary triumph — and a psychological one at that — is considered to be a direct result of consuming a "wonder" food, and the discovery is passed on to the next person wishing to be transported to new heights of sexual capacity.

A further psychological influence is the strong association between hunger and sex as the most powerful of physiological drives. To be sure, highly nutritive foods are essential to optimum physical well-being and functioning. For certain sensuous people there is, in fact, a distinct aphrodisiac effect in a gourmet meal that is served leisurely and elegantly in an atmosphere of candlelight and lovely music. (The German nutritionist Dr. Hans Balzli wrote, "After a perfect meal we are more susceptible to the ecstacy of love than at any other time . . . .") The sex drive of most men and women, however, decreases significantly after a meal, especially a heavy one. Furthermore, it has been demonstrated time and again that those who are overweight and consistently overeat suffer from decreased sexual drive and ability.

The only persons for whom food can act as an aphrodisiac are the nutritionally deprived and those whose hunger is severe and threatening. Studies made during World War II, for instance, have shown that sexual drive decreased in direct proportion to the degree of hunger that the individual was experiencing. As hunger became a more and more relentless companion, food became almost an obsession, crowding out sexual thoughts entirely.

In recent years two drugs have acquired a considerable reputation as aphrodisiacs. The first, *cantharides* (Spanish Fly), is derived from dried and pulverized beetles. It causes an irritation of the urinary tract which, in turn, causes blood to accumulate in the irritated region. This accumulation is often sufficient to produce an erection, sometimes an unpleasantly protracted one and usually unaccompanied by sexual desire. This reaction to cantharides may be quite valuable in the effort to mate reluctant cattle, who then copulate mainly to relieve their great discomfort, but the treatment is hardly recommended for humans. Furthermore, Spanish Fly is poison; when it is taken by men in sufficient dosage to produce an erection, its effects may be not only unpleasant but deadly as well.

The other drug is *yohimbine*, derived from the bark of a tree that is native to Africa. Its primary use in most nations has been as a diuretic and in the treatment of such disorders as neuritis and meningitis. But yohimbine also stimulates the lower-spine nerve centers controlling erection and has long been used by African natives for sexual arousal. As one might suspect, authorities are divided in their opinion of its effectiveness as an aphrodisiac. In any case, the drug is obtainable only upon prescription.

One also hears of the aphrodisiac qualities of both arsenic and strychnine, which, when given in the proper (very small) doses, are said to heighten sensitivity to several stimuli. A drop too much, obviously, and the problem ceases to be one of mere sexual sluggishness. There are, of course, claims made for the aphrodisiac effects of various addicting or habituating drugs — hashish, opium, morphine, cocaine, marijuana, and LSD. These drugs, like alcohol, release inhibitions, which are at the root of many problems of impaired sexual functioning. But, like alcohol, drugs taken in large enough quantities usually have the opposite effect of an aphrodisiac. I do not propose to go into the medical and psychological aspects of drug-taking because of their wide coverage elsewhere. It should be sufficient to say that their use as an aphrodisiac or for any other purpose is illegal, except upon a medical prescription. I might also add that it is illegal throughout the United States to administer any alleged aphrodisiac for the purpose of seducing another person.

The most successful means today of dealing with faulty sex drives come under two headings. First and by far the most important is the psychological approach; for although erection and orgasm are physical phenomena, the forces controlling (or hindering) them are in the mind. Second is the physical approach; there are some sexual conditions (although not nearly as many in healthy people as is commonly thought) that may be successfully treated with medication or hormone therapy.

Recently there have been intriguing reports of the accidentally discovered aphrodisiac effects of two drugs used for quite different purposes. One, called PCPA, has been used experimentally to treat schizophrenia and certain types of tumors. The other, L-dopa, is being prescribed, no longer experimentally, for patients suffering from Parkinson's disease (called "the shaking palsy"). Many L-dopa patients have shown dramatic remission of their disease symptoms, but the side effect in some 2% of them has been hyper-sexuality — e.g., some elderly male patients who had not had coitus in five years began engaging in it daily. Similar results have been reported in the use of PCPA.

Unfortunately, optimism about the aphrodisiac qualities of both PCPA and L-dopa must be tempered with several notes of caution. They are both powerful drugs, and all their effects and side effects have not yet been fully measured. The large-scale experimentation needed to determine their specific aphrodisiac potentials has been conducted only with animals, and the extrapolation of these experimental results to humans is not warranted. However, human experimentation appears justified in the case of these two drugs, although one is wary of the usual excitement attending anything new that is alleged to be aphrodisiac. Perhaps in this era in which man has walked on the moon, yet another impossible dream will be realized — alleviation of the tragic afflictions of impotency and frigidity through the use of a true sexual stimulant.

———————

FALLACY:

ONCE A MAN OR WOMAN IS STERILIZED, SEX DRIVE DIMINISHES.

FACT:

The most common form of sterilization for women is an operation known as a salpingectomy, a procedure in which the tubes leading from the ovaries to the uterus (Fallopian tubes) are cut and tied. This prevents the woman's eggs (which are released by the ovaries into the tubes) and the man's sperm from uniting, thus preventing pregnancy. Women also become sterile when they undergo a hysterectomy, an operation in which the uterus (as well as the ovaries, sometimes) is removed. In comparison with a salpingectomy, a hysterectomy is a much more drastic surgical procedure and is rarely performed solely for purposes of sterilization.

Following a salpingectomy there will be no noticeable change in a woman's sexual function, other than her inability to conceive a child. When the uterus only is removed in a hysterectomy, menstruation ceases, but there is no change in hormonal functioning. In those relatively rare cases in which the ovaries are removed as well, certain vital hormonal production also stops, and the woman's sexual desire may decrease. But these adverse effects can be counteracted with hormonal treatment. Otherwise, with the fear of unwanted pregnancy permanently removed, it is logical to expect that sterilization might strengthen a woman's sex drive. Furthermore, coitus may now take on a greater spontaneity, since it is no longer necessary to anticipate the event with jellies, foams, or daily contraceptive pills, preparations that may well have been irksome to her or her husband through the years.

With respect to men, the usual method of sterilization is a vasectomy — also a cutting and tying of tubes, in this case the vas deferens, which transport sperm from the testicles. Since the incision is made through the scrotum, men frequently fear that they will be castrated by vasectomy. (Following castration, which means the removal of the testicles, sexual desire typically dwindles over the years unless hormonal therapy is administered, because natural production of male hormones in the testicles is, of course, no longer possible.) The fear is totally without foundation; sterilization and castration are *not* the same thing. Although the incision in a vasectomy is made through the scrotum, the testicles are in no way touched in the course of the surgery. Vasectomy is a quick, simple, and extremely effective method of birth control. It can usually be performed in the doctor's office, and if the patient follows a sensible routine for a few days, he should suffer no bad effects. Despite much lower percentages quoted by certain investigators, most authorities — including many from Planned Parenthood — state that a vasectomy can be undone with 60% to 80% chance of success if a man should decide later that he wishes to father a child.

As in the case of a woman who has undergone sterilization, one can logically expect that a man's sex drive might increase after a vasectomy. He no longer need be fearful of impregnating his wife — fear being a notorious detractor from sexual pleasure. Furthermore, he is either relieved of the obligation to pay careful attention to contraception himself, or is spared the unattractive aspects of his wife's contraceptive measures. Spontaneity, that great rejuvenator of sexual interest, is completely free to reenter the picture.

As a matter of fact, one survey, a typical one, revealed that of the vasectomized men interviewed, 74.2% experienced no change in sex drive, whereas 17.9% experienced an increase in desire. Only in a scant 7.9% was a small decrease noted.

FALLACY:

CASTRATION COMPLETELY DESTROYS THE SEX DRIVE.

FACT:

It is strange that castration is usually regarded as an event affecting only men. This assumption is incorrect, since, medically, castration means removal of the gonads of either sex — that is, a man's testicles or a woman's ovaries. In either case, the development of the reproductive cells — the male sperm or the female ova, or eggs — is permanently halted, as is the production of sex hormones. More women than men, as a matter of fact, undergo castration, yet they seem not to undergo the drastic changes in sexual responsiveness that men sometimes do. The male's sexual integrity appears to be greatly more threatened by castration than the female's is, which may possibly explain why castration is viewed as an ordeal afflicting only men.

Several physical conditions may necessitate the surgical removal of a man's testicles, notably cancer of the testes or of the prostate. The proliferation of prostatic cancer, as an example, is likely to be accelerated as long as the testicles continue to produce male hormones. Or, a man may have been the victim of an accident — war injuries immediately come to mind. When castration occurs after maturity, and nature is left to follow its course *without the supplemental assistance of hormonal injections* (notably testosterone), there is a gradual diminishing of potency and desire over a period of several years. In the absence of male hormones, there is also a degree of feminization. Ejaculation becomes less frequent and reduced in volume; it is the first male function to disappear, to be followed by inability to achieve erection and, finally, by loss of interest in sex.

The sexual waning in the castrated man is no doubt considerably aggravated by the emotional upset caused by the operation or accident. That an emotional upset or shock can prevent an erection in an uncastrated man, or cause an existing erection promptly to collapse, is well known. If the man feels that part of his manhood has been taken from him, if he is distressed over the fact that he cannot father a child, if he is embarrassed in the bedroom or locker room by his altered appearance, it is almost certain that his potency will be adversely affected. It takes a wise surgeon (who, incidentally, will often insert prosthetic testes in the patient's scrotum) and an understanding wife to overcome these assaults on the castrate's self-image.

If a man experiences castration after he has reached full sexual maturity, his sex drive will decrease only gradually over the years (in the absence of hormonal injections). This is especially true if the man has had considerable sexual experience. If, however, a youth is castrated before maturity, he will never develop a sex drive, nor will he be able to function sexually. The earlier the age at which castration occurs, the more drastic are its effects on sexuality.

The gradual decrease in a man's sex drive following castration often can be controlled by hormonal injections, as has been stated previously. Even so, hormonal production does not cease completely with the removal of the testicles, since other glands, notably the adrenal, continue to manufacture hormones in small amounts. This production should be supplemented by hormone therapy, however, whenever it is not contraindicated by the condition for which the castration was performed.

Castration in women is, in effect, a surgically induced menopause.

Whether the process is by knife or nature, when the ovarian production of female sex hormones ceases, the physiological effect is identical to that in the male whose testicles have been removed. Why then, one wonders, do women not experience more frequently the same change in responsiveness that men undergo?

In the Kinsey group's original study of the human female, the sampling included one hundred twenty-three women who had undergone surgical removal of the ovaries. From these women's histories, the researchers could find no evidence that the absence of normal hormonal levels affected their sexual interest, activity, or capacity for orgasm. Some of them, as a matter of fact, noted that their sexual desire had increased, perhaps because the threat of pregnancy had been permanently removed.

Kinsey went on to compare these castrated women with a slightly larger group of women who had gone through the menopause naturally. It is interesting that, in comparison with the castrated women, a larger percentage of the naturally postmenopausal women noted a decrease in sex interest and a smaller percentage of them experienced an increase in sexual responsiveness. Although Kinsey offered no explanation for these differences, the reason might well be that the castrated women were younger when they had the operation and had immediately begun sex-hormone therapy. Being younger, furthermore, they were likely to have younger husbands whose sexual vigor might have served as a stimulus to their own sexual interest to a greater extent than might be the case in naturally postmenopausal women.

The sexual activity of the postmenopausal women in Kinsey's sampling followed the same pattern of decline as that of the general sampling of women of the same age (including those who had not gone through menopause). His conclusion was that a woman's subsiding sexual activity after menopause either reflected her husband's declining interest in sex, or indicated that she was using the menopause as an excuse to stop the sexual activity she had never enjoyed in any case. It is fair to say that castration is sometimes blamed for sexual unresponsiveness when the cause, actually, is advancing age.

Among uncastrated men, there is a gradual diminishing of coital frequency as the years go by. The average twenty-year-old married male, for instance, engages in sexual intercourse 3.2 times a week; by the time he is sixty, the frequency has dwindled to 0.8 times a week. Of the men reaching fifty, 7% are already impotent and sexually unresponsive. Many castrations, therefore, occur after the man is descending the far side of the hill.

Some investigators contend that impotence is not an inevitable consequence of castration, even when hormonal treatment is withheld. They therefore hold that castration is an unreliable method of curbing sexual criminals and deviates. Potency may be reduced while desire is not, producing frustration that breaks out in yet further unacceptable sexual behavior.

From his research, Kinsey concluded that following castration many men (not all) retained sexual interest and potency, and that frequency and intensity of response may or may not be affected. These observations bring us to the consideration that the psychological aspects of the operation must be crucial in determining the man's postoperative sexual interest. Does a man become impotent and lose erotic desire after castration because he expects to be so cursed? Or, perhaps, because he wishes to be relieved of monotonous sexual obligations at home? Or because he was largely impotent even before the operation? One conclusion is inescapable: castration need not be a matter of despair to the man faced with it. Hormonal treatment and a positive attitude may very well be all he needs to assure his continued potency.

FALLACY:

MENOPAUSE OR HYSTERECTOMY TERMINATES A WOMAN's SEX LIFE.

FACT:

Kinsey and other researchers have shown that a woman's sexual desire usually continues undiminished until she is sixty years of age or older. This age is long after the age of menopause and its accompanying changes, and these findings clearly demonstrate that, ordinarily, no physical reasons exist for a woman's sex life to end because of menopause or hysterectomy.

It is understandable that, in the relatively unenlightened medical world of the 1880's, physicians would reason that, since the ovaries dwindle in their production of female sex hormones at and after the menopause, women's sex drive would accordingly decrease. It is now known that a woman's sex drive often does not diminish even when the ovaries are surgically removed. Hormones are only one of many factors affecting the capacity for sexual response; more crucial factors are the woman's emotional stability and attitude toward sex.

Total hysterectomy is the removal of the uterus; panhysterectomy is the removal of uterus, Fallopian tubes, and ovaries. In the first instance, there would not be even the physiological reason of hormonal imbalance to account for loss of sex drive; and, if the woman's surgeon carefully explains the effects of the operation, she should not experience any waning of sex drive because of psychological factors. If any change does occur, in fact, it might be in the direction of increased drive, since fear of pregnancy is removed. If ovaries and tubes are also removed, some hormonal changes will occur, although medication can make up any deficiencies.

Considering all the factors, a woman can expect her sex drive to remain at approximately the same intensity from the age of about thirty to sixty, despite menopause or hysterectomy. The main cause for the general decrease in a woman's sexual activity in the later years of her life is that either the husband's interest in sex is lukewarm, or he desires intercourse too infrequently to allow her all the sexual expression she needs or wishes; or there is no male sexual partner available. Given a sexually interested, active partner, the sex drive of a woman following menopause or hysterectomy will quite likely remain unimpaired.

FALLACY:

>SEX DESIRE AND ABILITY DECREASE MARKEDLY AFTER
>THE AGE OF FORTY TO FIFTY.

FACT:

Marital coitus among older men and their wives occurs considerably more frequently than is commonly realized. Of all men between the ages of sixty-five and sixty-nine, about 75% experience satisfactory coitus, as do about 60% of men between the ages of seventy and seventy-four and 48% of men between the ages of seventy-five and ninety-two. If that fails to inspire hope in all of us, consider the experiences of the subjects in one Kinsey investigation: one white male, aged seventy, still averaged seven ejaculations a week; and an eighty-eight-year-old man and his ninety-year-old wife reported that they still maintained an active sex life.

Seven out of ten healthy married couples who are sixty years of age or older remain sexually active, and the clinical observation is consistently made that those men and women with the strongest sex drive during their youth retain the greatest drive in their old age. It is a further clinical observation that maintaining a consistent pattern of sexual intercourse through the years of marriage is the best means of retaining vigorous sexual capacity in later years. Once interest is allowed to wane, it is difficult to rekindle. (It is interesting that elderly physicians seem to have one of the highest rates of impotency, while elderly clergymen, as a group, have one of the lowest.)

Studies of older men show that frequency of marital intercourse ranges from one to four times a month, with about 25% engaging in coitus four times a month. Even the 25% of older men whose sexual potency is unsatisfactory report that they engage in sexual intercourse three or four times a month. Over 60% of men seventy-five years or older report having occasional morning erections, and 17% report that the condition recurs frequently. It has generally been found that, among older people, Negroes are more sexually active than whites, and persons from low socioeconomic levels are more sexually active than those from the higher ones.

The sexual drive of older people generally follows their overall pattern of health and physical performance. It is true that from the age of forty, women begin to experience a sharp decrease in the secretion of the female sex hormone estrogen, a decrease that continues gradually for the remainder of their lives. Secretion of the male sex hormone androgen decreases from 55 units per 24 hours when a man is thirty years of age to about 8 units during the same period at the age of sixty; the secretion remains fairly constant thereafter. However, over 90% of the older men studied reported that they had no physical disability that interfered with sexual frequency. The factors that most often deter sexual activity in older men are such psychological agents as feelings of shame and guilt for having sexual needs and drives at their age, and the erroneous notion that older men are naturally unable to perform sexually.

It should be remembered that the decline in frequency of marital coitus after the first two years of marriage does not mean that there is necessarily a decline in interest in other forms of sexual activity. The incidence of female masturbation and nocturnal dreams involving orgasm increases after marriage and remains fairly steady at its maximum level until wives become sixty years of age or even older. Between the ages of twenty-one and twenty-five, 89% of a married woman's total sexual outlet is derived from marital coition. After the age of twenty-five there is a gradual but consistent decline, so that by the time she reaches the age of seventy, only 72% of her total sexual outlet is provided by marital coitus.

There is little evidence that aging produces any decline in the sexual capacity of women until, possibly, quite late in life. Apparently women struggle, with some success, through the years of marriage to throw off the inhibitory shackles forged by the taboos of their early sex education; and once they reach the maximum peak of sexual interest (between the ages of thirty-one and forty), they maintain this level. By this time, however, the husband's interest in sexual intercourse typically begins to slacken, with the unfortunate result of all-round frustration that frequently leads the wife to seek other means of sexual gratification. From the late teens to the age of forty-five and thereafter, the incidence of masturbation increases for all groups of women. The incidence rises from about 35% to 65% among single women, from 30% to 60% among the postmarital group, and from 25% to 45% among married women.

Older women, like older men, are quite capable of sexual intercourse and other forms of sexual activity. About 85% of all women aged fifty and 70% of those aged sixty continue to have intercourse with their husbands. Even of those women who no longer have husbands, 37% of the fifty-year-old group, 29% of the fifty-five-year-old group, and 12% of the sixty-year-old group continue to experience coitus.

Many women past sixty avoid having an orgasm because of the painful uterine cramping they often experience afterwards. This pain can be relieved by their taking the proper combination of estrogen and progesterone to correct the imbalance in the sex-steroid level caused by the aging process. However, despite some obvious and predictable physical changes resulting from aging, there are apparently no physiological agents that should prevent a woman in her postmenopausal years from continuing satisfactory sexual expression with the frequency of her younger years.

———

FALLACY:

THE PSYCHOLOGICAL NEED FOR SEXUAL EXPRESSION IS OF LESS IMPORTANCE IN THE LATER YEARS OF LIFE THAN DURING THE EARLIER YEARS.

FACT:

In the past, society's failure to recognize the sexual needs of its older members was a serious matter, but not a critical one. Today, there are more than 25 million people in the United States who have reached sixty-five years of age, and that figure is expected to reach 35 million by 1975. We cannot, therefore, afford any longer to support a pyramid of myths concerning the absence of sexual interest and capacity in such a large segment of the American population.

At the base of this pyramid of misconceptions about sex and the aged is a basically Victorian form of asceticism regarding human sexuality. This asceticism would impose sexual self-denial on those persons in our society who are beyond their reproductive years. According to this philosophy, it is "not quite nice" for older people to have sexual yearnings. (And the people subscribing to this philosophy quite likely never accepted the idea that their own parents had sexual intercourse.) On the level of idealism, there is yet another attitude prevalent in our society that works against sexual expression among older people — namely, the concept that links sex, love, and romance, holding that all three are provinces belonging solely to the young.

But older people *do* have sexual yearnings, and these desires are perfectly normal. Is it any wonder, though, that the older person is frequently bewildered by his sexual drive and is ashamed of it? The Victorian ethic pervading American sexual mores says that he should live in a sexless vacuum. His children very likely say, voicelessly, "Sex is for the young. Act your age." And it is entirely possible that the physician compounds his elderly patient's confusion and bewilderment by answering any questions having to do with sex by saying, "Well, what do you expect at your age?" Unless a physician is convinced of the psychological importance of sexual expression in the later years of life, he can do irreparable damage to his geriatric patient's sexuality, to say nothing of his general mental and physical health.

These older people are already unsure about their roles in this stage of life, which they have entered with very little preparation. Their children are gone from home and lead lives quite independent of their parents. The husband is often forced to retire from his job or profession before he is physically or mentally ready to do so. Quite likely both he and his wife are shoved aside as the young take over in social and community affairs.

From this enforced inactivity develops, understandably, the equation: "Young is good; old is bad." Thus is the cult of youth perpetuated and, along with it, the idea that "old" is a dirty word.

The key word in this discussion is *old*. But just how old is old? In terms of optimism, flexibility, and contribution, we all know people whom we judge to be old at twenty-five; conversely, would we not all agree that Picasso and Pablo Casals are young at ninety? When does the aging process actually begin? To grow old is certainly inevitable. And it may justifiably be said that the science of geriatrics begins where the science of pediatrics leaves off, for many of the alarming changes in body and mind that one commonly associates with advancing age often have their roots in earlier emotional and physical disorders that were never dealt with appropriately.

In these circumstances, senior citizens could obtain great psychological benefit from continued sexual-affectional relationships with their marriage partners. They are boxed in at this level because of the prevailing American attitude that equates the aging process with sexlessness. The resulting isolation and sexual frustration that many old people feel strike hard at their self-image, complicating and distorting all their interpersonal relationships. The public's tendency is to view aging as a disease, rather than as a normal process. This bias has not been altered to any great extent by the studies done of the aged, because these studies have focused on hospitalized or institutionalized older people, rather than on a sample of persons who are less afflicted with problems of physical health, emotional stability, or economics.

As I have already pointed out, the aging man has perhaps been forced to retire before he is ready. Along with the loss of his customary position of prestige, there may also be a loss of a healthy self-concept. He begins to *feel* old, sometimes long before he has begun to age significantly. A successful sexual relationship at this critical time of his life can provide him with much-needed warmth and comfort, and can be a highly effective source of self-assurance. After menopause, a woman also may find great reassurance in the sexual relationship with her husband. The feeling of being needed and loved at this time of her life is of great importance to her mental well-being; so also is the realization that she possesses the capacity of giving needed love and affection.

Since there is so much to be gained from continued sexual activity, and since intercourse is certainly physically possible in the later years of life, why, then, do so many older people shrink from it? For many of them, the popular attitude that the older person is sexless becomes a self-fulfilling prophecy. By extension, the elderly become uncertain of their sexual capacities and their power to please a sexual partner. For some older people, of course, sex has never played a very important part in their lives in any event, and the aging process conveniently provides them with a logical excuse for giving up the sexual activity that has always been, very likely, a source of anxiety to them.

The question naturally arises: Why hasn't present-day psychology done more to correct our society's prevailing attitude toward the aged and the aging process? The answer is probably that psychologists are as much caught up in the hang-ups of the society in which they live as doctors are. We must face the fact that we are a nation that is afraid, ignorant, and guilt-ridden about sex. We hear a great deal about sex education in the junior and senior high schools; it is probably needed as badly in night schools for adults.

Reproduction and Birth Control

Judging from the number of illegitimate and other unwanted pregnancies that occur in the world, it is obvious that much remains to be learned on the subject of how one becomes pregnant, the circumstances that make it likely, and how it can be prevented.

In this section, I shall discuss a few of the dangerously false beliefs that could lead to an unwanted pregnancy. With one exception, I do not propose to discuss the various techniques of contraception here, with their attendant advantages and disadvantages. The choice of a contraceptive is an individual matter, one best decided upon by each couple in consultation with a doctor. (I think that the husband should assuredly be part of the decision, because certain methods may be as irksome or distasteful to him as others may be to his wife. In either instance, the dissatisfaction will inevitably result in a corrosion of the couple's sexual enjoyment and adjustment.) If there is no doctor in whom the couple have sufficient confidence to consult on so personal a matter, then the logical place to seek information about contraception is the Planned Parenthood Center in their community.

The one contraceptive that I have discussed here is the Pill. This most effective of all contraceptives has recently fallen under suspicion because of questions raised in the Senate's hearings about its safety. The controversy has received wide publicity — understandably, because so many American women take the Pill. But both sides of the issue were not always fully stated in the news media. This lopsided presentation seems unfair because it has caused many women to abandon the Pill in alarm, thinking that what threatens the health of an extremely small minority of women poses an equal threat to all women. I have therefore attempted to evaluate birth-control pills in the context of their safety and possible side effects.

Other subjects having to do with birth prevention are also examined in this section. For example, a great deal of folklore has sprung up about the circumstances considered to be uniquely favorable or unfavorable to conception. Some girls think that conception is impossible if they hold themselves back from orgasm during intercourse; others think that restricting intercourse to a certain time of the menstrual month offers guaranteed safety against unwanted pregnancy. Still others think that as long as there is no penile penetration in sex play leading to ejaculation, conception is an impossibility.

Other aspects of conception and pregnancy are also discussed. The sex of a child is a matter of chance, although recent research has shown how to lengthen the odds before conception occurs that the baby will be of the sex desired by the parents. Nevertheless, many people cling to the belief that a variety of totally unrelated factors influence the sex of the unborn child. Still other mythology that enjoys extensive acceptance is the "marking" of a baby through some event, traumatic or otherwise, occurring before his birth. Most people have heard that the baby born two months prematurely has a better chance to survive than the baby born only one month early. Many of us have also heard, from those who allegedly had read of it in some obscure scientific journal, of strange creatures resulting from the union of a human and an animal. Or perhaps we have assumed the possibility because of childhood fascination with stories of Minotaur, mermaids, satyrs, or the race of centaurs; or because of the rare person — Tarzan, in literature, and the "wolf children" of India — who were human, but who grew up exclusively among animals.

———————

FALLACY:

THERE IS AN ABSOLUTELY "SAFE" PERIOD FOR SEXUAL INTERCOURSE INSOFAR AS CONCEPTION IS CONCERNED.

FACT:

The rhythm method of birth control is based on the premise that restricting intercourse to certain times of the menstrual month is a safeguard against conception. The premise is founded on four considerations: (1) that a woman can become pregnant only around the time of ovulation — the time of the month at which the ovum, or egg, is released by the ovary; (2) that ovulation usually occurs about fourteen days before the next menstrual cycle or period begins; (3) that the egg lives only about twenty-four hours after its release from the ovary; and (4) that sperm live only about forty-eight hours after their discharge into the vagina during intercourse. On the assumption that the menstrual cycle lasts twenty-eight days, it would then appear that the best time for conception is the fourteenth day of the cycle, plus a day or two before and after it. These extra days are added in order to take into consideration the life span of both sperm and eggs. Theoretically, one could thus assume that it is only during these vital five days — the two days before ovulation, the day it occurs, and the two days afterwards — that pregnancy can take place.

The theory is good, but, unfortunately, in practice it does not always work. Many women have such irregular periods that it is extremely difficult, if not impossible, to predict with any reasonable hope of accuracy the date of the next ovulation. Furthermore, the more irregular the cycles are, the greater the number of days that must be declared "unsafe" — much to the chagrin and frustration of these women and their husbands. The unreliability of the theory prompted the riddle: "What are people who use the rhythm method called?" To which the answer is: "Parents." Despite its low batting average as a successful birth control method, for religious reasons the rhythm method is the only acceptable one available to many people, causing some disgruntled couples to refer to it as "Vatican roulette."

It is thought that the menstrual cycles of 50% of all women vary in length as much as ten days. For that reason eminent researchers into ovulation in the context of a method of birth prevention — e.g., Ogino of Japan and Knaus of Austria — insist that any woman using this method of birth control must keep accurate records of her menstrual cycles for six to twelve months before embarking upon its use. Furthermore, it is essential that these records be interpreted by a doctor with some experience in the rhythm system or its allied method of "natural" birth control, the temperature system. This latter method requires that even more exacting records be kept. In addition to noting the date of each menstruation, a woman must make a daily recording of her temperature, at the same time of day, preferably upon awaking. The premise upon which the temperature system is based is that a woman's temperature drops sharply at the time of ovulation, and then makes a dramatic rise to a level above what it had been earlier in the month. It remains at the higher level until menstruation starts, at which time it drops to its preovulation level.

When allowance is made for fluctuations in the time of ovulation, plus the two days before and after, the time left that is considered "safe" against conception amounts to two-thirds to one-half of the month. But even a rigorous observance of the calendar or diligent recording of temperature is no guarantee of protection against unwanted pregnancy. Available data indicate that the rhythm and temperature methods offer 86% protection. This means that eighty-six of the hundred pregnancies that would have occurred among couples using no form of birth control would be prevented. The fourteen pregnancies that would occur, however, compare unfavorably with the results among couples employing certain other methods of birth prevention. For example, the Pill offers virtually 100% safety against unwanted pregnancy, while an intrauterine device, such as the loop, offers 97% to 98% protection.

Even the menstrual cycles of those women who are unusually regular can be thrown off by physical or psychological changes. Illness and shock, or even a change in altitude, for example, are known to bring about ovulation at a time that it would not normally be expected to occur.

It is well known that certain animals — notably the cat, rabbit, mink, and squirrel — ovulate only under the stimulation of copulation. It is now believed that some human females also respond to sexual excitement by discharging an egg — a reflex ovulation, as it has been called. This ovulation may occur at any time of the month, even though the woman may already have ovulated at the predictable time of the menstrual cycle. Furthermore, women who normally ovulate about the fourteenth day of the menstrual cycle can, for no apparent reason, ovulate at quite an unexpected time of the month. Such lack of cooperation on the part of nature may definitely thwart the most conscientious and motivated efforts on the part of the couple using rhythm or temperature as a birth-control means.

FALLACY:

SIMULTANEOUS CLIMAXES ARE NECESSARY IF
CONCEPTION IS TO TAKE PLACE.

FACT:

The best proof of the error in this belief is that a woman can be made pregnant through artificial insemination, at which time no orgasm — alone or simultaneous — occurs. The presence or absence of orgasmic response on the part of the woman has nothing to do with whether or not she becomes pregnant. If she produces a mature healthy egg that is penetrated by a normal sperm, conception has taken place.

Because of the coincidental occurrence in man of the sexual climax and the ejaculation of seminal fluid, it is sometimes mistakenly believed that a woman similarly does not produce an ovum and cannot become pregnant except at the time she reaches orgasm. Ordinarily, of course, a woman discharges an ovum on about the fourteenth day of her menstrual cycle; ovulation will take place whether or not she has an orgasm, or any other form of sexual response, for that matter.

Since ovulation usually takes place only once a month, orgasm — whether it occurs once a month or several times a day — will not ordinarily cause a woman to discharge additional eggs. Her fertile period is, therefore, usually (although not always) limited to the few days just before, during, and immediately after ovulation, as was discussed under the last fallacy. It is in no way related to her having an orgasm, either alone, or simultaneously with her partner.

Although only remotely related to the discussion at hand, an interesting incident concerning an ovarian transplant is alleged to have occurred recently in England. A woman with nonfunctioning ovaries received one from another woman. Eventually the transplanted ovary functioned normally and discharged an egg. The transplant recipient then became pregnant and gave birth to a child. The courts, however, ruled that the child was illegitimate, because the egg in its unfertilized state was already in the ovary when the transplant was made; the actual mother of the child was therefore judged to be the donor of the ovary. Since the donor was not married to the man who fertilized the egg, the court ruled that the child was born out of wedlock. One might conclude from this bit of legal skulduggery that a single act of sexual intercourse produced a climax for one woman and a conception for another. One can only speculate whether or not the story is true. But the laws of England and America (and of almost any other country, for that matter) are sufficiently unrealistic to cause just this sort of muddle and injustice.

FALLACY:

URINATION BY THE WOMAN AFTER COITUS, OR HAVING SEXUAL INTERCOURSE IN A STANDING POSITION, WILL PREVENT PREGNANCY.

FACT:

Since a woman's bladder does not empty through the vagina, urine cannot possibly wash out sperm deposited in the vaginal canal during sexual intercourse. There is some remote possibility — certainly not a probability — that the position assumed for urination, should a woman void immediately after coitus, might cause the sperm to flow from her vagina rather than enter the uterus. But the act of urination itself will not prevent impregnation. Neither does the position assumed in sexual intercourse have much to do with preventing impregnation. Coitus, whether experienced in a lying, standing, sitting, or some more unusual position, can produce a pregnancy. Sperm are deposited at or near the cervix upon ejaculation and almost immediately afterwards begin to move toward and into the uterus. As in the case of being seated to urinate after coitus, the standing position in intercourse is not likely to cause the sperm to spill out of the vagina.

Perhaps one reason for the persistence of the fallacy that urination after coitus can serve as a birth-control method is a largely invalid notion that links urination and venereal-disease prevention. Most men have heard that if, after intercourse, they will urinate, they will (hopefully) cleanse the urethra of any infection that might have been contracted. They must also, so the rumor goes, bathe the exterior penile surface with urine. Indeed, the salt content of the urine may cause a burning sensation if any skin breaks or open wounds exist on the penis, which the uninformed may interpret as evidence of its germicidal action. It is only a short step for these people to believe that urine may also serve as an effective spermicide — an agent lethal to sperm. But even if urine were a spermicide, it is discharged through a woman's urethra (as was discussed earlier), not her vagina, and therefore can serve no useful purpose as a birth-control means. Couples who have relied upon this "method of contraception" report it to be about as successful and rewarding as French-kissing a water-moccasin!

FALLACY:

ABORTION IS ALWAYS A DANGEROUS PROCEDURE.

FACT:

The relative truth or fallacy of this allegation depends entirely upon what kind of abortion one is talking about. In those countries in which abortion is legal and is performed in hospitals, the mortality rate is, as Dr. Selig Neubardt points out, less than in normal deliveries of babies and is about one-fourth that in tonsillectomies. The most common form of hospital abortion is a surgical procedure, lasting twenty minutes or less, wherein the cervix is gently dilated and the implanted embryo scraped from the wall of the uterus with a spoon-like instrument called a curette. The process is called dilation and curettage or, more popularly, a "D and C." It is understandable that such a simple procedure, when performed by a competent surgeon and under the antiseptic conditions of a hospital's operating room, poses practically no risk to a woman.

But that is a legal abortion, the kind which, tragically, constitutes only a very small proportion of the vast number of abortions that are induced — that is, are not spontaneous — each year in the United States. (It has been estimated that there are approximately two million induced abortions each year in this country.) I say "tragically," because I believe the maxim that if a woman wants an abortion she is going to get one. If she is a resident of a state or country in which abortion is forbidden or is permitted under only the most serious of conditions (e.g., to save the mother's life), she has three alternatives: she can travel to another country or state known for easy abortion; she can seek an illegal abortion in her own state; or she can resort to do-it-yourself techniques.

In the first two instances, all it takes is money — usually lots of it. It is a fortunate woman to whom money is no object. She can fly to some country such as Mexico or Puerto Rico, where abortion is illegal, yet traffic in abortion is enormous; or she can fly to Japan or Hawaii — and now New York — where abortion laws are liberal; or, if she makes enough discreet inquiries, she can very likely find a doctor in her own city who will perform the abortion in his office — for $600 to $1000 (or even more) in cash.

In many of the latter instances there are not, of course, the safeguards provided by a hospital; but the woman is at least seeking the services of someone with medical training. The danger here is that some such doctors are addicted to drugs or alcohol; or, guilty of some infraction that has caused them to be "defrocked" by the medical profession, are therefore operating in the twilight zone of medical ethics and expertise. Although one hears periodically of the death of a woman aborted by such a practitioner, one has to conclude that the incidence is nonetheless quite low, if one accepts the estimate that some two million illegal abortions are performed annually. A risk nonetheless exists. This is not to say that some well-respected and highly competent physicians do not perform abortions. Lured by the easy money (and in some instances by feelings of compassion), they do indeed. Such doctors can often convince hospital administrators of the need for a "therapeutic" abortion, and they are thereby able to perform the operation in the safe confines of the hospital. Studies have shown, for example, that women who can afford the charges in private wings of hospitals are able to procure many more "therapeutic" abortions than those women lying in the charity wards of the same hospitals.

Abortion, then, poses its greatest dangers to those women who have no grounds for a legal abortion and who do not have several hundred dollars with which to pay a medically trained abortionist for an illegal abortion. These women, unfortunately, constitute the majority of those seeking abortion. As Dr. Neubardt puts it, the $35 abortion is the basic method of family planning in the slums of this country's big cities and among the peasantry of South America; and the $35 abortion is the one that kills. When the woman goes to an untrained abortionist, four things are against her: his lack of medical training; the unsanitary conditions — often hideously so — under which the abortion takes place; the crude physiological principles upon which these abortions are based; and the detrimental psychological effects that all these wretched circumstances have on the woman, and perhaps on the father as well.

The $35-abortion "technicians" quite likely do not scrape out the uterus by means of a D and C; instead, they kill the embryo in one of several manners and leave it to the body's natural processes to expel the remains of the pregnancy and to heal the wound in the uterus. Most of the time the methods work, amazingly, to great or less degree of discomfort or infection in the woman (10,000 such post-abortion infection cases reach the hospitals of New York City each year, according to Dr. Neubardt). These women can only be considered lucky; the unlucky ones are those who took the same chance and lost — their health, permanently, or perhaps their lives.

Those women who try to bring on an abortion themselves through such terrible means as crochet hooks and coat hangers — incurring in the process the possibly lethal danger of puncturing the uterus, bladder, or rectum — or by jumping off high places, are taking the same chance, of course. Swallowing such things as pills to "take care of late periods," diuretics, emetics, or alcohol in excessive amounts produces nothing except, perhaps, a case of nausea and diarrhea. They are probably not dangerous to life or health; but neither are they effective methods of abortion. Swallowing such substances as quinine, ergot, lead, and arsenic is based on the premise that the embryo or fetus is weaker than the mother and will therefore perish first — but who can establish the margin of safety for the mother? Vaginal insertion of such medications as disinfectant tablets can cause extensive damage to the woman's internal genitalia, but no abortion.

Despite the remedies for unwanted pregnancies that have passed by word of mouth through the centuries, there is no generally available medication that will produce an abortion without also posing an unacceptable threat to the health and life of the woman. Medical researchers are presently working on an abortion pill that reportedly is completely effective, yet does not threaten the mother's health. Although federal authorities are not yet ready to release this pill for general use, from the point of view of simplicity and the lessening of emotional impact, it appears to hold much promise.

Since abortion *can* be simple, safe, and inexpensive, one wonders why such misery and trauma must surround so many incidences of it. The moral dilemma created is obvious and is serious for some: when does a conceptus become a human being and hence murderable? Centuries of religious thinkers have been unable to come to a consensus on this question. One has to question, however, the wisdom, propriety, or feasibility of relegating a moral issue to legal regulation. American public opinion seems strongly against abortion, except under special circumstances. Yet the widespread practice of aborting an unwanted pregnancy reveals a distinct hypocrisy. Should not, then, the matter of an unwanted pregnancy be left to the individual conscience, and removed entirely from the purview of lawmakers — who are, one must concede, primarily men, the inseminators and not the bearers of children (as authoress Marya Mannes puts it)? It appears that only then will those women determined to become unpregnant be able to do so in almost total safety. It also appears to me that the woman involved, and she alone, should make the decision about whether or not to continue a pregnancy. Should she decide negatively, then the safest, least expensive, most effective abortion known to medical science should be easily available to her.

FALLACY:

> FRIGID WOMEN, PROSTITUTES, AND PROMISCUOUS WOMEN
> ARE NOT SO LIKELY TO CONCEIVE AS WOMEN WHOSE
> SEXUAL RESPONSE OR ACTIVITY IS MORE NORMAL.

FACT:

Since frigidity in women is practically always based on psychological factors, and since conception has nothing to do with whether or not a woman enjoys sexual activity, it is obvious that there is no foundation to the first part of this myth. If, in an attempt to prevent conception, a woman holds herself back from orgasm or remains passive and indifferent during coition, she is still running the risk of pregnancy. Neither orgasm nor active participation in coition is in the slightest degree necessary to conception.

Prostitutes who allow themselves to become pregnant are putting themselves out of business. One would naturally, therefore, expect them to take extra precautions against such an eventuality, which they probably do. Furthermore, some prostitutes are sterile because of present or past venereal infection. But frequent sexual intercourse of itself will not lessen the likelihood of these women becoming pregnant, nor strengthen the possibility of their becoming sterile.

If promiscuous women, like prostitutes, do not appear to become pregnant as readily as the average woman does, it is because they take better precautions against the possibility. Sometimes promiscuous women begin their coital activity at a very early age, even before they produce mature ova. They are not, of course, able to conceive at that time of their lives, which perhaps leads to the false notion that a woman's "sexual excess" will cause her to be sterile.

Men do, by the way, lower *their* ability to impregnate by frequent ejaculations, because their sperm count are thereby reduced. The average man requires about thirty or forty hours to regain his normal sperm count after ejaculation.

FALLACY:

THERE MUST BE TWO ACTS OF SEXUAL INTERCOURSE TO
PRODUCE TWINS, THREE FOR TRIPLETS, AND SO ON.

FACT:

It is true that twins can be the result of two acts of sexual
intercourse. The babies can, in fact, have different fathers. Such an
occurrence implies that the woman has ovulated (discharged an egg) twice in
one month, and that each of the ova has become fertilized by a separate
sperm. Even so, when two ova are discharged during a single menstrual cycle,
it is usually at very nearly the same time of the month. The eggs, therefore,
would normally become fertilized as the consequence of a single act of sexual
intercourse. The twin babies conceived from two eggs are called *fraternal*, or
dizygotic, twins. Because they came from two different ova that were
fertilized by two different sperm, the children will not necessarily be of the
same sex, nor will they be any more alike than any other two youngsters in
the same family.

Twins are born once in about every eighty births, but only two-thirds of
them are fraternal twins. The other third are called *identical*, or monozygotic,
twins, having resulted from the fertilization of a single egg by a single sperm.
The fertilized egg in some way manages to split, with each half developing
into a separate baby. Because they are the product of the union of the same
egg and sperm, their heritage of genes is identical. These babies will invariably
be of the same sex and will be alike (or nearly so) in all other respects. Later
environmental influences, of course, will have a great effect on whether they
remain psychologically, mentally, or even physically alike. There is also some
speculation that the longer the fertilized egg takes to split, the less alike the
babies will be.

Triplets, occurring approximately once in 6400 births, can be the result of
a single fertilization (the ovum splits, and then one of the halves splits again);
or the result of the separate fertilization of two ova, one of which then splits;
or the result of the separate fertilization of three ova that are discharged
within a single menstrual cycle. Once again, the release of two or three ova
would be expected to occur at or about the same time of the month, which
means that they could very easily have been fertilized as a result of a single
act of sexual intercourse.

A variety of patterns of fertilization is possible when quadruplets are
conceived, with one to four ova being involved. Perhaps the most widely
publicized multiple birth in the last fifty years, that of the Dionne
quintuplets, was unique not only because all the infants survived a somewhat

precarious beginning (the kitchen oven served as the immediate incubator), but also because the girls came from a single fertilized egg. There have been other reports in recent memory of the birth of quintuplets, and even larger multiple births. Recently, for example, there have been several reports of seven children born at one delivery, one delivery of eight infants, and one of nine. But the survival rate in multiple births has been exceptionally poor; the uterus typically cannot maintain more than one baby in residence at one time long enough to assure both (or all) full maturity at birth.

In all these instances of multiple births, then, the babies could have been conceived at different times of the month in separate acts of coition — which may account, for instance, for the fact that some twins are born days or even weeks apart. But to say that twins or triplets can only be conceived after as many acts of coition is clearly erroneous.

————

FALLACY:

SPERM FROM ONE TESTICLE WILL PRODUCE MALES AND FROM THE OTHER, FEMALES; OR THE OVA FROM ONE OVARY WILL PRODUCE MALES, AND FROM THE OTHER, FEMALES.

FACT:

The only truth in this statement is an implied one: that men normally have two testicles, and women, two ovaries; and that there are two sexes. Nothing else in the statement is correct, for the determination of a child's sex is in no way dependent upon the east or west location of the gonads producing the man's or the woman's germ cells. Sex is determined by chromosomes.

Except when it is defective, every human cell contains twenty-three pairs of chromosomes. Of these, twenty-two pairs are called nonsex chromosomes; they contain the some 30,000 genes that determine everything from the tilt of the nose and the whorls of the fingerprints to certain personality traits. The chromosomes are, in effect, the blueprints of the future individual. The twenty-third pair of chromosomes are called sex-determining; in the male, one is an X and one a Y, whereas in the female, both are X chromosomes.

At sexual maturity, the gonads of a boy and girl begin the manufacture of germ cells: the testicles produce sperm, and the ovaries, ova, or eggs. Both germ cells go through an intricate, unique process of change and development before they reach maturity and unite with one another. At an early stage in its development, each splits "down the middle," as it were, into two separate germ cells, each of which receives one-half of the chromosomes contained in the parent cell. In the case of sperm, one of the newly formed cells receives the X chromosome (female producing), and the other, the Y chromosome (male producing). Thus X- and Y-bearing sperm are always produced in exactly equal numbers.

The process of division in the female's egg is the same. Because the sex-determining pair of chromosomes is XX, however, after the "split" the new cells each contain only the female X chromosome (in addition, of course, to the twenty-two nonsex chromosomes). Both cells thus formed proceed to develop, although at different rates (some fail to develop at all), into mature eggs, a woman producing approximately four hundred to five hundred during her lifetime.

All ova, therefore, can contain only the female X chromosome, no matter which of the two ovaries produces them. Of the sperm — which are produced in vastly greater quantity than ova (some 200 to 500 million are normally contained in each ejaculate) — half are X and half Y, as I have described. Since the mature ovum and sperm contain only one-half the chromosomal component of all other human cells, neither can develop further until it has joined with the other in the act of fertilization. When they do not unite, both atrophy and die. When they do come together — when the sperm penetrates the ovum — then all chromosomes pair up. And the sex of the conceptus is determined, instantly, by the twenty-third (or sex) chromosome of the sperm. An X sperm plus the X egg means a girl, a Y sperm plus the X egg means a boy.

It might be mentioned in passing that, through a mechanism not fully understood, only one sperm of the many millions contained in the male's ejaculate can penetrate and fertilize the ovum. The ovum then becomes completely resistant to the entry or influence of any other sperm in the ejaculate. The sex of the conceptus, therefore, never becomes confused by the presence of more than one sperm.

Except under the circumstances discussed later in this section (Predetermining the Sex of a Child), the sex of the newly conceived child is thus a matter of pure chance. A woman's ovaries produce only female components, and the sperm are always produced in exactly equal amounts of male- and female-bearing components. Which sperm reaches and penetrates the ovum first is all that matters. The fallaciousness of the notion that the egg or sperm from one gonad will produce children of only one sex is further borne out by those men and women with only one testicle or ovary who nevertheless produce children of both sexes.

FALLACY:

THE WOMAN DETERMINES THE SEX OF THE CHILD.

FACT:

As I pointed out in the previous discussion, every ovum, or egg, produced by the woman that has matured sufficiently to be ready for fertilization contains twenty-three chromosomes — those substances that determine all such inherited characteristics as blood type, color of hair, and shape of body. Of these chromosomes, twenty-two are nonsex chromosomes and one is the sex chromosome, which is *always* X, or female.

The male sperm penetrating the egg contributes a matching set of twenty-two nonsex chromosomes, which pair with those of the egg. The twenty-third is also the sex-determining chromosome and can be either X or Y. If it is X and unites with the X of the ovum, an XX, or female, child is conceived; if it is Y and unites with the X chromosome of the ovum, an XY, or male, child is conceived.

The responsibility for determining the sex of the child, then, rests solely with the male's sperm. Whether the fertilization results in a boy or a girl also represents a fantastic roll of the dice under ordinary circumstances, in that only one sperm of the entire 200 to 500 million contained in the typical ejaculate will succeed in penetrating and fertilizing the ovum. The race indeed goes to the swiftest; and it is the father, not the mother, who supplies the contestants.

It has been calculated that approximately 180 male children are conceived for each 100 females. However, from this time onward, the female of the species proves to be sturdier than the male. By the time the fertilized egg makes its way through the Fallopian tubes and into the implantation site within the uterus, the ratio has decreased to 120 males to 100 females; by the time of birth the ratio is approximately 105 males for each 100 females.

FALLACY:

A WOMAN'S DIET WILL HELP DETERMINE A CHILD'S SEX.

FACT:

The child's sex is fixed from the first moment that the sperm and egg unite, as was detailed in the two previous discussions. Its sex is determined solely by whether the sperm's twenty-third chromosome is X or Y. Nothing can change the sex of the conceptus after that moment, although unusual hormonal activity, natural or artificially induced, may influence the appearance and structure of the genital organs. For example, the development of the external genital structure of both sexes occurs between the sixty-first and seventy-first day after conception. If there is a sufficient amount of male hormones present during this vital ten-day period to influence an XY (male) embryo, a normally developed male child will be born. If the quantity of male hormones is insufficient during this crucial time, or if the male hormonal influence is delayed beyond this time, the sex organs will develop improperly. An intersex child (one with the organs, poorly developed, of both sexes) will be the result.

The idea that the baby's sex is "up for grabs" in the first weeks after conception possibly arises from the knowledge that its sex cannot be distinguished until about the second month after conception. Prior to that time, the genital areas of both male and female embryos are nearly identical folds of tissue. This fold is called the genital ridge, and it follows the same course of development both in the male and the female. The development into an identifiable boy or girl infant occurs at about six weeks, when the undifferentiated genital mass begins development into the male testes, which will one day produce the procreative "seeds" called sperm, or into the female ovaries, which will produce the ova, or eggs.

Until the turn of the century, scientists did in fact generally believe that the fertilized egg remained neuter — that is, neither male nor female — until some environmental force during its development determined which of the two sexes it would become. Among these developmental conditions, one assumes, was the mother's diet. Until then, the chromosomal content of human cells, including the sex-determining chromosomes X and Y, was not understood.

Even without an understanding of the roles played by the X and Y chromosomes, however, one can perceive through a comparison of identical and fraternal twins that sex is determined immediately upon conception, rather than by circumstances occurring during the pregnancy. Identical twins, who develop from a single ovum, are invariably of the same sex, whereas two-ovum twins may or may not be. If only environmental factors are at work in sex determination, one would naturally expect that twins — whether identical or fraternal — would always be of the same sex.

A well-balanced diet, one of high vitamin, mineral, and protein content, is of course absolutely essential to the health of the expectant mother and the child. Indeed, poor maternal health and nutrition are the leading causes of premature births; the mother's system simply cannot maintain the pregnancy. But eating foods like bananas and oysters because they are shaped like the penis and testicles, in the hopes of having a boy (or perhaps eating pêche melba and lady-fingers if a girl is wanted), cannot have the slightest effect on the sex of the child, as that was determined from the first moment of conception.

FALLACY:

NOTHING CAN BE DONE TO INCREASE THE POSSIBILITY OF PREDETERMINING THE SEX OF THE CONCEIVED CHILD.

FACT:

In very recent years noticeable differences between the X (female) and the Y (male) sperm have been discovered. The Y-sperm has a small round-headed body with a long tail, while the X-sperm has a large oval-shaped body and a short tail. Dr. Landrum B. Shettles of Columbia University, a leading scientist in this important area of research, believes that by use of this information the sex of a child can be removed from the realm of mere chance and can be predetermined by controlling the time of sexual intercourse. (Dr. Shettles supports his theory by research findings, although it should be noted that there is hesitancy on the part of some scientists to accept the reported differences in the X and Y sperm.)

Ordinarily each ejaculation contains millions of both X and Y sperm, although the sperm count per ejaculate tends to diminish as the frequency of intercourse increases. The higher the sperm count is, the greater the proportion of male sperm, and, conversely, the lower the sperm count, the greater the proportion of female sperm. Male sperm are more fast-moving and agile than female sperm, but lose their vitality more quickly, especially in the acid environment of the vagina. Female sperm are stronger and live longer than the Y sperm.

The mature ovum is met and fertilized by a sperm in the Fallopian tube. It is reasonable to assume that the smaller-headed, longer-tailed Y sperm would move from vagina to ovum at a faster rate than X sperm do. It is also reasonable to assume that the larger-headed, heavier female sperm is stronger and will live longer — or will at least maintain its vigor longer than the male sperm. The first healthy sperm penetrating the ovum fertilizes it and fixes the sex of the child.

For a couple wishing a boy, Dr. Shettles suggests that a preliminary alkaline douche be taken by the wife (two tablespoons of baking soda in a quart of water), and that the couple abstain from intercourse until just *after* the time the wife expects to ovulate. The alkaline douche neutralizes the acid environment of the vagina, thus lessening the threat to the sperm. Abstinence appears to increase the proportion of male sperm, for one reason or another; also, timing intercourse to follow ovulation allows the faster-moving male-producing sperm a better chance to reach the waiting egg first.

For a couple wishing a girl, Dr. Shettles suggests that a preliminary acid douche be taken (two tablespoons of vinegar to a quart of water). There should be no abstinence from intercourse; however, intercourse should take place two or three days before ovulation is expected (and then cease) so the weaker male sperm will die off before the egg arrives on the scene.

For some reason that is not clear, artificial insemination results in a marked preponderance of males. When the semen to be used in the artificial insemination is allowed to stand in a container for a time before being injected in the uterus, the heavier (by about 4%) X (female) sperm settle to the bottom of the container, whereas the lighter Y (male) sperm rise to the top. Samples of the top one-third of such a collection of semen reveal an approximate 80% Y, or male, content, whereas the lower one-third contains about 80% X, or female, sperm. The middle one third contains roughly equal amounts of male and female sperm.

———

FALLACY:

A FETUS SLEEPS DURING THE DAY AND IS AWAKE AT
NIGHT (AND KICKS).

FACT:

Late in the fourth month of pregnancy, the expectant mother becomes aware of indistinct abdominal fluttering, which she soon identifies as being the movements of the baby within her uterus. In the fifth month, the baby's muscles grow much stronger, and the fluttering changes into punches, kicks, and much maneuvering of the body. These activities alternate with periods of quiet. This early movement of the fetus is known as "quickening," and in the distant past it was considered to be the time at which the conceptus within the woman's body became a human being. Abortion, for example, was sanctioned in certain societies as an acceptable method of birth control if it was performed before quickening. Abortion performed after the first fetal movements were felt was considered murder.

It is apparently true that unborn babies go through periods of waking and sleeping, just as newborns do. During these periods they settle into their favorite position — or "lie," as it is called; and they can in fact be awakened or stirred into action by vibrations outside the mother's body — for example, very loud music — although they are unable to hear, as such. Because the baby is so tiny in the early months after conception, and because he is quite active after the fifth month, he can turn somersaults, twist, and move rather freely; but by the eighth or ninth month, his living quarters are much more cramped, and his movements are largely restricted to elbowing, shoving, jabbing, and kicking, leaving the poor mother often wondering if it is a baby or an octopus with brass knuckles that she is carrying.

Since the unborn child's sleeping habits are somewhat the same as those of the newborn, it is logical to assume that these habits are in no way dictated by the time of day. We all have at least an idea of the erratic and unpredictable nature of newly arrived infants. Witness the frantic parents who are convinced that their offspring will never settle down to a reasonable, predictable schedule of sleeping and being awake. And so it is with the same infant before he is born. Even if the fetus were not in a totally dark environment, his eyes are closed, in any case, as a kitten's are, until about the seventh month of fetal life.

The idea that an unborn baby reverses night and day in its sleeping and waking patterns probably arises from the fact that the mother is too much absorbed in her activities during the day to be particularly aware of its movements, other than the more pronounced punches in her ribs. In the still of the night, however, the mother becomes more attuned to all sensory stimuli, especially so because her sleep is disturbed in the process. She is therefore much more conscious at night of the baby's cavorting than she is during the day.

The unborn baby's waking-sleeping habits are dictated, as they are with the newborn infant, by the alternating need for rest and exercise. He simply does not have the scope for movement within his crowded lodging that he will have after birth.

FALLACY:

A SEVENTH-MONTH BABY HAS A BETTER CHANCE OF
SURVIVAL THAN AN EIGHTH-MONTH BABY.

FACT:

The most common cause by far of death among newborn infants is
physical immaturity. Such a baby is born prematurely, before the completion
of the nine months of uterine life designed by nature to prepare his body to
function independently of its mother. In the year 1958, as an example, over
half of the babies dying soon after birth weighed less than five and one-half
pounds, the weight agreed upon by the World Health Organization as being
minimal for a mature infant.

In evaluating the possibilities for survival of a seven-month fetus, as
opposed to those of the fetus at eight months, it is important to examine the
degree of development at both stages. At the end of the seventh month, the
baby weighs about three pounds and is only sixteen inches long. It is very
thin, and statistically, it has only a 50% chance of survival. The primary
danger is that the layer of fat essential to the preservation of heat in the body
is absent (it does not appear until the eighth month), meaning that the infant
is extremely sensitive to reduced temperature and to temperature changes.
His vital organs may not be well enough formed, so that his lungs have
difficulty absorbing sufficient oxygen to support life. His digestive processes
may be poor, causing him to lose some of his precious weight, and he is very
much subject to infection, not having absorbed a sufficient number of his
mother's antibodies to protect him against various infections and diseases.

The eight-month fetus, on the other hand, weighs about five pounds, most
of the weight gain having come from the addition of a layer of body fat,
which will keep him insulated after birth. The development of his organic
system is virtually complete, and his chance of survival is statistically about
90% — obviously much higher than that of the seven-month baby.

The full-term nine-month baby, in contrast to the one born one or two
months prematurely, has better than a 99% chance of survival. His breathing
and digestive systems are fully functional. He now has not only the vital
protective layer of body fat, but also the full quota of his mother's
antibodies, affording him protection for about six months against the
diseases to which she has immunity (but only those) — for example, polio,
chicken pox, and even the common cold. These immunities build up during
the last three months of prenatal life; so naturally the baby born at nine
months has maximum protection from infection. And so, in turn, has the
baby born at eight months greater immunity than the one born at seven
months.

It is obvious that the closer the pregnancy approaches full term (two hundred and eighty days, or forty weeks, from the last menstruation; or two hundred and sixty-six days, thirty-eight weeks, from the last ovulation), the better the odds are that the baby will live. Yet most of us have heard the old wives' tale that the seven-month fetus is better off than the one born after an eight-month pregnancy, although I do not recall that any rationale for the assumption was ever offered.

Medical writers have suggested that the error was originally made by the great physician Hippocrates, whose writings and oath of medical integrity have long influenced the profession. Perpetuating the error through the ages, however, has perhaps had a practical value. When a couple marry as quickly as they can after discovering that the girl is pregnant, the baby typically arrives seven months later. It takes about two months to determine that the girl is pregnant, to calm hysterical parents, and to make arrangements for the wedding. It obviously saves face to declare a full-term baby to be a seven-month prematurity. So what is really being compared is a nine-month to an eight-month fetus, rather than seven- and eight-month fetuses. Perhaps flippantly, but nevertheless accurately, "Dear Abby" summed the case up perfectly when she said to a correspondent, "The baby wasn't early, the wedding was just late."

FALLACY:
> AN UNBORN CHILD CAN BE "MARKED."

FACT:
> Because of the close connection between fetus and mother, it is understandable why many people assume that such experiences as sudden shocks or fright to the mother would cause her baby to be born with some physical or emotional "mark," most commonly a birthmark. There is, however, no direct connection between the nervous systems of mother and fetus, or between their blood systems, and the idea of prenatally "marking" the child in the manners mentioned is, therefore, completely false.

Most often when a child is born with an unusual birthmark — for example, a skin discoloration in the general shape of a bird — the parents' faulty memory processes will cause them to "remember" an incident during the pregnancy wherein the mother was attacked or in some way frightened by something of that shape.

Misinformed scientists have also been party to perpetuating the "marking" myth. For example, in 1836 eight physicians made a report, which appeared in an American medical journal, of a man with a face like a snake who could coil and uncoil his arm in a snake-like fashion. These phenomena were allegedly the result of the man's mother having been frightened by a rattlesnake in the sixth month of pregnancy.

It is true, of course, that the mother supplies nourishment for the fetus; her diet and chemical intake can have a direct effect on certain physiological reactions of the child before its birth, and afterwards, if she breast-feeds the baby. For example, if a woman during pregnancy grossly overeats certain foods, an allergic condition is sometimes produced in the child that continues after birth. It is also well known that the physical condition of infants whose mothers smoked tobacco during their pregnancies will be affected by the smoking. Prematurity, for instance, is higher among babies of mothers who smoke than among the babies of nonsmokers. However, these reactions are not the same as those ordinarily considered when one discusses "marking" a baby. The latter theory is a physiological and psychological impossibility, so far as scientific investigation has been able to determine.

FALLACY:

"VIRGIN BIRTHS" (PARTHENOGENESIS) DO NOT OCCUR IN HUMANS OR ANIMALS.

FACT:

"Virgin birth," or parthenogenesis, concerns the development of the female's egg into a new being without any possible previous contact with male sperm. This phenomenon is a common occurrence in lower animals, such as the honeybee, and is the sole method of reproduction among certain other insects. Experimentation in parthenogenesis with various animals has shown that a great number of stimuli will induce the same process of development that fertilization does. For example, cooling the Fallopian tubes of rabbits, heating the eggs of certain moths, and even applying saliva of human males to carp eggs have sufficiently irritated the eggs to prompt their development. A very high percentage of the eggs of virgin turkey hens undergo parthenogenesis in experimental circumstances, although the early death rate among the hatched birds is very high.

The obvious question arises: is this phenomenon possible in human beings?

There has been considerable disagreement among investigators, past and present, and there is no definite answer to the question at the present time. One aspect is a certainty, however. If parthenogenesis were to occur, the offspring must invariably be female because of the way chromosomes are arranged in men and women. Since women have only one type of sex-determining chromosome (X), only the X chromosome could be passed on.

In a study of four hundred human ova, Dr. Landrum B. Shettles, mentioned in a previous section, observed that the first stages of developmental processes had begun in three of the eggs, even though there could have been no contact with sperm. The logical conclusion would seem to be that if developmental processes in the human ovum can begin spontaneously, they should be able to continue to term. Only further research can uncover the answer.

The phrase "virgin birth" ordinarily conveys the idea of human pregnancy and subsequent birth without a previous act of sexual intercourse followed by union of ovum and sperm. In this context, the possibility of a true virgin birth has never been scientifically established. Impregnation without penile penetration, however, is a real possibility, a phenomenon that occurs more often than many realize. If, for instance, a man were to have his penis near or on a woman's vulva and ejaculate during sex play, semen could enter the vaginal opening and make its way through the vagina into the uterus. Or if a man were to ejaculate, get sperm on his hands, and soon thereafter manually manipulate the woman's genitals — especially if he inserted a finger into the vagina — he could introduce sperm into the vaginal canal. Were impregnation to result in either of these instances, and if the girl's hymen remained intact — or, more accurately, if she had never had sexual intercourse — the subsequent parturition might accurately be called a "virgin birth."

FALLACY·

> THE BIRTH CONTROL PILL WILL EVENTUALLY CAUSE A
> WIDE VARIETY OF ILLS IN ANY WOMAN USING IT FOR ANY
> LENGTH OF TIME.

FACT:

The birth control pill, a combination of synthetic estrogen and progesterone that prevents ovulation, is considered to be the most effective contraceptive known to man — apart from total abstinence or surgical sterilization. Because of the success of the Pill as a method of birth control, it is not surprising that eight and one-half million women in the United States alone are estimated to have taken oral contraceptives in 1969. Yet, the list of known side effects that users of the Pill have experienced is extensive, ranging from nausea and breast changes to mental depression, higher blood pressure, and blood clots. Statistically, then, what medical risks do women run in using the Pill?

Dr. Alan F. Guttmacher, director of Planned Parenthood-World Population, testified before a Senate subcommittee in March of 1970 that blood-clotting problems are the only proven serious risk associated with oral contraceptives. Death from clot complications, he said, occurs in only three out of every 100,000 women taking the Pill. By contrast, he pointed out, the risk involved in unwanted pregnancy is far greater: the mortality rate in the United States from the consequences of pregnancy is 22.8 deaths per 100,000 women every year; what is even worse, there are 100 deaths per 100,000 abortions performed illegally by unqualified persons.

Four medical studies, three in Great Britain and one in the United States, have revealed that there is a relationship between use of the Pill and blood clot disorders. The researchers involved in these studies conclude that users of oral contraceptives are several times more likely than nonusers to have thrombophlebitis (blood clots in a vein) and pulmonary embolism (an escaped blood clot lodging in the lungs). Once the user discontinues the Pill, the risk disappears. It should be noted, however, that an eight-year study of some 9600 women in Puerto Rico (where the Pill has been in use longer than anywhere else in the world) failed to uncover any evidence linking deaths from blood clots with use of the Pill.

How about the other side effects usually associated with taking the Pill? The most commonly experienced ones, such as nausea, weight gain, breast tenderness, and change in sex drive, usually tend to disappear within three months. Almost half (41%) of the women using the Pill report having experienced no side effects or complications at all, according to a Gallup Poll conducted in February, 1970. Studies are presently under way to investigate the much more serious charge that the Pill can cause cancer, or that it may reduce a user's fertility after she stops taking it. As yet, however, there is no evidence to confirm or refute either claim.

How much risk does a woman run in using the Pill? If she has a medical history of blood clots, breast cancer, strokes, heart disease, impaired liver function, or an undiagnosed abnormal genital bleeding, her physician quite likely will not prescribe the Pill for her. Any woman with a history of high blood pressure, asthma, diabetes, epilepsy, migraine headaches, or episodes of mental depression needs careful medical supervision if the Pill is prescribed for her. But if she is healthy and has none of these danger signals in her history, then the risk of possible complications in her using an oral contraceptive is small indeed.

Furthermore, in the light of its proven effectiveness, ease of use, and esthetic superiority over all other forms of birth control, rejection of the Pill because of the extremely remote possibility of its side effects is most unfortunate. And, in light of the Pill's superior effectiveness over other birth control methods, discontinuing its use would pose a disastrous problem for our already overpopulated world. I am not saying that all caution should be thrown to the winds in the taking of the Pill (or of any other medication). I feel, rather, that its use should be a completely individual matter based upon the woman's preference and the doctor's evaluation of her physical condition. One might draw an analogy between use of the Pill and the use of penicillin and cortisone. Both of the latter are known to cause bad reactions in certain patients. Yet it would have been a tragedy for many, many more patients if, because of the few, those drugs had been deleted from the list of available medications.

The conclusion of a study made for the British Medical Association seems to me appropriate. Statistically, the Pill is less of a hazard to life and health than is smoking, driving, or swimming.

———————

FALLACY:

TAKING THE PILL WILL DELAY A WOMAN'S MENOPAUSE.

FACT:

Rather than preventing the union of sperm and any egg that the woman's ovaries may have released, as other contraceptives do, the Pill works in quite a different way. It prevents ovulation (the release of eggs) from occurring at all by imitating the hormonal activity of a woman's body during pregnancy, when ovulation, of course, no longer occurs. If there is no egg for the sperm to fertilize, obviously there will be no conception.

An old theory has it that menopause occurs when the supply of eggs in a woman's ovaries has been depleted. If this were true, it would be logical to assume that preventing the release of ova would lengthen her childbearing years and thus delay her reaching the menopause.

Not so, say modern medical authorities. By way of illustration, endocrinologists have pointed out that some women have given birth to as many as seventeen children in fifteen years. With pregnancies occurring so often, these women ovulate only once or twice a year for many years, since ovulation does not take place during pregnancy. (Each pregnancy can be considered the equivalent of ten months on the Pill.) Yet these women enter menopause at the expected time. The age at which menopause occurs appears to be related, like the menarche (beginning of menstruation), to an inborn genetic factor and to general health. It is not dependent upon the maturation and discharge of all the eggs contained in the ovaries.

A female baby arrives in this world with an incredible number of undeveloped eggs (between 200,000 and 400,000) in the follicles of her ovaries. By the time she reaches puberty, the number is reduced to a mere 10,000! Since she will ovulate about thirteen times a year for a period of some thirty-five years, only about 450 of these undeveloped eggs will mature and be discharged. Every woman, then, whether she is childless or has borne many children, reaches menopause with thousands of immature eggs still remaining in her ovaries. And all women go through their menopause at approximately the same time in their lives — if their doctors have not shortened nature's timetable, either through removal of the ovaries (thus bringing about menopause by surgical means), or through hormonal treatment intended to continue the menstrual cycle indefinitely. The use of the Pill may in some instances cover up the onset of menopause, but there is no evidence that its use will delay it.

FALLACY:

HUMANS AND INFRAHUMAN ANIMALS CAN CROSSBREED.

FACT:

Undoubtedly, our knowledge of the wondrous creatures of Greek and Roman mythology — the centaurs, sphinxes, mermaids, and satyrs — has given status through the years to the myth that humans and lower animals can interbreed. Not only is it impossible, however, for humans to crossbreed with infrahuman animals, but interbreeding among the various genera of lower animals is also impossible, although members of different species of the same genus may produce crossbred offspring. A man and an ape cannot interbreed, nor can an ape and a tiger; but two members of different species in the cat family, for example, may crossbreed.

Even animals in the same family but of different species seldom crossbreed of their own volition. They prefer to make their choice from among members of their own specific grouping. A lion and a tiger have been known to breed, the offspring being called a *liger*; and recently a news account reported the crossbreeding of a donkey and a zebra (the offspring, a *dobra*). Mixed breeding of animals of the same genus but of different species is more successfully performed in the laboratory through artificial insemination than through the natural breeding habits of animals.

Lack of sophistication in understanding sexual needs, sexual behavior, and sexual functioning of both man and infrahuman animals has also undoubtedly contributed to the confusion that exists concerning crossbreeding. The fact that some human beings at times involve themselves sexually with lower animals (in an act referred to as bestiality and, sometimes, as sodomy), and that a man may be able to ejaculate within the vaginal canal of the animal (or an animal within a woman) is accepted by some uninformed people as evidence that offspring from such a union is possible. The efforts at organ transplants from one human to another have been largely unsuccessful to date, pointing up the great difficulty that science has encountered in uniting the tissue and chemicals of two humans. By extension, efforts to create a creature from the sexual union of a human and a lower animal must perforce be doomed to failure.

Homosexuality

Speak the word homosexuality to a random sampling of people and the reactions will include almost every emotion in the psychologist's hand book — contempt from the self-righteous, condemnation from the moralist, curiosity from the academician, shock from the timid, ribaldry from the coarse and ignorant, compassion from the thoughtful, perplexity from the behaviorist, and conflict within the homosexual himself. Of all forms of deviant sexual behavior, homosexuality is probably the most widely discussed — and the least understood by the general public.

Most behaviorists would describe homosexuality as an abnormality. They would also agree that most homosexuals are extremely resistant to therapeutic efforts to change their life style. This prognostic gloom about the homosexual and his departure from the norm of sexual expression is further compounded by the lack of knowledge of what really causes the abnormality.

In the atmosphere of doubt and conflict among the "straight" community, among professionals in medicine and psychiatry, and within the homosexual himself, is it any wonder that as much misinformation as information exists on the subject of homosexuality? Is the problem moral, psychological, medical, or legal? That it could be a matter of moral defect alone seems unlikely. If the homosexual seeks psychiatric help, should the psychotherapist direct his efforts toward helping him join the "straight" world, or toward helping him adjust to his homosexuality? Can there be some endocrinological factor that predisposes one individual more than another toward homosexuality? Is the cause environmental? Or is there a particular combination of these last two factors that makes one person more vulnerable than another? Is homosexuality a matter that requires legislation by penal codes? Or should the homosexual be left alone to pursue his sexual *inclinations as long as adults only are involved, no force or threat is used, and no affront to public decorum exists?*

Despite all that is not understood about homosexuality, a large fund of factual knowledge has been collected by researchers and clinicians. Yet misconceptions about both male and female homosexuals have a way of perpetuating themselves. Some of the stories one hears are ridiculous, others are gross exaggerations, and many do injustice to this poorly understood segment of our society. This section is intended to provide a factual basis for a clearer perception and understanding of homosexuality.

FALLACY:

HOMOSEXUAL OFFENDERS ARE A MENACE TO SOCIETY.

FACT:

A recent poll conducted by CBS-TV revealed that two-thirds of all Americans regard homosexuals with such negative emotions as discomfort and disgust; and that the majority regard homosexuality as a greater menace to society than abortion, prostitution, or adultery. Why?

The public's attitude of fear and revulsion toward the homosexual stems primarily from four sources: fear that he will attempt to seduce the young to his "perverted" way of life; belief that he will use force, if necessary, to secure a sexual partner; distaste for the blatant, often bizarre mannerisms of some of the more obvious homosexuals, whose behavior is thought to be typical of all of them; and a conviction that he is a detriment to his community. These points deserve examination in the light of several studies made of homosexuality.

In the Kinsey investigators' *Sex Offenders* (1965), the subjects of the imprisoned homosexual himself and of the homosexual's relationship to his partner were carefully studied. A large number of these homosexuals had come from broken homes, or had lived in homes in which the relationship between the parents was very bad. The incidence of childhood illness was high among them. They had been very well socialized in childhood, however, and had had a large number of girl playmates. They had also indulged in a high degree of both homosexual and heterosexual sex play as children.

About one-third of the homosexuals in this Kinsey sampling had been the object as preadolescents of sexual advances from males. The number is high, to be sure, in comparison with the homosexual advances reported by the

Kinsey control sampling — that is, men who had never been in prison on any charge — of whom only 8% reported having been the object of homosexual approaches as youngsters. (In both groups, however, only 20% to 28% of these advances had culminated in overt physical contact.)

The prisoner-homosexuals' record of childhood sexual contact with adult males suggests that these experiences may have disposed some of these boys to later homosexual activity. Certainly a child thus involved in sexual contact with a man will have the lasting impression that men can achieve sexual gratification with boys — especially if the experience was a pleasurable one for the child. Nevertheless, preadolescent exposure to homosexual men usually came after homosexual contacts with other children; thus the cause-and-effect paradox arises: did the homosexual tendencies or the homosexual contact with adults come first?

The Kinsey investigation also examined the degree of participation of the youngsters who were involved with homosexuals in the sampling. Of the child partners under the age of twelve, 70% were agreeable to the sexual contact, or at least passive about it. Of the minor boys (twelve to fifteen years of age) 83% either encouraged the homosexual advance or were passive. These figures seem extraordinarily high if the assumption is made that the young boys were exhibiting nothing more than normal curiosity about homosexual experience; or that their behavior was the sporadic, episodic homosexuality which occurs in so many men's lifetimes. Certainly the figures appear disproportionately high when one remembers that the original Kinsey study of male sexual behavior revealed that only 37% of all men had experienced some form of overt homosexual activity to the point of orgasm; and that 50% had experienced some sort of homosexual response.

It is unusual and atypical for homosexuals to use force or threat in their offenses against boys. The degree of participation or acquiescence of the homosexual partners in the Kinsey study certainly bears this statement out; in fact, the incidence of force or threat was but 10% when children were involved, and only 4% in cases involving minors.

The homosexual offenders against adults had the lowest incidence (2%) of threat or violence of all the imprisoned sex offenders in the Kinsey study. In fact, the great majority (93%) of their partners either encouraged the contact, or were passive about it. When homosexual rape did take place, it usually occurred in a prison or hobo jungle. Even in these cases, however, the rape was only incidentally homosexual; the aggressor in all likelihood would have preferred a female victim, but only a male was available.

It comes as a surprise to most people that only about 15% of male homosexuals (and perhaps 5% of lesbians) are identifiable from their appearance. The effeminate, limp-wristed "pretty boy" types and the homosexual "toughs" with a fondness for leather belts and chains may offend us by their appearance. But so also do they offend each other — and a great number of other homosexuals, who are sensibly dressed in the grey-flannel uniforms of their business and junior-executive positions. Some homosexuals are, in fact, married and have children, although sometimes only in a desperate attempt to disguise their deviation. In some professions — notably interior design, fashion, hairdressing — homosexuality probably does not matter, since the men work so closely with a female staff and female clientele, who are less likely than a male staff and clientele to be repulsed or upset by their homosexuality. (I am by no means implying that these professions abound in homosexuals; they are simply more likely to be accepting than some others of the worker who happens to be homosexual.) Various government agencies and industries, however, still do not regard homosexuality with an attitude of indulgence or compassion, so it is necessary for the homophiles in their employ to recede into the shadows and remain as inconspicuous as possible. Most homosexuals, then, cannot be identified by any characteristic, or combination of characteristics, of manner or dress. They cannot afford to be.

His sexual proclivities notwithstanding, the homophile hardly presents the picture of a man who is in any way a detriment to his community. Of all sex offenders, he has the highest socioeconomic status and is the best educated. Drugs and drink are not factors in his behavior. He is the least likely of all to deny his guilt when faced with legal charges of homosexuality. The number of homophiles convicted of offenses other than the sexual ones is the smallest of all the sex offenders in the Kinsey study. The conclusion of the Kinsey investigators is that homosexuals are neither dangerous nor criminal. "They do not damage society; they merely do not fit into it."

Under the sponsorship of the National Institute of Mental Health, in October of 1969 a fourteen-member panel (led by Dr. Evelyn Hooker of UCLA, a leading authority on homosexuality) completed a far-reaching investigation into the subject of homosexuality. The panel concluded that the hostility and suspicions harbored by so many Americans toward the homophile are unfounded, that he poses no threat to public morals and decorum. The report said further that the infamy and contempt that the public attaches to homosexuality do more social harm than good and go beyond the limits necessary to the preservation of order and decency. The report continues: "Homosexuality presents a major problem for our society largely because of the amount of injustice and suffering entailed in it, not only for the homosexual, but also for those concerned about him."

The NIMH report went on to recommend that the United States follow the example of England, which in 1968 made legal any homosexual act performed discreetly between consenting adults. There have been no discernible ill effects suffered by the British public. (Any forcible homosexual contact or one involving minors remains, of course, a criminal act.)

The implication of the Hooker report is that we are highly unfair in our attitude toward homosexuals, and that the legal sanctions imposed against them are equally unjust. We have jeopardized their mental health by driving them underground into a life shrouded by fear of discovery and the ever-present danger of blackmail. The techniques of entrapment used by the police are often degrading. The homosexual is discriminated against in government and in many private-industry jobs, although most are good citizens and productive members of society. Homosexuality is an undesirable way of life to members of the "straight" world. But this in no way implies that all homosexuals are undesirable members of society — or that all heterosexuals are more desirable because they are "straight."

The suggestion that homosexuals in top-level governmental jobs are poor security risks and should therefore be fired upon discovery may be well taken; but, tragically, not for the reasons usually offered to support it. Because his sexual preferences are different from those of the average heterosexual man, the homophile is judged to have a flawed character, and to be lacking in the virtues of trustworthiness and loyalty. It is assumed, therefore, that at the first opportunity — or at least with little pressure — he is ready to betray his country. Knowing that with the revelation of his homosexuality he will be shamed before his family, discharged from his position, and — depending upon what state he resides in — perhaps subjected to legal prosecution, the homosexual understandably might yield to threat and commit an act of disloyalty rather than face public exposure. It is the threat of blackmail, then, that makes the homosexual somewhat vulnerable to corrupt pressures, rather than an innate tendency to disloyalty.

In not allowing the homosexual the same freedom of sexual choice that is granted the heterosexual, we "normal" citizens are the real culprits when a homophile succumbs to the blackmailer. If there were public — or at least legal — acceptance of his homosexuality, the possibility of blackmail (at least on the grounds of sex) would be removed; and the homophile would be no more of a security risk than his heterosexual fellow employee.

FALLACY:

>PEOPLE ARE EITHER TOTALLY HOMOSEXUAL OR TOTALLY HETEROSEXUAL.

FACT:

The Kinsey research figures — which remain about the most valid on the subject — show that 50% of white men have been sexually aroused by another male at least one time in their lives. When homosexual activity is sporadic or episodic, it does not suggest significant homosexual leanings in the individual but, rather, motives of experimentation, or the results of a situation in which he or she is deprived of the companionship of the opposite sex. In prisons, and occasionally in the services and in boarding schools, men may turn to homosexuality; yet they revert to unwavering heterosexuality when women are once again available to them. Women in prison also form lesbian attachments in their efforts to make prison life more bearable, but they almost always return to a heterosexual way of life when they are released. There are also those men and women who enter into a brief escapade of homosexual contact out of sheer curiosity.

One can hardly label as homosexual that man or woman who has had a single homosexual experience in his or her life; or who perhaps had a homosexual episode that lasted a year or two, after which homosexual activities were abandoned forever. Yet obviously there must have been some slight homosexual inclination, or these experiences, albeit extremely limited, would never have taken place at all — an observation that has led some sexologists (though certainly not all) to conclude that a certain degree of homosexual tendency exists in everyone. Conversely, the man or woman now living an exclusively homosexual life may have had sporadic heterosexual contacts at some period. There are also those people who are truly bisexual, functioning sexually with equal pleasure (or nearly so) with their own or the opposite sex. Or perhaps they led a heterosexual life for a number of years, and then their amatory interest shifted to their own sex. None of these individuals can be called an exclusive heterosexual or homosexual.

The Kinsey workers established a seven-point scale to demonstrate degrees of sexuality. At one extreme they placed exclusive heterosexuality, in which no homosexuality is involved. This is followed by predominant heterosexuality with only incidental homosexuality. Then follows predominant heterosexuality, but with more than incidental homosexuality. At midpoint, there is sexual functioning at equal heterosexual and homosexual levels. Still further along the continuum is predominant homosexuality, but with more than incidental heterosexuality; then predominant homosexuality with only

Incidental heterosexuality; and, finally, exclusive homosexuality with no heterosexual leanings at all.

The statistics amassed by the Kinsey researchers illustrate the impossibility of categorizing people as being, simply, either homosexual or heterosexual. In *Sex Offenders*, the assertion is made that three-fifths of the homosexual offenders against adults in their sampling had been or were married. Of all men, 37% have experienced homosexual contact to the point of orgasm, and 50% have been at least sexually aroused by another male, as was mentioned. Of women, 13% have experienced orgasm at least one time in their lives through a homosexual relationship, while 28% acknowledged having had "intense feelings" for another woman at one point or another (other researchers have set this last figure as high as 50%).

The Kinsey group state further that 8% of men are exclusively homosexual for a period of at least three years of their lives, and 4% remain so all their lives. Only 1% to 3% of women are exclusively homosexual all their lives. Ten percent of married men have homosexual relations, some being more homosexual by preference than heterosexual, even though coitus with their wives continues. Wardell Pomeroy, formerly a Kinsey associate, mentions a man who claimed homosexual contact with some 10,000 different males (apparently the gentleman kept a record — as well, quite likely, as establishing one) while having had coitus with a mere 700 or 800 women. Yet Dr. Pomeroy classifies this man as more heterosexual than homosexual because the frequency of his contact with women was much greater than it was with his male contacts, and his response to them much stronger.

The ancient Greeks, in contrast to many societies, had an indulgent attitude toward homosexual practices and espoused the premise that man is bisexual by nature. They placed high value on the development of both body and mind, on sensuality, pleasure, happiness, and beauty, the latter tending naturally toward the glorification of the naked human body. The Greek view of the individual as a bisexual being is evidenced in the worship, in Cyprus, of the god Hermaphroditus, who was depicted as having the outward appearance of a man, but wearing the clothes of a woman. Although the intellectual and sensual attachment between an older and a younger man was idealized — the older one being something of a counselor, and the relationship being not necessarily erotic — any sexual relationship with a young boy was punishable by law.

Socrates, as an instance, was married and fathered three sons; yet he was tried in the Athens courts for corrupting youths. (One wonders if his relationships with these youths helped him tolerate his wife, Xanthippe, who was reputed to be of foul temper.) No less a giant than the biographer Plutarch, himself an excellent husband and father of many children, felt constrained to emphasize in his apologia for matrimony, *Amatorius*, that girls as well as boys are capable of inspiring passionate love in the hearts of men.

One has only to peruse a shelf of biographies to understand the degrees of overlapping sexuality that exist in many men. Probably the most publicized example in the last seventy-five years of a man whose life was spent both homosexually and heterosexually was Oscar Wilde. He affected an esthetic, artistic, almost effeminate way of life in his Oxford days. But he fell in love, courted extravagantly, and married a beautiful, gentle, and well-born woman. Constance Wilde loved her husband deeply and bore him two sons; even after his eventual disgrace, she refused all blandishments of her family to divorce him. In the beginning, he adjusted fairly well to marriage and fatherhood, although a life of Victorian domesticity was hardly compatible with his highly intellectual, sophisticated nature. His growing discomfort with routinized heterosexuality is no doubt reflected in his epigrams regarding marriage: "When a man has once loved a woman, he will do anything for her, except continue to love her"; "In married life three is company and two is none." About seven years after his marriage, he formed an intense emotional relationship with Lord Alfred Douglas, the son of the redoubtable Marquis of Queensberry, whose name is attached to boxing rules. The relationship ultimately sent Wilde to prison (from whence his *Ballad of Reading Gaol* was written) on a conviction of sodomy. The scandal destroyed his career and almost certainly shortened his life.

The marriage of the renowned French author André Gide to his cousin Madeleine lasted for forty years; on both sides were genuine love, admiration, and tenderness. Yet it was a tragic marriage for both of them because of Gide's predominant homosexuality — a fact made all the more paradoxical by his fathering of an illegitimate child before his wife's death. Madeleine may, in fact, have died a virgin. Gide considered his greatest work to be *Corydon*, which was an apologia for homosexuality and also — brave for 1924 — a public avowal of his private sexual philosophy. Here we have a man who was obviously not exclusively homosexual, even though essentially so.

Somerset Maugham said that he had tried to convince himself that three-quarters of his nature was normal, and only a quarter queer; but that in retrospect he had come to realize that it was the other way around. His marriage of eleven years terminated in divorce after he met a young American man who became his secretary. The clash of temperaments, however, between Maugham and his wife was probably sufficient to cause trouble in the most heterosexual of marriages. Maugham's association with his male American secretary lasted 30 years — until the younger man's death.

Michelangelo, in company with Leonardo da Vinci, has long been identified as a homosexual; but such a diagnosis of his sexual bent appears to be a bit simplistic. For the first sixty of his ninety years of a fantastically productive life, this giant among Renaissance artists was literally too involved in his work to form close personal relationships, male or female. In his later years — his long old age, really — he found himself needful, as he never had been earlier, of the solace of close relationships. There were men, to be sure, who filled the need; but how much these passions were part of his near-religious obsession with the beauty of youth and how much were sexual can only be guessed at. Indeed, some of his love poems were written to these young men. But there was also the poetess Vittoria Colonna, to whom he expressed himself in magnificent sonnets. When her name was mentioned to Michelangelo after her death (their relationship, whatever it was, lasted eleven years), "he often remained dazed, as one bereft of senses."

Of Julius Caesar it was said that he was the husband of all women and the wife of all men. He was married three times, and no less a woman than Cleopatra was at one time his mistress. One could conclude that Julius Caesar was neither homosexual nor heterosexual — he was just sexual. He took his sex wherever, whenever, and however he could find it.

Finally, there was the recent (and painful) example of ambisexuality in a personage close to the President of the United States. It constituted a case in point, at least in broad outline, of the premise that most humans, no matter what position in life they hold, have the proclivity to love both man and woman. The incident was also a tragic demonstration of the destruction of life and career that typically attends the revelation of homosexual tendencies. Our society, having little understanding of human sexuality in all its ramifications, still shrinks in horror of homosexuality. Its vengeance is cruel and relentless, its compassion and understanding almost nonexistent. I sometimes wonder why so much space is given to the controversy over sex education of the young. The parents often appear to stand in greater need.

―――――

FALLACY:

MEN (AND WOMEN) ARE HOMOSEXUALS BECAUSE THEY WERE "BORN THAT WAY."

FACT:

This mistaken idea rests on the belief that some hormonal imbalance or genetic defect has caused a man or woman to veer away from the opposite sex and toward members of the same sex as love objects. The advocates of this belief argue that the homosexual tendency must be inborn, because ours is a heterosexual world, and because from birth we are oriented toward heterosexuality. The theory is a popular one, having the support of many learned persons as well as those who gain their knowledge of scientific "facts" from tabloids. Neither hormones nor genetics, however, has ever been proven to cause homosexuality.

Our maleness or femaleness is determined by sex hormones, although each of us has a certain allotment of the hormones of the opposite sex. It is therefore understandable that hormonal imbalance — an overgenerous supply of the wrong hormones or a paucity of the right ones — should be suspected as the causative factor in homosexuality. However, a more critical examination of the body's reaction to the presence or absence of these unique substances tends to refute the theory. The castration of the male, for example — which means removal of the testicles, thus halting forever the major production of male hormones — fails to make a homosexual out of a heterosexual. Similarly, the surgical removal of the ovaries — a much more common occurrence — signals the end of major female-hormone production but creates no lesbians. Neither does injection, for therapeutic purposes, of female hormones in the male cause a previously heterosexual male to become homosexual. In fact, injection of a homosexual male with male hormones may merely serve to strengthen his homosexuality by intensifying his sex drive.

If a defective genetic process were responsible for homosexuality, one would expect the homosexual male to exhibit some distinct physical characteristics of the female and, conversely, the female homosexual, male traits. But such is not the case. As surprising as it may seem, only a scant 15% of the male homosexual population and about 5% of all lesbians are detectable from their mannerisms. And mannerisms — which are learned rather than inherited characteristics — are hardly the same as the physical characteristics of a particular sex.

In sum, neither present-day endocrinological tests nor microscopic or clinical examinations have revealed any physiological differences between the heterosexual and homosexual individual. There are therefore no grounds for the assertion that homosexuals are "born that way" based on their anatomical or physiological endowment at the time of birth, or upon their later physical development.

It appears far more likely that homosexuality is an outgrowth of childhood and adolescent conditioning. A child *learns* to identify with a particular sex, whether it is the genetically correct or incorrect one, and the most powerful influence is obviously the home. Many psychological pressures may act together or separately to veer a boy toward homosexuality, and similar forces steer a girl toward it. The father may have been a weak, aloof, and ineffectual force in his son's life, leaving the boy to develop an excessive attachment to the mother that he never outgrows. He then may feel that a serious involvement with another woman is a gross disloyalty to his mother or, worse, is tantamount to incest.

A more common father-son interaction that can culminate in the son's becoming homosexual, however, is one in which the father is harsh, overly aggressive, and too much of a "tough guy" to allow his son to enter into a close relationship with him. The boy does not identify with his father and does not learn the masculine role in life. This sort of father frequently is attempting to teach his son to be a real "he-man." But he prevents the very thing he wants for his son by not establishing a relationship with the boy rooted in the tenderness, acceptance, understanding, and love that are necessary to a healthy association between father and son. Thus, the son may become frightened of the "masculine" role epitomized by his father, or is otherwise unable to accept it, and he may go in the opposite direction. That is to say, he identifies with the feminine role, with its implications of warmth and understanding, as a defense against the unfortunate relationship he has with his father.

Other causative factors in homosexuality are to be found in the home. A boy's parents, wanting a daughter, may have rejected his sex from birth. Or the child's sex education may have been so faulty and larded with guilt, or the relationship between the parents so bad, that homosexuality provides an escape from the feared and contemptible example of heterosexuality that he or she has witnessed in the home. In the case of a girl, there may be a deep-seated hatred of the father. Or, frozen out by a cold mother, she may seek in another, older woman the maternal love that she was denied as a youngster.

The dynamics behind homosexuality are not generated solely in the home, however. Other sociological forces upon particularly vulnerable adolescents can be equally damaging. For example, a boy's relationships with girls may have been so unsatisfactory and threatening that he seeks instead the companionship of his own sex in order to avoid a repetition of his failures. Similarly, a sensitive girl who has been callously rejected by a man she loves may decide never again to run the risk of another rejection, and therefore turns to women for warmth and acceptance.

If a parent or teacher catches an adolescent sexually experimenting with another boy (such experimentation is quite common and normal) and calls him a "queer," the lad may come to the conclusion that he alone in the world is guilty of such a "crime," that he is different, that he is a true homosexual. In this age of emphasizing the importance of success on the sporting fields, the physically small, attractive boy who is athletically disinclined may be labeled "sissy." The power of suggestion is so strong, says psychologist Evelyn Hooker, that he may come to the conclusion that he is indeed homosexual, even though he has never been sexually aroused by a male.

In sum, whether the home or society, or the two in combination, exert the primary pressures that produce homosexuality is not known. Most authorities feel, however, that the child who develops such a problem has undergone a series of emotionally disturbing experiences over a period of several years that ends eventually in his turning homosexual.

Since the homosexual was not "born that way," one would expect that psychotherapeutic efforts to alter sexual inversion would meet with the same degree of success that treatment of other types of emotional problems does. Unfortunately, this is not the case. As long as the causes underlying homosexuality are not fully understood, the prospects of converting the homosexual to the "straight" life will never be spectacular. Homosexuals themselves typically do not wish to abandon their deviation, and, not wanting help, they are scarcely likely to profit by psychotherapy. It is the opinion of many therapists that those who do seek therapeutic help are not true homosexuals. These people, the therapists argue, actually prefer members of the opposite sex but are afraid of heterosexual relationships. Because of severe hurt or threat, and not because of true inversion, they have turned to their own sex for warmth, love, and affection.

―――――――

FALLACY:

HOMOSEXUALS ARE MORE CREATIVE THAN HETERO-SEXUALS.

FACT:

To the heterosexual world, it often appears that the fields of music, art, the dance, fashion, interior design, theatre, and the like are dominated by homosexuals. It is probably true that, in these areas, a homosexual in authority will try to help homosexual friends. But this favoritism is scarcely different from the nepotism existing in many businesses, nor does it differ from the ethnic, religious, or political considerations that often prejudice the hiring (or not hiring) of "straight" people in other enterprises.

Giants such as Leonardo da Vinci and Michaelangelo, who happened also to be homosexual (to some degree or other), appear to be the exception rather than the rule in their stratosphere of genius. The demand for true talent being as great as it is, the "gay" boss cannot afford to pass over a worthy, but straight, candidate in favor of a mediocre gay one, or he would soon be out of business. Furthermore, the charge that the world of the arts is a homosexual closed shop, a sort of artistic mafia, is no doubt quite frequently made by the straight loser who, lacking the talent, must seek a scapegoat.

A noted psychiatrist, Samuel B. Hadden, who has had extensive experience in the treatment of homosexuals, offered an interesting commentary on the prominence of homosexuals in arts, letters, and fashion. Writing in *Harper's Magazine*, Dr. Hadden commented that in his experience the typical homosexual was aware very early in his life that he was "different." His school years are lonely, so his mother buys him a fiddle or paint box and sends him off to take lessons; not being part of a group, he has plenty of time to practice. "The prominence of homosexuals in the arts, in my view, does not reflect any special talent among them but rather the fact that they have been deprived of the rugged but distracting avocations of normal boys and turn to the arts to attain some significance."

Somerset Maugham offered another view — and perhaps he should know better than most — when he commented that "however subtly [the homosexual] sees life, he cannot see it whole"; that he lacks the ability to take with great seriousness those things "that normal men take seriously. . . . He has small power of invention, but a wonderful gift of delightful embroidery. He has vitality, brilliance, but seldom strength." (How incisive Maugham's opinion is, it is difficult to say. Perhaps it is nothing more than one peevish, egocentric writer's view of other writers, straight or gay.) The late psychiatrist Dr. Edmund Bergler held similar views, as he found homosexuals to be caught up in the turmoil of conflict, thus sapping "so much of their energy that the shell is a mixture of superciliousness, fake aggression, and whimpering." A psyche thus sapped obviously cannot devote its full energies to the development and flourishing of a talent.

———

FALLACY:

ORAL-GENITAL SEX BETWEEN A MAN AND A WOMAN
INDICATES HOMOSEXUAL TENDENCIES.

FACT:

Homosexuality involves sexual contact between members of the same sex. The choice of a partner of the same, rather than of the opposite, sex is the determinant in homosexuality, *not* the technique used in sexual activity. Some of the most genuinely masculine of men and feminine of women often enjoy oral-genital contact. But unless that type of outlet is preferred with a member of the same sex, it is no more an indication of homosexual tendencies than if sexual intercourse were the technique of choice.

Probably this idea is an outgrowth of the fact that homosexuals often employ oral-genital techniques in their sex-play activities. It does not follow, however, that the same technique cannot be employed by heterosexual partners with pleasure and without the implication of the slightest trace of homosexuality.

Techniques of sexual stimulation, arousal, and intercourse vary from culture to culture and from person to person and are in no way related to heterosexuality or homosexuality. All couples who have maintained an active and interesting sex life for any period of time have tried variations of all known sexual acts and positions and have probably added variations of their own to the variations, including any and all forms of oral-genital sex. Such experimentation is especially prevalent among persons of higher education, yet the incidence of homosexuality is no higher — if as high — among these people than it is among those with less education.

Such specialists as psychologists, psychiatrists, and marriage counselors point out that couples who limit their sexual activity to a single method of outlet, even though that method be sexual intercourse, are afflicted with more sexual inhibitions and conflicts than those who enjoy a wider range of outlets. From clinical and research findings one can easily judge that oral-genital sexual contact between a man and a woman is an adventuresome, positive form of heterosexual behavior and therefore actually stands in contradiction to the suggestion that it has homosexual overtones.

FALLACY:

THE MAN WHO ENJOYS HAVING HIS NIPPLES STIMULATED
HAS SUPPRESSED HOMOSEXUAL DESIRES.

FACT:

It is axiomatic that there is much less difference in sexual response
between man and woman than there is among various members of the same
sex.

This statement is particularly true when the matter of erogenous
zones — those areas of the body particularly sensitive to sexual stimulation — is considered. The supply of nerve endings especially responsive to
such stimulation is the same in both men and women. In the genital area, the
male's penis and its counterpart, the female's clitoris, are the most sensitive.
And of the nongenital erogenous zones, the most sensitive are usually the
breasts, particularly the nipples.

Even though some parts of the body are more sexually sensitive than
others, there is no such thing as an abnormal erogenous zone in either sex. If
a man or woman becomes sexually aroused through the stimulation of some
part of the body that would ordinarily be considered somewhat unusual, the
arousal must be regarded as the result of conditioning. It is *not* the product of
any suppressed, perverted, or inverted tendencies. If, for instance, a woman
has experienced intensely gratifying sexual encounters while having her
eyebrows blown upon, she becomes conditioned to being sexually aroused
just by her lover's blowing on her brows. Yet this is not commonly regarded
as a sexual stimulus, and a subsequent lover might think that he has become
involved with some kind of nut if she asks him to blow upon her brows as
part of their love play. Furthermore, individuals are differently endowed in
their supply of sex nerve endings in different parts of the body; heredity,
therefore, also plays a role in what is and is not an erogenous zone in a
particular person's body.

In their meticulous clinical examination of the many ways in which
humans respond to sexual stimulation, Masters and Johnson noted that 60%
of all men experience nipple erection during sexual excitation, and that the
erection persists for a considerable period of time after orgasm has occurred.
The man's nipple erection may occur spontaneously, or because of the
female's caresses.

Women also experience nipple erection, of course, together with enlargement of the breasts during sexual excitation. But it is interesting to note that
only about 50% of them become sexually aroused through having their
breasts manipulated, whereas 75% of men themselves become sexually

aroused when they view and stimulate their partner's breasts. This is another instance of the superiority of psychological over physiological factors in sexual matters.

Although a woman's skin is far more sensitive to the touch than a man's is (which should serve as a warning to new husbands to guard against overstimulating their brides), the supply of nerve endings in both their bodies is, in general, the same. There is sound physiological basis, therefore, for a man's experiencing sexual excitation when his wife touches or stimulates his nipples, just as there is if she caresses his penis: the particular part of the body that he especially enjoys having stimulated is largely a matter of his particular distribution of nerve endings and of conditioning. In no way does his liking the sexual stimulation of any part of his body constitute evidence of homosexual (or heterosexual, for that matter) leanings, or of his being in any way less masculine than the man who is indifferent to this sort of stimulation.

———————

FALLACY:

A CHILD CONCEIVED THROUGH REAR-ENTRY COITUS WILL BE HOMOSEXUAL.

FACT:

The curious notion has arisen that, if a couple conceives a child in the course of coitus in which penile entry is made from the rear of the woman, that child will quite probably grow up to be a homosexual.

This distorted idea probably is an outgrowth of the fact that many male homosexuals achieve orgasm through anal intercourse — which means, of course, that the homosexual most likely makes his sexual contact from the rear. Carrying this fact into the realm of fallacy brings some people to the conclusion that anyone who approaches his sexual partner from the rear is *ipso facto* homosexually inclined, and that any child thus conceived is accordingly "marked."

The possibility that a genetic abnormality can be the cause of a person's becoming a homosexual has never been proved and has, in fact, been almost wholly discounted by present-day investigators into the subject. These researchers say, instead, that almost certainly it is environmental pressures in the person's childhood and adolescence that veer him from "straight" to "gay." Even if the father were homosexually inclined, there is no way that this abnormality could be *genetically* transmitted to his offspring.

This is in no way to suggest that a man or woman who engages in rear-entry coitus is homosexually inclined. It is a coital position assumed by many strongly heterosexual couples for reasons of preference, convenience, or health, or simply because they wish to add variety to their sexual maneuverings.

Intromission from the rear can be accomplished while the woman sits, kneels, lies flat on her stomach, or lies side by side with her husband. Many women find it unsatisfactory because, in comparison with other coital positions, there is considerably less stimulation of the clitoris when this position of intercourse is assumed. Many men find it unsatisfactory because there can be no deep penile penetration. Both the couple may object to it because the face-to-face intimacy, which is important to them, is missing. Even so, it is a useful position for a woman who is in advanced pregnancy, and it is a relaxing one for the couple who are old or ill.

Intromission from the rear while both the partners assume a knee-chest position is especially enjoyable to some couples. At the same time, however, many people find it repugnant, because it most closely approximates the position of anal intercourse taken by many homosexuals.

That this "guilt by association" exists is unfortunate. Many couples deny themselves much pleasure in their sexual interchange by allowing a dull and eventually, perhaps, a deadly routine to characterize it. There should be a sense of adventure in the sexual relationship; not everyone *has* to enjoy rear-entry coitus, as a case in point. But many couples might find it satisfactory in a time of debility when they might otherwise forego intercourse; or they may discover that it provides the particular excitement that comes from experiencing something new. The experimentation is the important thing; even if a coital position enjoyed by a couple is an unusual or even bizarre one, the only important thing is that it is *mutually* satisfying and pleasurable. If a couple finds the rear-entry sexual position — or any other position – fun and exciting and in no way harmful to either of them, they should engage in it, even if it is so unconventional as to have them swinging by their heels from the chandelier. The emotional future of the child resulting from intercourse in any coital position is protected, because there is no possible way that parents can thus "mark" him.

FALLACY:

ANY LESBIAN WOULD PREFER A MAN, IF HE IS A "REAL MAN" AND IF HE WOULD USE THE RIGHT TECHNIQUE.

FACT:

This statement may be true in the case of a bisexual woman — the woman who enjoys sex equally, or nearly so, either with another woman or with a man — or in the case of a woman who more correctly should be labeled a pseudolesbian than a lesbian, because she enters into emotional relationships with women for reasons other than sexual preference. When, however, one is considering the true lesbian, the assumption is false that she would prefer a man if only he would use the right sexual technique. This woman would never choose a man as a sexual partner in preference to a woman, no matter how great his charms and persuasiveness, or his skill in making love. The true lesbian resents, distrusts, or dislikes men for a variety of reasons, some of which I shall describe below. She resents society's insistence on her playing the passive, submissive role in most areas of a woman's life. Her pride in herself, as well as her resentment toward the male of the species, cause her to turn her back completely on a sexual or otherwise deeply emotional relationship with any man.

The lesbian may have been severely deprived of maternal warmth and affection as a child and adolescent. Her erotic needs as an adult, therefore, can perhaps be satisfied only by establishing a warm daughter relationship with an older woman, who provides a substitute for the emotional nourishment she failed to receive from her own mother.

It may well be that certain women have turned from men because of disappointment. (But perhaps, as the renowned French authoress Simone de Beauvoir points out, the disappointment grew from the fact that such women really preferred another woman.) The lesbian may have been subjected to such a traumatic sexual experience in her young days that she has come to evaluate woman's role as being that of the sexual prey or plaything of the man. Therefore, she cannot accept the idea that a man is capable of mingling love and tenderness in his sexuality, believing that only another woman can combine these qualities in sexual expression.

The lesbian's psychosexual development may have become arrested, as I have mentioned earlier, thus freezing her in sexual immaturity. When she reaches physical maturity, an intimate association with a man is as unthinkable to her as it was when she was a girl. She remains at that pubescent stage in which the primary interest and affections of almost all girl children are directed toward other girls, or to certain older women whom they admire.

Her lesbianism may have been formulated by the observance of her parents' bad marriage, or because of the terrible, terrifying things her mother told her through the years about her father (and, quite likely, about men in general). She may have witnessed brutal or alcoholic behavior on the part of her father toward her mother. The home is the symbol of the world to all children; and the parents' marriage epitomizes to them all marriages, since children have little opportunity, generally, to observe other marriages closely. A girl therefore can easily develop an aversion to marriage because of her childhood exposure to a bad heterosexual relationship, and hence an aversion to men as sexual partners. Men are seen as creatures to be mistrusted, afraid of, and avoided.

In none of these instances can a man's technique — or lack of it — have the slightest influence on changing the woman's lesbianism. She has rejected *all* men as sexual and emotional partners. She is probably a thoroughgoing proponent of "male protest," as Freudian analysts would call it. She is, as the public considers it, a man-hater. Nothing short of a will to change, coupled with intensive psychotherapy, will alter the lesbian's inversion. And, unfortunately, even with strong motivation on her part and the best of professional help, the prospects of reversing her homosexual tendencies after she has reached adulthood are unpromising.

———

FALLACY:

MOST PROSTITUTES ARE LESBIANS.

FACT:

To evaluate this oft-quoted statement fairly requires an examination of the underlying causes both of prostitution and lesbianism. Why did this woman turn prostitute, and why did that one become a lesbian? The dynamics of the two conditions are usually different, but it is not impossible for them to overlap, or, in fact, to be nearly identical. One must concede from the outset that it is not unknown that a lesbian becomes a prostitute — or that, in time, a prostitute becomes a lesbian.

Typically, a lesbian's psychosexual development becomes arrested, or fixated, in that stage of adolescent development at which all girls (and boys as well) are far more interested in members of their own sex than they are in those of the opposite one. Or the lesbian as a girl may have developed an unusually strong attachment to a father or brother, so strong that sexual contact with another male would constitute disloyalty, or, worst of all, incest. Perhaps her father was so harsh or cruel in his treatment of his wife and children that she has turned against all men. Perhaps the parents' marriage was so unhappy or corrosive that it has set her against marriage. A woman may look to another woman for warmth and affection because she feels that she is unattractive to men, or has been rejected by them. There are those who become "situational lesbians" in such instances as confinement in a penal institution. (It has been estimated that one-half to three-fourths of women in prison have homosexual experiences.) In the prison milieu, most of these women form lesbian contacts not so much for sexual outlet as for affectional bonds and a means of "belonging," thus making prison life more tolerable. Most will again become sexually interested in men, and exclusively so, upon their release.

A woman becomes a prostitute for a variety of reasons. Many view it as the road to easy money (unfortunately, they have not reckoned with the ugly prospect of payoffs to corrupt officials, pimps, or blackmailers). Some, indeed, are so indolent or mentally deficient that they cannot hold down regular jobs. Only a very few are so highly sexed that they actually enjoy the contact with many men. There are also those who go into prostitution as a means of rebellion against parents or society. A great many girls regard prostitution simply as an expedient means of solving a financial crisis. And once they are out of financial difficulty they retreat into their usual occupation of housewife, salesgirl, or teacher.

Let us now look at those instances in which lesbianism and prostitution do, in fact, overlap. The reasoning is very likely subconscious; but if a woman has lesbian tendencies, she may go into prostitution as a means of proving to herself that she is indeed heterosexual. Psychoanalyst Wilhelm Stekel, for one, believed that many women enter prostitution because of latent homosexuality, fearing that it might break into overt lesbian behavior. In the course of their exposure to many men, especially to those who are brutal or perverted, their revulsion for men grows and, ironically, drives them toward women for love and warmth. Thus are they caught up in the very sexual pattern that they had sought to escape — homosexuality.

It is axiomatic that most prostitutes receive no sexual satisfaction from their customers. The occupational necessity of having to have sex relations with many men who hold no attraction for them, or who are downright repulsive, could therefore quite logically in the course of time cause prostitutes to develop a distinct aversion to men. It follows that, being lax about social taboos anyway, they then would turn to other women for the warmth, affection, and sexual expression that they had been unable to find with men.

Dr. Frank Caprio made an extensive investigation of prostitutes living in brothels in the Americas, Europe, and the Orient. He reported in his book *Female Homosexuality* that the majority of prostitutes interviewed maintained that they "obtained satisfactory sexual gratification either through solitary masturbation or through sexual intimacies with another prostitute." The noted sexologist P. H. Gebhard, on the other hand, claims that, in his sampling of prostitutes, the percentage of those having orgasmic responses to their husbands or boyfriends was greater than that among married women in general. (I assume that his sample was mainly composed of call girls, who are far more independent than "house girls," since brothels are fast disappearing from the American scene.) Throughout the world many brothels, quite lucratively, stage lesbian performances for customers. The performances, however, are designed for the titillation of the viewer and certainly not for the benefit of the prostitutes involved, despite the fact that showmanship demands a display of heaving passion so that the customer will feel he has had his money's worth. Furthermore, one cannot overlook the unusually high fee which the prostitutes themselves receive for their performance. The prostitute, therefore, is probably not motivated by lesbian tendencies to participate in these displays; money is the thing.

The notion that most prostitutes are also lesbian would appear to have grown from these "spectacles," and from the reasoning that prostitutes are not normal sexually (otherwise they would have chosen another profession) and that, per se, they must be homosexual. It is interesting to note what Polly Adler, the famous New York madam, has to say on this subject in her book, *A House Is Not a Home*: "Inevitably, I had a few lesbians . . . . I have no figures on the incidence of female homosexuality, but it's my observation that it occurs in every walk of life."

Harry Benjamin and R. E. L. Masters in *Prostitution and Morality* state flatly that "substantial evidence would be required to persuade us that any large percentage of prostitutes are homosexual, latently or overtly, at the start of their careers." These writers admit that they did encounter much lesbianism in their investigations, but tabulated no data on the total amount of sexual outlet that prostitutes obtained from homosexual contacts. They theorized that lesbian activity among prostitutes probably stemmed from a desire for something new, disillusionment with the male sex, and the like. These researchers were obviously writing about women living in bordellos, who have much less freedom to pick and choose their customers, and who have many more of them, than is usually the case among call girls.

FALLACY:

THE TYPICAL CAREER WOMAN IS A SUPPRESSED LESBIAN.

FACT:

The role of woman in our culture, other than that of childbearing and lactation, is not one that is fixed by her genes. Anatomically, males and females are far more similar than dissimilar, and what physical differences do exist are often further blurred by similarities of dress and hair styles.

The customs of her particular cultural environment, then, determine what role woman shall play. In our society she is told that she must be a submissive and passive creature and that, in effect, she is inferior to the male. If she is to be regarded as truly feminine, truly desirable, she should have few personal aspirations not oriented toward the home — "the woman's place." All her intellectual and emotional needs should be satisfied through her husband, children, and household. (That women in increasing numbers are coming to recognize the fallacy of this contention is wholly another story.)

When the female's role is thus so narrowly defined, what of the woman whose talents are along "unfeminine" lines — the woman who wishes to be a geologist or an engineer, a doctor or a business executive, long regarded as provinces belonging exclusively to the male? Such a woman must of necessity be strong-willed (nonpassive), determined (nonsubmissive), and intelligent (almost certainly meaning that she has rejected the premise that emotional fulfillment is to be found in the repetitious performance of menial household chores). She must be competitive in a peculiar way, and an unfair one: she not only has to prove that she is as talented as the similarly gifted men with whom she is in competition, but she must also overcome the prejudice, perhaps hostility, of men toward her, a woman, for having invaded what they consider to be their exclusive domain.

Her teeming ambition may be, of course, solely an expression of the intellectual side of her nature, and have nothing whatever to do with the sensual. Simone de Beauvoir has pointed out (*The Second Sex*) that in some cases a woman may be so caught up in her narcissism (that is, an absorbed interest only in herself and her career) that she is "incapable of a warm attachment to other women; she sees in them only enemies and rivals." No doubt her emotional reaction to men runs along the same lines. Her consuming passion is not for an affectional relationship with either man or woman, but for her profession. Other women, made to feel uncomfortable in a male world in which their talents force them to compete, attempt to compensate by altering their dress and appearance, and in some extreme cases by adopting the vocabulary of a seasoned sailor. Because of this pseudo-masculinity, such a woman is judged to be a lesbian, and one who plays the male role in her lesbian relationships.

These extremes in dress and behavior are rare among today's career women, however. Most are considerably above average in appearance and, in fact, usually impress one as being quite feminine in manner. Although — unfairly — a professional woman may have to be more aggressive than the average woman in her competition with the men in her profession, at least until she has proved her worth or talent, the aggressiveness in no way implies homosexuality. Neither does aggressiveness in her business dealings mean that she cannot or does not participate as freely in sexual intercourse, and with as much pleasure to herself and her partner, as do more passive or "typical" women.

Another common basis for believing that women with careers are largely lesbian is that there are fewer marriages among career women as a group than among those women who do not pursue careers. The myopic view is that, if a woman is not married, she must be unsuited for marriage; and if not suited for marriage, then, ipso facto, she must be lesbian. Such crooked thinking fails to take into consideration the fact that the successful career woman is not pressured by economic necessity to marry. And if she does marry, but the marriage proves unhappy, she is not forced by economic dependency on her husband to stay married, as is too often the case with women who have no careers. One might say that the career woman perhaps marries less but enjoys it more!

A final word. The "butch" lesbian — the one who tries to make herself look as tough and mannish as possible — is considered by most people to be typical of female homosexuals. To the contrary, however, she is quite atypical and is probably as offensive to most other lesbians as she is to the "straight" community. Only a very few lesbians can be identified from their appearance — probably not more than 5%. It is as unjust to label a woman as being lesbian simply because she is not particularly feminine in dress and manner as it is to label a man as being homosexual because he is small, delicate, or unaggressive.

———————

Sexual Disorders and Sexual Abnormalities, Real and Imagined

In this section I have chosen for discussion a few of those subjects about which the individual suffers the most self-doubts and despair, and over which he displays the greatest tendency to project feelings of guilt or shame onto others. Consider the long-held view that the sex drive of men and women differs in strength. The truth of the matter is that there is little difference, in general, between the sex drive of men and women; the widest variation in drive is among members of the same sex. The danger of believing otherwise becomes a real threat in a marriage in which, for instance, there is a distinct variance in the needs of the partners. The less needful partner protects his or her ego by deciding that the other's sexual desires are abnormal.

Examination of the statistics on those who masturbate and those who do not shows without a doubt that masturbation is one of the most natural of human sexual activities. Yet many people are still burdened with the conviction that masturbation is grossly abnormal and will inevitably exact a dreadful toll in physical or psychological ills. Others firmly believe that there is only one way in which marital sexual intercourse should be conducted; embellishments upon the act of penile-vaginal coitus suggest a degree of perversion, as does any departure from the national coital average of 2.135 times a week!

The woman who is uninhibited and exuberant in her enjoyment of sex, or who does not wait for her husband to initiate sexual overtures, tends to be put on the list of suspected nymphomaniacs.

Sexual inadequacies and incompatibilities cause much unhappiness, often needlessly. Many people are unaware that there is help to be had for many *problems of sexual malfunctioning, as well as for those cases wherein a couple's sexual desires differ. Often only a proper understanding of what is truly normal in sexual behavior — or, more often, what things are definitely not abnormal — will suffice to bring about the ease of mind necessary to successful sexual functioning.*

―――――

FALLACY:

MASTURBATION IS KNOWN TO CAUSE LUNACY, ACNE, AND A CONSTELLATION OF OTHER PHYSICAL AND PSYCHO-LOGICAL PROBLEMS.

FACT:

The list of maladies attributed to "self-abuse," as it has been darkly referred to, would fill a billboard. Masturbation has been alleged to weaken body and mind; to cause acne; to cause warts or fine hair to grow on the palms of hands, and hair to fall out; to produce frigidity, impotence, and deformities in future children; to "use up" the individual's predetermined allotment of ejaculations, so that sex life is shortened; and to endanger future marital adjustment.

Surveys indicate that possibly 60% of women and easily 95% of men masturbate, or have done so at one point in their lives (the cynics declaring that the other 5% of men are probably lying). If, therefore, masturbation causes so many mental and physical disorders, one would logically expect that most of mankind is doomed to spend time under medical or psychiatric care because of it. Obviously this is not the case.

Masturbation never hurt anyone, although the guilt feelings one has about it can cause much anguish. In the opinion of the vast majority of authorities, masturbation, rather than being sinful or a peril to health, is normal and beneficial, part of growing up, part of self-discovery, a stepping-stone toward the youth's eventual role as an adult sexual being, and is actually a normal and beneficial act. It cannot be called abnormal in any case, since the practice is so widespread. Solitary masturbation is an indicator that something is wrong only if it is used as the exclusive sexual release, even when heterosexual relationships are possible; or if it is used excessively to reduce tensions and conflicts in other areas of life — school, family, and peer-group relationships, as examples. In these instances, masturbation is not the cause of the difficulties but a symptom only.

It is not too difficult to perceive how the unlikely relationship between masturbation and the phenomena of acne and pimples was established. The time of greatest masturbatory activity is adolescence, which is, coincidentally, the time of the hormonal upheavals producing the skin eruptions typical of puberty. Moralists could then seize upon this "evidence" in their efforts to deter the young from masturbation. The argument is easily destroyed when one considers that, if self-stimulation to orgasm could truly cause skin disorders, orgasms resulting from sexual intercourse between man and woman would quite rightly be expected to cause the same disorders.

The linking of masturbation to lunacy is a bit more subtle. Those anxious to "prove" the dangers or sinfulness of masturbation are quick to point out a severely disturbed mental patient whose excessive behavior patterns include masturbation. They do not understand (or do not wish to admit) that a mental patient's excesses may well be in other directions — nonstop, senseless talking, or the endless counting of a handful of buttons, or refusal to walk anywhere except along a wall. What is important is this: behavior such as excessive masturbation does not cause mental disorders; the mental disorder causes the inappropriate behavior.

The only psychological problems caused by masturbation arise from the individual's feeling guilty about it. Many religious denominations warn that masturbation Is wicked and merits hellfire; parents and teachers voice their strong disapproval by saying it is a disgusting and "unmanly" act, betraying a lack of self-control; the peer group warns that ejaculation is a drain on the fixed supply of semen. No wonder a youngster feels guilty and anxious; and until the guilt can be resolved — which assuredly it should be by some enlightened adult — he is well advised to leave off masturbating.

I recall the only formal sex "education" that I received in my own school days. It consisted of an annual lecture from a local minister who (it is now obvious) was beset with more than his rightful share of sexual problems. He thundered away that not only was masturbation sinful, but that also it would cause hair to grow in the palms of our hands and our shoulders to become rounded. The result was a roomful of students with ramrod-straight posture who could scarcely concentrate on the following classes for making so many stealthy glances at the palms of their hands — and who continued, I am sure, to masturbate as before.

It is curious why masturbation should have fallen under such a shroud of condemnation in the first place. The answer probably lies in the history of the ancient Jews, when great emphasis was placed, understandably, on strengthening individual tribes. Hebrew men were enjoined to "increase and multiply"; wastage of sperm was therefore considered sinful. The dictum declaring women "unclean" during menstruation and for five days thereafter would seem to have been based on the effort to conserve the husband's sperm till a time of the menstrual cycle when intercourse would be more likely to produce conception.

"Spilling of seed" is the theme of one of the most famous accounts in the Book of Genesis. Onan refused to follow the Hebraic tradition of impregnating a dead brother's widow, apparently using withdrawal as the means of preventing conception. God struck Onan dead; and through the centuries God's action has been misinterpreted as evidence of His wrath over the "spilling of seed" rather than over Onan's defiance of the law. "Onanism" somehow became equated with birth control and, eventually, with masturbation. Although the condemnation of birth control on religious grounds has largely dissipated during the past fifty years, masturbation remains under the cloud of misinterpretation.

Long prior to the birth of Hippocrates, the "Father of Medicine," down through the ages to 1900, the medical world was rather ignorant of cause and effect in all areas of sexual behavior. Objectivity and a scientific approach were notoriously lacking in those paltry investigations that were made. Occasionally some brave scientific soul would reach out for enlightenment, but such men were few. Struggles through these dark ages toward an understanding of human sexuality were dealt a near deathblow in the mid-18th century when S. A. D. Tissot of France wrote his *Onana, a Treatise on the Diseases Produced by Onanism*. Projecting his personal problems into his writings, to say nothing of his superabundance of ignorance, Tissot wrote of the viciousness of self-abuse, attributing most of the known medical disorders — including consumption, epileptic seizures, gonorrhea, and insanity — to the loss of semen through masturbation. It was Tissot who introduced the fatuous and totally unscientific idea that the loss of one drop of seminal fluid causes more bodily damage and weakness than the loss of forty drops of blood.

Tissot's writings and theories captured the attention of many countries, influencing medical men and laymen alike. Other "authorities" added their views to those of Tissot, until even today there still persist irrational social prohibitions against the perfectly normal, and probably beneficial, act of masturbation. Fortunately, the vast majority of people are almost ready to accept masturbation for what it is — a not immoral and certainly harmless act of sexual stimulation and relief. The tide of ignorance concerning masturbation began turning in 1891, when Dr. E. T. Brady became one of the first authorities to challenge the concept of masturbation as a pernicious act; but even Brady considered self-stimulation somewhat dangerous. The hysteria over masturbation reached such a pitch in the late 1800's that "depraved" women who resorted to it were frequently forced by their families to submit to a clitoridectomy as a method of control.

In the light of today's prevailing opinion that masturbation is not harmful, it seems unrealistic that certain people and institutions still declaim against it as a dangerous and evil practice. For example, the United States Naval Academy regulations of June 1940 state that evidence of masturbation is adequate grounds for refusing to admit a man as a candidate to that institution. Considering the prevalence of masturbation among men, one wonders how the Naval Academy has managed to fill its ranks.

To be sure, maximum sexual fulfillment is not intended to be a lonely pursuit. Perhaps the one danger of masturbation, although a remote one, is that through it one might come to view sexual release as a solitary, rather than a shared, experience. Nevertheless, even in an adult's life there are those periods of loneliness, aloneness, or illness, whether one is married or unmarried, when masturbation is the only acceptable means of releasing sexual tensions. Masturbation in these circumstances, as well as in the developmental period of adolescence, can be considered neither harmful nor evil, but, rather, as that thoughtful minister and author, Dr. Charlie Shedd, put it, "a gift of God."

FALLACY:

UNUSUAL OR EXCESSIVE SEXUAL PRACTICES CAN LEAD TO MENTAL BREAKDOWNS.

FACT:

This argument demands the immediate answer to two questions: who is the person saying so, and what are his definitions? The people who pass along this fallacy are classically those who know little or nothing of man's sexual makeup or capacity, or whose peculiar religious convictions cause them to view the relationship between God and man in terms of sin and punishment, rather than in the terms of love, understanding, and forgiveness that Christ constantly urged. For such people, pleasure is defined as sin, and what is sinful must be punished. Their reasoning goes something like this: sex, being pleasurable, must consequently be bad; what is bad is the devil's handiwork, for which God demands punishment; if the mind is evil enough to harbor sexual thoughts, then it merits the wrath of God, who punishes it by destroying it in whole or in part by madness.

Parents and religionists who wish to prevent their charges from engaging in premarital petting or intercourse warn that such self-indulgence and lack of self-control are heralds of a fast-approaching mental breakdown. Or, confusing cause and effect, they may point to a mentally defective neighbor who mindlessly but openly fondles his genitals (very likely not to the point of orgasm), and warn that similar mental deterioration awaits the person who masturbates.

These arguments come not only from those with a pleasure-sin obsession, but also from those who wish to control the sexual behavior of other people. Consider the person who feels that the sole purpose of sexual activity is reproduction and that such activity should therefore be confined to efforts to beget a child. To such a person the couple equipped with a generous supply of the Pill and enjoying coitus nightly appear to be selfish pleasure-seekers, who will no doubt pay for their excessive behavior by a general breakdown in their mental health.

Categorically, there is no form of sexual behavior nor any degree of its frequency that can in any remote way cause mental disorders. The connection between sexual activity and emotional difficulties exists only in those cases in which a person is *made* to feel guilty about sex. Lacking the proper education in such a supersensitive subject, a young person can easily absorb a freight of guilt feelings (from parents, teachers, and the community) about *any*thing sexual. The important thing to remember is that sexual activity of itself does not cause such upset or worry; the condemnatory attitude of other people is responsible. Also, the person whose sexual behavior is contrary to the mores of his community — for instance, the homosexual or the compulsive exhibitionist — typically suffers from anxiety and personal conflict growing out of a fear of discovery, if not fear of arrest. Here again, the emotional unrest is brought about by the society in which such a person lives, not by his behavior. If an invert lived in a culture tolerant of homosexuality, or the exhibitionist in a community not given to wearing clothes anyway, there would be no soil in which such sexual anxieties and fears could germinate. "There is nothing good or bad but thinking makes it so."

The person who judges others' sexual behavior as being unusual must be considered something of a sexual autocrat — bigot is probably a better label. Only what he or she personally approves of as being "normal" is considered acceptable; everything else is considered "unusual" and hence suspect. Penile-vaginal intercourse in marriage, then, becomes the only normal form of sexual expression; everything else becomes sexual excess or abnormality. Intercourse must always take place in bed; the man's proper position is invariably on top (a position, incidentally, so strange to certain "primitive" societies that it is referred to as the "missionary position"); the woman should be a relatively passive participant; talking about sex with one's spouse, or daydreaming about it, is a little depraved; sex is not intended to be fun, something to be laughed about, as it is deadly serious business; sexual foreplay is an unnecessary, juvenile pursuit and, if carried on for any length of time, is probably perverted.

Is there really any such thing as too much sex? There are, to be sure, those husbands and wives who want intercourse far more frequently than their spouses do. But this is a matter of a distinct difference between the two in sexual desire and interest. It is not indicative of excessive sexual desire on the part of the more needful partner. In fact, when the body has functioned to the point of complete sexual satisfaction, it rebels, shuts down, and says, "No more." It is therefore impossible — at least for the man — to have too much sex. And if having too much is an impossibility, how can having his physiologically normal quota cause the individual to come apart mentally?

———

FALLACY:

VAGINAL-PENILE INTERCOURSE IS THE ONLY NORMAL METHOD OF SEX RELATIONS.

FACT·

There can be nothing basically wrong, morally or physically, with any form of sex play. The only criteria to be applied are these: does the behavior heighten sexual pleasure and bring a great measure of emotional fulfillment to the partners, and do both partners enjoy and desire the specific play? A particular form of sex play becomes wrong if one partner does not like it; if it causes discomfort or pain; or if it is sadistic or masochistic in motivation, thus injuring the partner's integrity or personality; or if it is conducted within the sight or sound of an unwilling observer.

The center of the most intense sexual pleasure is the male's penis and the female's clitoris and the vulval area surrounding it. Indeed, sexual arousal involving only these areas can be quite pleasurable. Other areas of the body are likewise intensely responsive to stimulation and, having been stimulated, can lift merely pleasurable sexual intercourse to the level of the ecstatic. Touching and being touched, looking and being looked at, hearing and being heard — these things are exciting in themselves to both giver and receiver; and as the partner observes the excitement of the other, so his or her own excitement grows. The flow washes back and forth, and each wave lifts sexual excitement to yet another peak of pleasurableness. Even the senses of smell and taste should be brought into play. In no other area of human behavior does the precept "anything goes" have more importance than in the sexual-love relationship. Each individual has the right to "do his own thing," and I do not necessarily mean masturbation.

Many married couples, however, refuse to consider any sexual experimentation or exploration, on the grounds that anything other than coitus is dirty and perhaps even perverted. It is easy enough to say religions are responsible for these attitudes, that they undertook the regulation of sexual practices, declaring what is natural and unnatural, with little or no insight into what motivates or directs man's sexual desire. But part of the blame for perpetuating unrealistic, often unjust regulation of man's sexual behavior also lies with lawmakers who, fearful that the registered voters of their area might consider them sexual liberals, refuse to work toward reformation of outmoded legal codes. It is hard to believe that in Indiana a man recently served three years in prison for having engaged in oral-genital sexual relations (sodomy) with his wife. (She swore the complaint against him in a moment of anger, tried later to withdraw it, but was not allowed to do so because sodomy is a criminal matter.) Another example of the need for legal reform: statutory rape in Texas means sexual intercourse with a girl under eighteen years of age, and the maximum penalty is death; in Delaware, by contrast, no crime is committed unless the partner is under seven years of age.

Fewer forms of sexual expression are more misunderstood or have been more roundly condemned than oral-genital contact. Many people, at least officially, continue to brand the application of the mouth to the sexual organs of one's partner (called fellatio if the act is performed on the man, cunnilingus if on the woman) as a perverted, obscene act. Yet practice and preachment seem to be at odds, since such a large majority of the population engage in it. It is considered by many to be immensely pleasurable and stimulating as foreplay, and is an excellent way to cause sexual excitement in a woman whose sexual drive otherwise is low or difficult to arouse and in a man whose potency is marginal.

There is a good physiological basis for the pleasure derived from mouth-genital contact: The mouth and tongue are erogenous zones common to nearly all people, and the genitals, of course, are very responsive to sexual stimulation. Furthermore, recent neurophysiological studies have shown that there is a close relationship between the parts of the brain concerned with oral functions (amygdala) and those parts concerned with sexual functions (septum and rostral diencephalon). Stimulation of an area of the brain affecting oral activity will readily produce a "spillover" into areas related to genital function. Since oral-genital contact is so pleasureful, one can only conclude that those who reject it out of hand are under the influence of the sort of puritanism that associates anything to do with the genitals (and, probably, with sex) with "dirtiness."

The proximity in the woman of the anus and the urethra to the genitals, and the fact that the male penis is both a seminal and a urinary outlet, are the physiological factors contributing to the concept of "dirtiness," but these do not constitute a logical objection to oral-genital contact. Certainly if one allows his body to become unclean and malodorous, especially in the anal-genital region, any type of sexual contact is likely to become objectionable. However, with the myriad supply of cosmetic and hygienic products currently on the market, there is really no excuse for an offensive odor emanating from any part of the body — including the anal-genital area.

People seldom enjoy even kissing someone when his or her breath is reeking, to say nothing of entering into more intimate physical contact with someone who needs a bath. If one has recently eaten, or suspects that the mouth might otherwise be offensive, then one is well advised to tackle the problem with toothbrush and mouthwash. The same sensible precautions should be taken with the genitals. Because the folds of skin that partially cover the surface of the genitals are natural receptacles for a collection of smegma and secretions, the region should be cleansed in such a way that there is no chance that any of the offensive material or odor lingers. In the same fashion used in cleaning the ear, a finger should move in and around the folds of the genitalia to cleanse them. If a couple give this sort of attention to keeping themselves clean and pleasant-smelling, making whatever use is indicated of "personal hygiene" and cosmetic products, the objection to oral-genital contact on the grounds of "dirtiness" is less than valid.

In spite of the fact that some people associate placing the mouth and tongue on the partner's genitals with homosexual practices or some other "perverted behavior," oral-genital contact is not abnormal. Masturbation, as I have discussed, is not abnormal. Sex foreplay that accidentally climaxes in orgasm before intercourse gets underway is not indicative of abnormality. Stimulating the anal area by caressing or tickling the anus, or even inserting a finger into the rectum, if this heightens sexual pleasure, suggests no perversion. Nor does stimulation that purposely leads to orgasm without coitus; the husband whose broken hip is in a cast and the wife on the verge of delivering a child cannot, or should not, have intercourse, yet they may be in definite need of sexual outlets.

This is not to say that any form of sexual activity is more fulfilling, or even nearly so, than penile-vaginal intercourse that culminates in orgasm for both the man and woman. The other forms of contact, however, are pleasurable in themselves, even if less so than coitus, and in certain circumstances some couples may actually prefer them to sexual intercourse. Whatever form of sexual contact a couple prefer, and for whatever reason, the choice should be based only on what best attunes every nerve of the body for the moment of orgasm, and should be restricted only by the criteria set forth in the first paragraph of this section. Preference for any form of sexual behavior is a matter of individual taste.

We all know that people can have sex without any love existing between them. We have all heard that love greatly enhances sexual satisfaction. What we hear less often, however, is the degree to which sexual satisfaction in marriage intensifies the love bond between a man and woman. The bed, then, should truly become a place of complete freedom to do whatever comes naturally.

―――――――

FALLACY:

WOMEN WHO HAVE STRONG SEX DRIVES, COME TO EASY CLIMAX, AND ARE CAPABLE OF MULTIPLE ORGASMS ARE NYMPHOMANIACS.

FACT:

The term "nymphomania" suggests, in sum, a woman of insatiable sexual appetite; a woman whose erotic impulses control her, rather than her being able to hold rein on them; a woman of blind indiscrimination in her choice of sexual partners. In the judgment and experience of behavioral scientists, however, a true nymphomaniac is an extremely rare phenomenon.

If a woman is accused of being a nymphomaniac *simply* because she is capable of quick, monumental, and numerous orgasmic responses, or because she is interested in sex and obviously enjoys it, one need not look at the woman for evidence of neurosis, but at the person levying the charge. About the most accurate one-word description for these girls is "lucky." When a woman's partner entertains as lively an interest in sex as her own is, and his attitude toward sex is healthy, he will almost certainly be delighted and consider himself most fortunate to have found such a woman. (As only Mae West could phrase it, "Sex is an emotion in motion.") But if he views her warm sexual responsiveness as evidence of nymphomania, then the unavoidable conclusion must be that the malady is in the eye of the beholder. He is the one with problems, not the woman. And if he refuses to change his thinking, he may quickly render the lady's "nymphomania" into frigidity, or perhaps drive her into the arms of another man.

One wonders what attitudes shape the man who would call a woman's active interest in sex nymphomania. First of all, he may have acquired the idea in his formative years that only "bad" girls — that is, prostitutes or other sexual delinquents — actually enjoy sexual relations. This belief was perhaps best exemplified in the Victorian era, when no "decent" woman was expected to enjoy sexual relations; sex was an ordeal to which she submitted to pacify the "animal nature" of her otherwise nice husband, or to conceive a child. Thus was the double standard formulated: men's sexual appetites are normal and acceptable, and they are permitted reasonable latitude in satisfying that appetite; all decent women, however, are "above" sexual responsiveness, and any form of sexual activity outside marriage is, naturally, unthinkable.

Such was, at least, the purported Victorian sexual code, to which nearly universal lip service was given in the English-speaking world. An example of the extent to which the effort was made to control women's sexuality in 19th-century England lies in what might be called the sewing-machine syndrome in garment factories. In many such factories, several matrons were assigned the task of wandering among the ladies seated at their sewing machines, which were operated by treadle, of course, rather than by electricity. If a matron were to hear a particularly rapid whirring of a treadle, she immediately rushed to the run-away machine to pour water on its operator, or otherwise to halt her rapid leg movement, which was considered masturbatory activity. It is a shame that these girls were not allowed the solace of experiencing an orgasm as they sewed (if, indeed, it were possible to achieve one that way), since they were so miserably underpaid for their — excuse the expression — piecework. One might argue that the real reason for such incredible policing of seamstresses was the fear that they would exhaust themselves and not be able to do their jobs properly. But the greater likelihood is that, given the moral climate of the times, the supervisors viewed themselves as saving their charges from the life of depravity and ruin that would almost certainly follow if a girl were to masturbate. Horrors!

The double standard of sexual behavior has persisted well into this century, and it is understandable that a man subscribing to it might expect the "good girl" he married to be disdainful of something so degenerate as an active, warm sexual response. Sometimes, furthermore, the double standard boomerangs, and the man discovers to his dismay that the words of the marriage ceremony had not dispelled his "good-girls-don't" attitude. Sex with his wife then becomes guilt-ridden and unsatisfactory, to the extent that he must once again turn for sexual pleasure to the nameless, faceless "bad girl" he picks up in a bar. He probably never recognizes that the fault for homemade sex being a flop is his own. His conviction is thus reinforced that women (or at least wives) are supposed to be sexually unresponsive creatures. Through early conditioning, this poor creature has been pushed into the trap of viewing women as either "princesses or prostitutes" or, more graphically (if less delicately), as "mothers or whores." Everyone thus becomes a loser.

Other men's misconceptions about nymphomania stem from their ignorance of the wide variations in the sexual drives of women, all of which almost certainly lie within the limits of normalcy. Such a man may be unaware that a woman is capable of several orgasms in a single sexual encounter and of her possible need for them. Or that the intensity of a woman's sexual responsiveness grows as she grows older, reaching its peak after her thirtieth year and remaining fairly steady thereafter. Or that his own sexual potency, by contrast, probably peaked while he was in his late teens and has been on a gradual decline — the skids, as he perceives it — ever since. Feeling a distinct threat to his masculine self-esteem when his wife fails to achieve sexual satisfaction from a single orgasm, or when she wants intercourse more often than he does, he protects himself by crying "nymphomaniac!"

The double standard and the lingering sexual ignorance of our society have come increasingly under assault in the last twenty-five years or so. The woman is rare today who does not expect and demand the same sexual satisfactions that her partner does. Men often appear to be in greater need of sex education, or re-education, than their ladies do. The reason possibly is that men have, in the main, more sexual conflict and guilt feelings than women, despite their time-honored passport to relative sexual freedom. Men need to understand the differences, as well as the similarities, between male and female needs and responses, and the changes wrought in them by time and maturity. A man who projects his feelings of inadequacy (which are very likely unjustified) onto his almost certainly normal wife by calling her a nymphomaniac solves nothing.

It is perhaps fair to say that not all charges of nymphomania are made by men. It is conceivable that a woman, sexually cold by nature and prudish by indoctrination, might regard her neighbor's outspoken, positive attitude toward sex as evidence of nymphomania. Perhaps also there is an element of jealousy over a fulfillment that she herself has been unable to achieve in her own sex relationships. Rather than admit to failure or inadequacy, she feels less threatened by convincing herself that the other woman is oversexed, and that her obvious enjoyment of things sexual is disgusting.

FALLACY:

NYMPHOMANIACS AND SATYROMANIACS ABOUND IN OUR SOCIETY.

FACT:

Who among us has not been awed, intrigued, or perhaps repulsed by tales of women who tumble freely into bed, boat, or meadow with any available pimply-faced youth or shriveled ancient capable of an erection? These women are called — usually without justification — nymphomaniacs. Their male counterparts are called satyromaniacs. We hear fewer stories of such men than of women, probably because our society, still embroiled as it is in the double standard, is inclined to gaze with more indulgence on the sexually libertine male. (Another reason for the public's unfamiliarity with the term may be that satyromania is a hard word to pronounce!) But in the sense that nymphomania and satyromania imply abnormally excessive sexual craving and uncontrollable sexual acting out, few words in the language have been more misused in the practical application.

To be sure, there are those men and women whose sexual behavior is unacceptably casual and promiscuous. However, those who are merely casual or promiscuous, or both, in their sexual encounters are usually not, by definition, nymphomaniacs or satyromaniacs. Men and women whose uncontrolled and uncontrollable sexual behavior truly merits these two labels are driven to their action in some extremely rare cases by endocrine or hormonal imbalance, or by pathology within the brain. More typically, the cause is neurotic compulsion. We have all heard of those compulsive people who constantly wash their already clean hands, or who steal what they have no use for, or who eat excessively what they neither relish nor need. The behavior of the compulsive is almost as if directed by an inner devil who has taken over his body. The compulsive finds no real satisfaction or pleasure in his behavior, only unrest or agitation if the pattern is broken. It is obviously disruptive, self-defeating behavior and evidences an emotional disturbance that interferes with the individual's functioning to his full emotional and intellectual capacity. Compulsion, then, controls the person. The person cannot control the compulsion.

Herein lies the big difference, as Albert Ellis points out, between those who can correctly be termed promiscuous in their behavior and those who, clinically, can be classified as nymphomaniacs or satyromaniacs. The promiscuous are in control of their actions and can indeed exercise discrimination in their choice of partners, even if they do so within quite liberal boundaries, and despite society's disapproval of their behavior. Control of action and discrimination are not characteristics of the compulsively sex-driven person, however, and these features are what distinguish the nymphomaniac (and her male counterpart) from the person who is merely promiscuous. Albert Ellis also lists the additional symptoms of self-hate and self-punishment when he describes the personality of the nymphomaniac. Lastly, there is the important difference in gratification derived from their sexual behavior: the nymphomaniac never finds any, whereas the promiscuous person typically does.

Nymphomania and satyromania are obvious neuroses; so also, it must be added, is the behavior of the promiscuous man and woman usually neurotic. In both cases the underlying motivation may be the same: an attempt to compensate for real or imagined emotional deficiencies, or the use of sex as a means of escaping from a disorganized or dull existence. The sexually promiscuous and the sexually compulsive may both feel a desperate need to be loved and accepted, and, having equated sex with love (although, perhaps, on the unconscious level), they set upon a reckless path of sexual activity to prove to themselves that they are lovable.

It cannot be overemphasized, however, that the incidence of nymphomania and satyromania is extremely small. I would hazard the guess that considerably less than one-tenth of 1% of all women are so afflicted, and that the number of men is even smaller. Indeed, in my own twenty-five-year practice I have seen only one true nymphomaniac (who, fortunately, could be helped by psychotherapy toward a more reasonable sexual life). I have never seen a satyromaniac and have heard of very few psychotherapists who have had one as a patient. It might also be added that the truly promiscuous are not a much more common phenomenon, since they constitute only 2% of the population.

Because the malady of nymphomania and satyromania is so rare, one wonders why the public is so free in branding a sexually active woman (especially) as a "nympho" and a man as a "sex maniac." Their only "fault" is that their sexual appetites are greater than what is popularly believed to be normal. The answer lies in the public's impoverished understanding of the human sex drive, and of the variations in sexual needs among individuals.

It is consequently easy for a man who is satisfied with relatively modest sexual activity to protect his ego against a woman whose sexual drive is greater than his own by calling her a nymphomaniac. (If her sex drive is somewhat less than his, he is likely to label her "frigid.") It is also easy for a woman with a low sex drive, or one whose attitude toward sex is unhealthy, to accuse her husband of sexual depravity, simply because he would like to have intercourse three or four times a week. Both attitudes are clearly unfair and, psychically, totally wrong. It is the consensus among psychotherapists that the vast majority of cases presented to them as being nymphomania or satyromania are nothing of the sort, although many men and women come to them *thinking* that they are abnormal. The cases represent, instead, very real differences between the sexual needs of the patient and his or her spouse, each of whose individual sex drive in all probability lies within the boundaries of normalcy.

―――――――

FALLACY:

IF ONE PARTNER DESIRES SEX MORE OFTEN THAN THE OTHER, NOTHING CAN BE DONE TO MAKE THE COUPLE SEXUALLY MORE COMPATIBLE.

FACT:

A crucial element in any successful marriage is the constant concern of each partner for the needs of the other in all spheres of life, including the sexual one. If one partner is disinclined toward sex on an occasion, the other should be made to understand why, in a manner that best protects his or her ego. At all costs a feeling of rejection in this most sensitive of human needs must be avoided. Sickness, fatigue, anger, or anxiety over matters having no sexual connection all can temporarily drain either partner's sexual interest. A serious illness or advanced pregnancy may make coitus inadvisable for a longer period of time. There are some men and women, however, who are genuinely "not in the mood" for intercourse much of the time. If a husband or wife consistently desires intercourse more frequently than the other, the usual reason is a distinct difference in their sexual needs.

In these marriages, the constant frustration and growing feeling of hostility in one partner because of needs not met, and in the other for what appears to be unreasonable demands for intercourse, can only have a corrosive effect on the couple's whole relationship. It is too much to expect that other areas of the marriage will flourish when underlying it all is one partner's suspicion that the other is a sex maniac, while the other is firmly convinced that he or she would find more warmth in frozen egg rolls. The expectation of Instant Expertise also plays havoc in sexual relationships. The woman expects her man to be a sexual athlete worthy of international competition, to have a sexual technique that would cause a marble statue to writhe, to possess the sexual stamina of a turned-on satyr, and to proceed with the skill and timing of a ballet master. The man, for his part, expects his lady to become fully aroused, sexually, to fever pitch in record time; to be capable of quick, monumental, and multiple orgasms; to be adept in every imaginable kind of sexual activity, especially those particularly favored by him; and to be completely satisfied, sexually, the moment he chooses to call it a night. (I almost said that the girl should be adept at any *conceivable* kind of sexual activity, but this lady is not supposed to conceive, except on demand.)

These expectations, particularly in early marriage, are unrealistic, to be sure. Yet the partners understandably feel bewildered, hurt, and rejected when their own needs and the expectations they held of the other are not met. What can be done? If the couple's sexual needs and desires remain chronically at odds, they need to talk as frankly as they can to one another. If conversation fails to help them to understand that the difference between their sex drives is not a sign of abnormality on the part of either — although each might be inclined to question the normalcy of the other — then outside help should be sought.

Many people do not realize how great are the divergences in sex drive among persons of the same sex, almost all of which lie within the wide range of normalcy. Most important (and discouraging) of all in the understanding of human sex drive is the recognition that an inequality exists between the sexual interest of men and women in the course of their life cycles — a quirk of nature that apparently must forever remain a mystery. The average man's sex drive is at its most powerful in his late teens and early twenties, after which it very gradually but steadily diminishes. The average woman's drive, however, peaks in her mid-thirties. It remains at that plateau fairly consistently thereafter, probably not diminishing until old age, if then.

Given the disadvantages of changing sexual needs imposed by nature on man and woman from the outset and individual differences in sexual needs (as natural as differences in need for sleep and food intake), as well as situational depressants or stimulants to sexual desire, the wonder is that so many couples do manage to achieve genuine sexual compatibility. Once a couple have recognized and accepted their divergent sexual needs, the next step is to look at the alternatives to sexual intercourse that might reduce the sexual tension in the more needful partner. In this connection, I like to compare the woman who seeks to satisfy her husband, even though she has no sexual need of her own at the time, with the woman who does not enjoy breakfast, yet prepares a good meal for her husband every morning because it pleases him — and because of the satisfaction she gets from pleasing him.

Women, of course, are usually able to engage in sexual intercourse even if they are not in the slightest degree sexually aroused. At times, however, their feelings are such that they want no part of coitus, no matter how urgent their husbands' sexual needs are. There are some men who, to gratify their wives, can attain and maintain an erection long enough to have intercourse, even though they have no interest in experiencing orgasm at that particular time. But, generally speaking, men who have no desire for sex are usually unable to perform the coital act, no matter how much they might wish to please their wives. It is these men and women, unable as they are to perform the act of sexual intercourse for whatever reason, who must resort to alternatives to coitus.

The alternatives to intercourse can be put into four categories: digital, manual, oral, mechanical. The partner with the greater sex drive may quite likely not find these noncoital avenues to orgasm as satisfying as intercourse, but they do serve a purpose. And within their limitations they can be quite satisfying if the experience is a shared one. For example, solitary masturbation can scarcely be expected to carry the emotional satisfaction that being brought to orgasm does through petting with someone one loves — especially when the orgasm is preceded by the loving play of hands and fingers caressing and stroking the whole body.

Oral-genital sexual contact is rejected by many people as being somehow sinful, dirty, or suggestive of homosexual behavior. It is none of these things, and should only be considered a possible sexual disorder when it is used as a sexual technique to the exclusion of all others. I do not mean to say that every couple *has* to enjoy oral stimulation of the genitalia; but because it has given great pleasure to many sexually well-adjusted couples, it seems sensible to try it — as a part of precoital loveplay and, especially, in the context of this discussion, to bring the partners to orgasm when coitus is not desired.

By mechanical means I am, of course, referring to the vibrator. This device is particularly useful when the wife is desirous or needful of a series of orgasms in one sexual encounter and her husband is unable to sustain intercourse long enough to satisfy her completely or even partially. It is also extremely useful, I might add, when a woman cannot reach orgasm through sexual intercourse or any other technique. The direct application of the vibrator to the woman's clitoral area by the husband as he fondles and kisses her seldom fails to bring her to orgasm. (One patient, the wife of a sexually indifferent man, did point out an unexpected drawback in the use of the vibrator. She claimed that "right in the middle of using it, I want to stop and kiss that sweet thing!")

In sum, none of the methods of sexual satisfaction discussed here is intended as a replacement for coitus. But their use as supplements or substitutes for coitus is sometimes clearly indicated and certainly valid. Objections to them are psychological in origin.

FALLACY:

PEOPLE SUFFERING FROM SEXUAL INADEQUACY CAN EXPECT VERY LITTLE HELP FROM TREATMENT FOR THEIR PROBLEMS.

FACT:

I am certain that many couples, still reeling from the disillusionments of a honeymoon and early marriage, upon which they embarked with unrealistic expectations both of themselves and of their spouses, have despaired that anything could be done to help them. The same feeling of hopelessness confounds those who entered marriage burdened with sexual difficulties to begin with, and who have experienced failure after failure, of one kind or another, each of which makes success more unlikely the next time sexual intercourse is attempted.

The types of sexual failure besetting both men and women are legion. A woman, for example, may suffer from vaginismus — a spastic, often severely painful contraction of vaginal muscles that prevents penile penetration, thereby interfering with coital function. In a man, failure or inadequacy may mean premature ejaculation — the inability to control ejaculation long enough during intercourse to satisfy the woman sexually in at least 50% of their coital experiences, according to definition. These are but two of the selected few sexual disorders discussed by Dr. William H. Masters and Virginia E. Johnson in their book *Human Sexual Inadequacy*.

These problems are ones that are not likely to respond to self-treatment — if, indeed, a couple know how to go about solving the problems themselves. But there *is* hope. Psychotherapy has long been recognized as being of great value in treating a wide variety of sexual difficulties and disorders. And now the work of Masters and Johnson offers renewed hope to those beset with difficulties that they seem unable to overcome in this most important area of their lives. The Masters and Johnson book, as its title suggests, deals exclusively with the problems and treatment of inadequate sexual functioning.

The authors report that they achieve roughly 80% success in treating all types of unsatisfactory sexual functioning that afflict both men and women. They say further that this percentage of success is reduced by only 5% or 6% after the passage of a full year following treatment. There is, of course, considerable variability in the degree of success achieved, dependent upon which type of malfunctioning is being treated. For example, Masters and Johnson report 100% success in treating women suffering from vaginismus. Of men who ejaculate prematurely, approximately 97% are successfully treated; whereas among those who suffer from primary impotence — the inability ever to achieve or maintain an erection firm enough to permit successful sexual intercourse — the percentage of success drops to 59%. Of all the types of inadequacy treated, primary impotence has the lowest percentage of successful outcome. Even so, 59% is an impressive figure (especially to those men who have been afflicted with this form of sexual failure).

Masters and Johnson find it crucial to ultimate success that therapists work with both husband and wife, because "there is no such thing as an uninvolved partner in any marriage in which there is some form of sexual inadequacy." In their research center, treatment is initially conducted by a male-female therapy team on a daily basis for a two-week period. In addition to taking a detailed sexual history, the team teaches the husband and wife how to find pleasure in their own and in each other's bodies — in other words, how to receive pleasure as well as to give it. The couple are given sex instruction aimed at dispelling the fears, guilt, and anger that so often are the causes or contributing factors in sexual problems, and that, in turn, spill over into the nonsexual areas of the couple's interrelationship and cause unnecessary difficulties there as well.

Men and women who are experiencing any of several problems in their sexual relationships are urged to seek professional help from a qualified psychologist, physician, or other trained person as soon as the difficulties become apparent. Early treatment increases the probability of a favorable outcome, and in a shorter period of time than when treatment is postponed. A major conclusion to be drawn, therefore, is that the sooner sexual problems are dealt with — professionally, if the difficulties cannot be overcome by the couple themselves — the better are the chances that happiness will return and that the marriage itself will survive.

FALLACY:

PREMATURE EJACULATION IS DUE TO PHYSICAL CIRCUM-
STANCES, SUCH AS AN ABNORMALLY SENSITIVE PENIS
CAUSED BY CIRCUMCISION.

FACT:

Until recent years, this fallacy found rather wide acceptance as a biologic fact. For example, one assumption was that the glans of the circumcised penis is more sensitive to the frictions of masturbation or coitus than is the uncircumcised penis; the circumcised man cannot, therefore, delay ejaculation as long as the man whose foreskin is still intact. Neurological and clinical testing of tactile discrimination (sensitivity to touch) has failed, however, to reveal any differences in the sensitivity of a circumcised and an uncircumcised penis. In most instances of the latter, the prepuce or foreskin retracts from over the glans during a state of penile erection, especially during coition, exposing the glans during the sex act to the same degree of stimulation experienced by the circumcised glans. But even in those cases in which the prepuce does not fully retract, the response to stimulation of the penis, circumcised or uncircumcised, is the same.

Control of ejaculation, or lack of it, is far more related to self-training and to emotional factors than to such physical conditions as an overly sensitive penis. From the outset of such a discussion, however, it is judicious to settle the question of what premature ejaculation is — and is not. To be sure, it is a condition causing anxiety and stress for many men and women; it frequently bedevils a marriage or seriously impairs a sexual relationship. Some authorities declare arbitrarily that ejaculation is premature if it occurs before penetration or within ten seconds thereafter. They say further that ejaculation occurring anytime after ten seconds of intromission, but not within the man's conscious control, must be considered "early ejaculation." Other authorities state that the man who cannot control his ejaculation for at least one full minute after penetration should be described as a premature ejaculator.

Another group of sex researchers define premature ejaculation in terms of the sexual requirements of the individual partners, and are not concerned about specific periods of time. Prominent in this group are Masters and Johnson, who designate a man as being a premature ejaculator if he cannot delay ejaculation long enough after penetration to satisfy his sexual partner in at least half of their acts of sexual intercourse together. Because of the prestige of these two sexologists, their definition will probably become the one accepted by scientists in the field of human sexuality.

Enough of definitions. Many men expect too much of themselves as lovers, and hence feel shamed and sexually inadequate if their "staying power" after penile penetration is minimal. Yet the Kinsey group found that perhaps three-fourths of all men ejaculate within two minutes after intromission. This is not to say that, because they are in the large majority, these men should not work at learning the technique of delaying ejaculation. For sexually aroused bed partners both feel cheated if orgasm occurs within mere seconds of penile insertion. Not only is the man's confidence in himself as a lover weakened, but also he has been denied the intense pleasure of prolonged penile plunging. As for the woman, if the couple depend upon intercourse to bring her to orgasm, she is left almost completely unfulfilled and most assuredly will feel frustrated. Repetition of this sort of bad timing can understandably spell quick death to what might otherwise have been a thoroughly satisfactory sexual relationship.

The penis, however, does not control ejaculation, premature or otherwise. The brain does, and usually unconsciously, via the spinal cord. The best evidence of this fact is that ejaculations can occur during sleep or while a man is unconscious. The psychological forces in premature ejaculation are legion, as one might suspect. It often has an element of revenge in it — toward the particular woman or toward women in general. Or the man may be unduly tense, tired, or lacking in self-confidence in his sexual abilities. Intercourse may have been preceded by an overlong period of sexual abstinence; or the man may have been under a prolonged period of sexual excitement because of foreplay, before intromission was attempted.

Only rarely does premature ejaculation have a physical basis. The glans may be abnormally sensitive because of, say, a chemical irritation. Or the prostate or the verumontanum (a part of the urethra) may be infected. But beyond these rare incidents, premature ejaculation is caused by emotional or psychological factors. Given the cooperation of his wife, except when the cause is purely physical, a man can train himself to withhold orgasm until both want it to happen. The main enemy is the fear and anxiety engendered in the man by previous failures. Once he gains confidence in his "staying power" and accepts the fact that all men face the problem at one time or another, the battle is half won. To assist him toward confidence in his abilities, several routes can be taken.

Some counselors recommend that a local anesthetic (e.g., Nupercainal) be applied to the penile glans — care being taken not to smear any on the woman's vulva — a few minutes before intercourse. The assumption is that the deadening effect of the anesthetic will decrease the sensitivity of the penis, thus delaying ejaculation. Others prescribe that one or more condoms be worn to reduce the stimulation generated by the friction, warmth, and moisture within the vagina. Since muscular tension is a notorious catalyst in ejaculation, the man's lying beneath the woman and thus taking a more passive role in coitus is believed by many to be helpful in controlling premature ejaculation. Some men also find that taking a drink or two before coitus helps, since alcohol is a deterrent in all physiological functioning. Other men claim similar success through concentrating on singularly unsexy thoughts, such as the income tax. (It is suggested, however, that these men take care not to let their women know of their diversionary thoughts, lest they be dumped from the bed before ejaculation, premature or otherwise.) Despite some writers' rather naive, out-of-hand condemnation of these methods, most psychotherapists who work with problems of ejaculation control find them quite useful when patients are undergoing a period of reconditioning during which they are striving toward greater confidence in themselves.

The technique of delaying orgasm *can* be learned, and probably the best method is one requiring the cooperation of both husband and wife, as I have said. Variations have appeared in several writings, most recently in the Masters and Johnson book *Human Sexual Inadequacy*. Self-treatment is possible, but, since the problem is a shared one, the best chance of success lies in both partners' consulting a psychotherapist. They will, first of all, be assured that premature or early ejaculation is a reversible phenomenon; they are then instructed in the somewhat complicated technique of bringing about its reversal.

The technique requires that the wife manually stimulate her husband's genitals until the point that he feels the very earliest signs of "ejaculatory inevitability." (This is the stage of a man's orgasmic experience at which he feels ejaculation of seminal fluid coming, and can no longer control it.) At that moment the female partner immediately ceases her massage of the penis. She then squeezes its glans or head by placing her thumb on the frenulum (lower surface of the glans) and two fingers on top of the glans, applying rather strong pressure for three or four seconds. The pressure is uncomfortable enough to cause the man to lose the urge to ejaculate. Such "training sessions" should continue for fifteen to twenty minutes, with alternating periods of sexual stimulation and squeezing. In later sessions, the husband inserts his penis in the woman's vagina as she sits astride him until he senses impending orgasm, at which point he withdraws and his wife once more squeezes the penis to stop ejaculation. Use of these techniques is continued in further sexual encounters until, progressively, the man is capable of prolonged sexual intercourse, in any position, without ejaculating sooner than he wishes.

In the many sexual histories taken by Masters and Johnson, as well as by other researchers, in the study of premature ejaculation, a consistent causal pattern for the disorder has unfolded. When the man so troubled is over forty years old, his first experiences in sexual intercourse typically were with prostitutes. A generation or so ago, the prostitute attempted to hurry her client along to orgasm as quickly as possible, perhaps to relieve his sexual tensions but primarily to make room for the next paying customer. After only two or three such experiences, the prostitute's client can easily become conditioned to a pattern of quick ejaculation. To his dismay, he later finds that this response pattern has carried over into his adult, mature sexual encounters.

Younger adults have not frequented houses of prostitution nearly so often as their fathers had done. Rather, their first sexual encounters were typically with girls of their own group. The experiences usually took place in a parked car, in the imminent danger of being spotlighted by the police; or on a couch in the living room of the girl's parents, while at any moment her father was liable to bound into the room, shotgun in his hand and blood in his eye. The anxious conditions of these copulations all served to condition many younger men to the pattern of quick ejaculation.

Another form of teenage sexual behavior also can help to condition the man to premature ejaculation. After extensive petting, the youth, possibly fully clothed, lies atop the girl, rubbing his penis over her vulval region by moving his body back and forth, as is done in intercourse, until he ejaculates. (Aside from the unfortunate conditioning of the male, the girl's unrelieved sexual tensions, and additional cleaning bills, about all one can say about this technique is that it prevents unwanted pregnancies, preserves the girl's virginity, and affords the lad some sexual release.)

There is also the man who has had wide sexual experience as a teenager, in the process of which he has developed a near-total lack of regard for women. The female exists, in his thinking, solely for his gratification, an instrument for his sexual release. Her needs and welfare are of no concern. Intercourse, in his selfishness, is truly a mounting process, in which delay of orgasm is neither necessary nor desirable. In fact, the most consistent and significant characteristic uncovered by Masters and Johnson in their study of the early sexual histories of premature ejaculators was that these men were concerned only with their own sexual gratification, to the utter disregard of whether or not their partners achieved any sexual release.

In any discussion of premature ejaculation, a word of caution must be injected. It is important to understand that at any one time or another almost every man has experienced ejaculation more swiftly than he or his wife would have liked. The essential thing is that the man not become anxious over possible future failures; otherwise, what is a normal, situational occurrence may become a chronic problem.

FALLACY:

REMOVAL OF THE PROSTATE SIGNALS THE END OF
A MAN'S SEXUAL ACTIVITY AND ENJOYMENT OF SEX.

FACT:

The prostate gland sounds insignificant enough in the description. It is a firm body about the size of a walnut and weighing about two-thirds of an ounce. Its prime functions are to assist the seminal vesicles in manufacturing the major portion of the seminal fluid in which the sperm cells are suspended — the fluid that is expelled at the time of ejaculation — and through its contractions to assist in ejaculation itself.

The male's sperm are produced in a continuing process by the testes, and they mature in the epididymis, a tightly coiled tube attached to each testicle. When sexual tension has mounted to a high peak and ejaculation is imminent, the sperm are speeded on their way by wave-like contractions of the vas deferens (vas). As climax is reached, the sperm that have accumulated in the seminal vesicles, in the enlarged ends of the vas deferens, and in the ejaculatory ducts — which are surrounded by the prostate — are suddenly discharged through the penis along with the seminal fluids.

It is a wonder that an organ as small as the prostate, whose functions are not spectacular, should cause men so much trouble, to say nothing of anxiety. Yet the prostate is destined to become enlarged in about 60% of men in their middle years and thereafter, although only 35% of the cases will require surgery. Why such a large proportion of men are so afflicted is not completely clear, except that prostatic enlargement is a part of the general aging process and is in some way related to the amount of male hormones produced by the testes.

Although prostatis — inflammation of the prostate — is not uncommon among young men, prostatectomy, the surgical removal of all or part of the prostate, is far more common among men past fifty. Since it encircles the neck of the bladder, any inflammation, enlargement, or infection of the prostate can make urination difficult, sometimes necessitating the surgical removal of part or all of the gland. If not corrected, the man may experience difficulty or pain in urination, incomplete emptying of the bladder, and, eventually, total urinary retention. Such secondary complications as serious bladder infection, kidney stones, and uremic poisoning often follow.

The problem of an enlarged prostate can sometimes be corrected medically. When surgery is indicated, the approach is made via the abdomen, or through the penis (a process called a transurethral prostatectomy), or from a point between the anus and scrotum (perineal prostatectomy), the procedure being decided by the seriousness or urgency of the condition. (Another procedure holding much promise is the cryogenic probe, which freezes the prostate or the offending enlargement in it, thus destroying it and leaving the dead tissue to be cast off by the body.)

But what of sexual potency after the removal of a noncancerous prostate? A study was recently reported in the *Journal of the American Medical Association* on the effects of the three major types of prostatic surgery in patients who had been potent before surgery. The results revealed that 95% of those patients who had undergone transurethral surgery, 87% with the abdominal surgery, and 71% with the perineal incision retained their potency. The reduced percentage in the third instance was attributed to the surgical approach having been made through sex-related nerve centers, which obviously involves the risk of damage to those nerves controlling erection. The selection of the operative procedure does not necessarily represent the free choice of the surgeon, however. It is primarily dictated by the seriousness of the case, as well as the age and physical condition of the patient.

When the prostate is cancerous, the possibilities of a man's retaining his potency after the prostatectomy are not so favorable. Surgery in this case is often of necessity a much more radical procedure, since tissue around the prostate must also be removed as a safety measure. Furthermore, advanced prostatic cancer, even when widespread throughout the body (it typically, and silently, spreads to the bones of the pelvis and spine before the patient is even aware that anything is wrong), may be controlled dramatically when castration is performed or the patient is treated with female hormones. Both these treatments, of course, militate against the patient's retaining his potency.

But about 80% of prostatectomies are, fortunately, performed to correct nonmalignant growths, and these patients have every reason to expect to retain their sexual vigor. Prostate difficulties are the inheritance of the man of advancing years, as I have said; and let us remember that, according to the Kinsey researchers, 27% of all men are impotent by the age of seventy anyway. When one does hear of a case in which potency was lost following a prostate operation, one has to question whether the cause was truly physical, or whether negative psychological forces were at work. Did the man *expect* to lose his potency, thereby almost guaranteeing its occurrence? Did his surgeon fail to discuss the sex-functioning aspects of the operation with him; or worse, did he perhaps compound his patient's silent fears by having him sign a paper relieving the doctor of responsibility in the event impotency followed the surgery? Had the man's sexual relationship with his wife prior to the operation become so dreary and unsatisfying that he welcomed an excuse to abandon it? Had his wife not properly understood the effects of a prostatectomy and, expecting impotency, appeared to reject him, thus precipitating his impotency? Or was she afraid to resume intercourse because she feared it might in some way endanger her husband's health?

Another matter that concerns men facing a prostatectomy is whether they will continue to enjoy intercourse even if potency is preserved. Because the structures within the prostate, notably the ejaculatory ducts emptying into the urethra, are as a rule unavoidably damaged (although less frequently with the transurethral than with the open approaches), it is no longer possible for the man to ejaculate normally. The ejaculate, instead of being expelled through and out the penis, may flow backwards into the bladder in a process called *retrograde* or *dry ejaculation*. (Semen are later discharged in the urine, and there is no harmful effect whatever on the man.) Some men very much miss the pleasant sensation of the pulsation of ejaculation, which lessens or is missing altogether after the prostate operation; but this is a loss that they quickly become adjusted to. As Dr. Joseph Trainor has pointed out, ejaculation has little to do with the pleasure of orgasm; too many people are conditioned to think of sex as a genital event only, ignoring all the other emotional and psychological components intrinsic in a satisfying sexual experience.

Because a vasectomy or tying of the tubes is often performed at the time of a prostatectomy as a precautionary measure against infection (primarily of the epididymis), and because ejaculation is usually "dry" after the surgery, the chances of the patient's fathering a child thereafter become slim. This is rarely a serious problem, as prostate surgery is typically the fate of the older man. But if it does befall a younger one, and a vasectomy has not been performed, it may be possible to extract some of the sperm from his urine, or take the sperm directly from the vas, so that his wife can be impregnated artificially.

It is no less important that men past fifty have a prostate examination once or twice a year than it is for women to have Pap smears. It is a simple, brief examination performed per rectum. Prostatic cancer is the second largest cancer killer of men. It is a "silent" cancer, rarely noticed by the patient until it has spread to other, unrelated, parts of the body, at which point its arrest or cure is much more difficult. In addition to the check for cancer in periodic examinations, the doctor can also catch nonmalignant prostate difficulties before they become serious ones.

Once a man's prostatic dysfunction is properly treated, his general health, well-being, and sexual performance will almost certainly improve as well. The attack on middle age, however, should not end with the prostate. Anything that improves general health will have a beneficial effect on sexual functioning as well. Hormonal or thyroid treatment may be indicated;

perhaps the thyroid gland, the body's regulator, can be made to function more efficiently by medication. If the older man's physical problems are complicated by a defeatist attitude toward the future of his sex life, then consultation with a psychotherapist might be greatly helpful. Especially after the age of fifty, a man should consult a urologist regularly. He should be careful, however, to choose one who understands the need in a man for regular and frequent sexual outlet and who will do whatever possible to ensure it.

===

FALLACY:

A TRANSVESTITE AND A TRANSSEXUALIST ARE THE SAME, AND BOTH ARE HOMOSEXUALS.

FACT:

The psychosexual disturbances of transvestism and transsexuality do bear a resemblance to one another in that they represent, in whole or in part, the rejection by the individual of his or her genetic sex. Indeed, the two conditions may overlap in the same individual, and it is conceivable that either the transvestite or the transsexual may also be a homosexual, or have been one at some point in his life. Nevertheless, the conditions are quite separate and different, despite the possible overlapping, and despite the similar causality in all three.

In this discussion, by the way, I shall speak only of *male, he,* and *his* — for the sake of simplicity, primarily, but also because the three aberrations are predominantly male afflictions. Just as there are female homosexuals, however, so also are there female transvestites and transsexuals.

The dynamics in *homosexuality* have been discussed in previous sections. In the context of the present discussion, however, it is important to emphasize only that the extremely effeminate homosexual, given to feminine mannerisms, intonations, and dress, represents a very slim proportion of the entire homosexual population. The rest are undetectable as they go about their business in their grey-flannel suits, blue collars, or slacks and turtlenecks. Only their choice of males as sex partners sets them apart from the norm.

Transvestites are those men who have an exaggerated liking for things feminine, and who gain some form of emotional or sexual satisfaction from wearing clothing appropriate to the opposite sex in their culture. The word derives from *trans*, meaning "across," and *vestis*, meaning "dress" —hence the more common term, "cross-dressing." The condition is also called *eonism*, after an eighteenth-century French nobleman, the Chevalier D'Eon de Beaumont, who was noted for his transvestite habits and who, in fact, served king and country well by spying for them while clothed as a woman.

Transvestism is obviously not a phenomenon new to the twentieth century. As a matter of fact, a pre-Revolutionary governor of New York, Lord Cornbury, had sufficient temerity to appear in public in female garb. Philippe, Duke of Orleans and brother of France's "Sun King," Louis XIV, was also a celebrated transvestite. Estimates vary, but transvestism exists today in possibly less than 1% of the population. The difficulty in making a more accurate estimate of its prevalence lies in the secrecy with which perhaps 90% of transvestites indulge in their cross-dressing habits.

The pattern of cross-dressing habits varies among transvestites. In one instance, women's apparel is worn only periodically, usually on special occasions. In another, the man has a fetish-like fondness for a particular article of women's clothing — e.g., panties or a brassiere — which he habitually wears under his own masculine clothing. In yet another, the yearning to wear women's finery may be so deeply ingrained that the transvestite discards men's clothing entirely to embark upon a lifelong masquerade as a woman.

Transvestites typically attest to a sense of pleasure and relaxation when wearing the clothing of the opposite sex, expressing a relish for the feel of the cloth and for the view of themselves thus attired in the mirror. A man's cross-dressing allows him to express the gentle, graceful, sensuous side of his nature, a part of him that has somehow become identified with the feminine gender and that society does not permit him to express as a man.

Authorities agree that the majority of transvestites are decidedly not homosexual. In fact, 74% of the two hundred seventy-two transvestites surveyed in one study were married, and 69% had fathered children; only 25% admitted having any homosexual experience at all. This last figure is especially interesting, since the Kinsey researchers found that 37% of all men have had at least one homosexual contact to the point of orgasm in their lives. The differences between the homosexual and the transvestite have probably been best established by an active transvestite, who writes and lectures extensively on the subject under the name of Virginia "Charles" Prince. Transvestism, Prince points out, is typically a secret pursuit involving only one individual; homosexuality obviously must involve two people, and, furthermore, to attract a partner, the homosexual must reveal himself as being one. The transvestite might be said to possess two personalities, one male and the other female, which alternately assert themselves. By contrast, the homosexual is always a homosexual, twenty-four hours a day, every day.

As with homosexuality, there is nothing in the present-day understanding of genetics to support the contention that transvestism results from an inborn, instinctive predisposition toward it. As with homosexuality, once more, the evidence is strong that transvestism is the direct result of a learning process, typically beginning in earliest childhood. The parents of transvestites (classically the mother) attempt to mask their great disappointment that the baby is not a girl by dressing him in girls' clothes, allowing his hair to grow long, and curling and beribboning it until he reaches school age. Sensing the beloved mother's approval of his feminine appearance, a boy can easily absorb the attitude that "girl is good." Another form of conditioning is a punishment whereby the boy is forced to wear some piece of little-girl apparel (the "pinafore punishment," as it has been called). In other cases, the father is so harsh or so demanding of hypermasculinity in his small, sensitive son that the boy retreats from him and identifies with his gentle, compassionate mother.

The problem in *transsexualism* is far more profound than that in transvestism. With rare exceptions, the transsexualist is genetically a male. The chromosomal content of his cells includes the XY pair designating the male sex; he possesses normal male genitals, internally and externally; and he is capable of impregnating a woman. In no instance is the difference between the *sex* assigned by nature and the *gender identity* acquired through social conditioning more dramatically demonstrated than it is in the transsexual. The man knows that he is a male, yet he rejects his maleness totally. Not content with dressing as a female, as the transvestite is, he wishes to go all the way and live the life of a woman — emotionally, physically, sexually. The male sex organs become such hated objects that attempts at self-castration or suicide are not uncommon among transsexuals. As Dr. Harry Benjamin — an endocrinologist and a recognized authority on transsexualism — puts it, the transsexual views his sex organs as a deformity.

The transsexual wishes to be loved as a woman by a "straight" man. He does not wish to be loved by a homosexual, whose love-sex object is another man. The transsexual is firmly convinced that some cruel caprice of nature has imposed upon him the body of a male while at the same time endowing him with the emotionality and mentality of a woman. It should be pointed out that transsexuals are not hermaphrodites — that is, they do not possess, even to a limited degree, the physical characteristics of both sexes. The problem is at the other end of the body. In his mind, the transsexual is convinced that he was given the wrong body.

The causative factors in transsexuality appear to be much the same as those in transvestism and homosexuality. The transsexualist's mother is typically an unhappy woman, who clutches her son to her bosom — literally and figuratively — entering into an intensely close relationship with him from which the father and the other children of the family are excluded.

The rejection of the sex assigned him by nature accounts for the dogged determination of many transsexuals to undergo a sex-change operation, despite the inherent legal and social difficulties attending such a procedure. (Imagine, for example, the passport problem when a transsexual goes abroad for such an operation as a man and returns as a woman.) It is logical to expect that most transsexuals would also be transvestites, and indeed they are, since they reject so completely the male role. Transsexuals wish to be responded to as women, not as men; hence their only hope to attract "straight" men is to present themselves to the world as female.

The transvestite, however, is seldom a transsexual as well. In fact, most transvestites, being otherwise normal sexually — most establish normal heterosexual relationships, as I have said — would cringe at the suggestion of a sex-transformation operation. They merely wish to be left alone to indulge in their cross-dressing habits.

There are perhaps 1500 people throughout the world who have undergone sex-reassignment operations. A guess is that about four hundred of them live in the United States although, for obvious reasons, the identity of very few is known. Until recently, American transsexuals had to go to Europe or Casablanca for a sex-change operation. However, fostered by the interest of Dr. Harry Benjamin, American medicine has in recent years given a reluctant consideration to the dilemma of the transsexual. Many doctors shrink from what is to them a mutilation of the human body. But, as Dr. Benjamin has pointed out, all forms of psychotherapy have been singularly unsuccessful in helping these people who, in company with the transvestite and homosexual, are notoriously resistant to change. Since the transsexual's mind cannot be made to adjust to his body, Dr. Benjamin contends, the only sensible and humane course to follow is to make the body adjust to the mind.

Undergoing a sex-reassignment operation is almost a technicality for the transsexual, since he has so thoroughly rejected his sex already. Among the few hospitals and clinics in the United States that will consider his application for the surgery are the Johns Hopkins Hospital and the Gender Identity Clinic at Harvard University, which perform a limited number of such operations after exhaustive consideration of each applicant. Primary requirements for consideration are that the individual has lived as a member of the opposite sex for a considerable time and has undergone female hormonal treatment. It is significant that persons approaching such operations — which involve, in the man, the removal of testicles and penis, leaving sufficient skin to form an artificial vagina — have not been known to get cold feet and back out. Their determination to shed the appendages of their hated genetic sex is that strong.

The Harvard Gender Identity Clinic has gathered data with respect to the postoperative lives of thirteen patients on whom the operation had been performed, in addition to four already operated on who underwent further reconstruction work at the clinic. Ten of these subjects had established a sexual association of some duration with a man (whom I shall refer to as the husband, although not all the couples had entered into a formal marriage). Of the seven husbands on whom data were available, all had had heterosexual experience before establishing the relationship with the patient, and two had been previously married. Concerning homosexual experience, one husband claimed to be bisexual and one admitted to a single homosexual contact at the age of fourteen; all the others maintained that they had had no homosexual contacts in their lives. Writing in the *Journal of Sex Research* (August 1970), Drs. John Money and John G. Brennan commented that "the transsexual male, though an incomplete and impersonating female, obviously projects at least the minimum of feminine cues needed to attract the erotic attention of a normal male."

Perhaps a word should be said about two other phenomena adding to the confusion surrounding transsexualism and transvestism, the *drag queen* and the *female impersonator*. The drag queen is that obviously effeminate homosexual whose appearance and mannerisms are perhaps the most offensive to the public and, it should be added, to most other homosexuals as well. He may wear makeup, go to excruciating pains to coif his hair (although the style remains essentially masculine), and attire himself in "mod" clothing, also essentially masculine. His whole appearance is aimed at proclaiming his homosexuality to the world and at accentuating, through abbreviated, uplifting underclothing and overly tight trousers, his genital attributes. So dressed, he is, in essence, "cruising," although he may be standing still.

The female impersonator, on the other hand, is first and foremost an entertainer. He may possibly also be a transsexual, transvestite, or homosexual — although a transsexual typically would not want to revert to the male role "after the show is over," and the transvestite typically desires to conceal his cross-dressing habits. The motivation in female impersonation is essentially that in any entertainment — the monetary gain and the psychological rewards coming from "the smell of greasepaint and the roar of the crowd." One might wonder, of course, why a man would choose to become this particular type of entertainer; one might also wonder why other entertainers choose to swallow flaming torches or to be shot out of cannons.

In sum, if a homosexual dresses effeminately, it is not because he wishes to be a woman; he wishes, rather, to attract other homosexuals. If a transvestite dons women's clothing, he does so alone and secretly, and only because of the emotional satisfaction it gives him. If a transsexual dons women's clothing, it is because he intensely desires to be a woman (or has actually undergone a sex-transformation operation), and wishes to be considered desirable as a woman; his only hope of attracting a "straight" man is to appear to be a woman socially.

════════

FALLACY:

HERMAPHRODITISM AND TRANSEXUALISM ARE THE SAME, AND BOTH REQUIRE THE SAME TREATMENT.

FACT:

It will be remembered from the last section that the transsexual possesses the completely normal internal and external sexual organs of one (and only one) sex. But he cannot accept the sex assigned him by nature, and he typically seeks a surgical operation to change his genital appearance to that of the opposite sex. The hermaphrodite, on the other hand, possesses the gonads of both sexes; that is, both ovarian and testicular tissue is present. Hermaphroditism and transsexualism are therefore clearly dissimilar conditions.

Cases of true hermaphroditism are extremely rare, with perhaps fewer than one hundred valid incidences appearing in the medical literature of the entire world. It would be possible, technically, for a hermaphrodite to impregnate as a male and also to conceive as a woman. Indeed, Brazilian doctors recently reported a case of a true hermaphrodite who had a developing fetus in the womb, and who also possessed a testicle capable of producing sperm. Furthermore, the person claimed to be both the father and the mother of the child! There is some doubt that this was an instance of self-impregnation, however, because the female hormones of the ovary would ordinarily sterilize the testis, making the person incapable of fertilizing ova.

Pseudohermaphroditism is a much more common disorder than true hermaphroditism is, some form of it appearing in about one of every 1000 infants born. The male pseudohermaphrodite has gonads that are testes, at least from a chromosomal standpoint, although he may exhibit varying degrees of external female characteristics. The gonads of a female pseudohermaphrodite are ovaries, but her external genitalia (and often other of her bodily characteristics) are primarily those of a male.

Because the pseudohermaphrodite usually has some rudimentary form of both male and female sex organs, his true sex is difficult to determine. And since his sex can be so easily misjudged, it is not uncommon for such a child to be brought up as a member of the wrong sex. Childhood influences quite naturally predispose the individual to assume the interests, attitudes, and sexual behavior of one sex, however much his physical characteristics are those of the opposite sex — another indication of the superiority of psychological over physiological factors in sexual matters.

When external physical characteristics cause any doubt regarding the sex of a newborn child, it is essential that the parents immediately seek the advice of specialists. Sometimes surgery is indicated, not only to alter the sexual characteristics of the child, but also to alleviate the emotional problems that typically develop as a result of such disorders. Early attention is crucial, since little success can be expected in re-educating the pseudohermaphrodite child in his correct sex role after he has reached school age.

Sex Offense

The greatest problem on this subject is one of definitions. It is a problem compounded by the public's assumption that in the extremely broad spectrum of sex offense there is a typical sex offender. The legal definition of sex offense does not clarify the issue, for what constitutes a grave violation of the law in one state does not even appear on the statute books of another. Definitions based on ethnic or cultural values are obviously invalid, because sexual mores vary vastly from one group to another. Even psychological definitions are not wholly acceptable, because they are based on concepts of mental or emotional defects which in themselves are subject to individual professional interpretation.

If behavioral scientists and legal codes do not offer definitive indices by which to identify a true sexual offense (or offender), it is small wonder that the public is confused. For purposes of this section, therefore, I shall arbitrarily establish that the sex offender is a person who has been arrested or convicted of a sex crime or offense. I shall then set about trying to correct a few of the most prevalent fallacies concerning the "typical" sex offender.

The second part of this section deals with pornography and obscenity, laws against which are aimed not so much at the perusers as at the purveyors thereof. There is little consensus in the public mind regarding what is truly pornographic. More important, there is great controversy over the capacity of such material to prompt sex-related crime or sexual acting-out, and over its potentialities for corrupting young minds. Nevertheless, there are a number of fears about the corruptive and dangerous effects of erotically stimulating pictures and literature that can be dispelled thoroughly by an examination of the results of several studies made in recent months and years. These findings, based on careful investigative procedures rather than on emotionality and semantics, are what I ask the reader to consider in forming his opinion on pornography and its dangers.

FALLACY:

A SEX OFFENDER CANNOT BE CURED AND IS LIKELY TO CONTINUE HIS UNACCEPTABLE BEHAVIOR THE REST OF HIS LIFE.

FACT·

The basic flaw in this argument is the inappropriateness of the catch-all phrase "sex offender," which in most minds is equated with a sexual deviate. Sexual deviation and sex offense are not, however, synonymous terms. If one considers sex offense purely from a legal (or legalistic) standpoint, the charge can, in some states, be levied against any male or female who has ever engaged in any form of sexual activity other than marital coitus. In such jurisdictions, then, the 95% of men and 62% of women who, according to the Kinsey research, have masturbated (to say nothing of those who have had intercourse outside of marriage) are thus rendered, legally, sex offenders.

One can shrug this suggestion off by saying "ridiculous" — which, of course, it is. But even those men charged with more obvious forms of unacceptable sexual behavior may not be true sex offenders or deviates but, rather, simply the victims of poor judgment, the double standard, or the prejudices of their community. Consider the man in a bar who succumbs to the charms of a seductive girl of obvious sexual experience, and who then discovers that she was "under the age of consent" as he faces her in a courtroom on charges of statutory rape. What about the man who carelessly displays his unclothed manhood at a window, to the shock and horror of some dear old soul passing by, who promptly calls the police and has him hauled off on charges of exhibitionism? Along these same lines, it is interesting to speculate on what would happen if a woman were similarly to display her nude body and be viewed by a man. She is not likely to be reported to anyone — except to friends of any male passerby who are called in to share the vision. Furthermore, if a man were caught in spellbound observation of such a sight, he would likely be charged as a "Peeping Tom," while the lady in question would no doubt go scot-free.

Consider further a news vendor living in a fundamentalist community; he may be jailed as a purveyor of obscene literature if he sells *Playboy*. No one is likely to bat an eyelash, however, at a fellow news vendor in Greenwich Village who, just as casually, sells *Screw* or similar sex-oriented periodicals. Both areas no doubt have laws against pornography, but the observance of such laws frequently differs according to local prejudice. In another example of evil being in the eye of the beholder: *Midnight Cowboy* was named the best film of 1969 by the Academy of Motion Picture Arts and Sciences, yet in the Texas town of Brownwood, a pornography suit was brought against a cinema owner for showing it. The complainant was a man who brought his family to the film, thinking it was a typical Western. (This family man has not only the right but also the obligation to see that his underaged children view only those films that he believes to be proper. But this obligation does not give him the right to extend his dictatorial powers into other families. While I think of it, he should perhaps be warned that the motion picture *The Boys in the Band* is not a musical.)

As an aside on the subject of pornography, one might also consider the plight of three Greek writers who in 1968 were charged with obscenity for having written that such ancient Greek luminaries as Alexander the Great, Zeno, and Sophocles were homosexual; their defense — successful, fortunately — was that their source material was papers written some years ago by Greece's present Minister of Education and Religion!

Because the people cited above have broken local statutes governing sexual behavior, they are deemed sex offenders. But can they conceivably be called sex deviates? The answer is clearly "no"; there is no mental pathology involved in any of these cases. I am not saying, however, that sex offense is nonexistent; but I do contend that there is a serious disparity between legal and scientific definitions of it. Most authorities in the field of human behavior define sex offense as an instance in which (1) there is harm or threat of harm to the victim; (2) an adult involves a minor in his sex acts, be it heterosexual or homosexual; or (3) the activity is conducted in public, or otherwise disrupts the community's concept of decent and sensible behavior. (In this last category a boy and girl may, without attracting undue attention, kiss on a park bench; but two homosexuals doing the same thing can, with all justification, expect the arrival of the paddy wagon.)

In the matter of sexual deviation, a distinction must be made between the doer and the act. According to the Kinsey researchers, 70% of American males will engage in some sort of "deviated" behavior at some point in their lives; and 60% will do so on a fairly frequent basis, at least for a period of time. Their behavior may be deviated, but these men cannot be considered sexual deviates unless that behavior becomes and remains the exclusive source of sexual gratification. Conversely, certain sexual behavior that you and I may call relatively normal becomes deviate if it is the only source of sexual outlet sought by the individual. Hence a married man who persistently masturbates, even though his wife is a congenial bed partner, or the woman who exclusively prefers cunnilingus to coitus, can be suspected of deviation, or at least can rightfully be suspected of having some problem in this area.

The majority of sex offenders who are caught in the toils of the law can accurately be categorized as a relatively harmless, ineffectual lot. They rarely become involved in nonsexual crime and, more important, do not progress from minor to major sexual offenses. The New Jersey Diagnostic Center investigated three hundred sex offenders who appeared consecutively over a fifteen-month period (thus a nonselective, 100% sampling), and the results were reported by Drs. Albert Ellis and Ralph Brancale. Of the three hundred, only 14% were considered psychologically "normal"; 29%, mildly neurotic; 34%, severely neurotic; and the rest as suffering from various degrees of psychosis, brain damage, or mental deficiency.

Even granting that the brain-damaged or mentally deficient probably can be helped in adulthood only minimally by psychotherapy (and that the normal obviously do not need this sort of help), why is the assumption made that the majority of sex offenders, most of whom are suffering from neurosis or perhaps psychosis, will be less responsive to therapy than a neurotic or psychotic person who has committed a nonsexual crime or has no criminal record whatever? If we showed this sort of pessimism about mental or emotional disturbance that never breaks into unacceptable sexual behavior, all efforts in the direction of improved mental health would be a farce.

The four largest categories of sex offenders in the New Jersey study were:

> The exhibitionist (29%),
> The statutory rapist (20%),
> The noncoital offender against minors (17%),
> The homosexual (16%).

It is worthwhile to examine what research, such as the monumental twenty-five-year study made by the Kinsey group (the results of which were published under the title *Sex Offenders*), has uncovered about the personalities of these four classifications of offenders and the prognosis in each case. More arrests are made for exhibitionism in the United States than for any other sex offense. The behavior of that inadequate and insecure creature, the exhibitionist, is thought to be largely compulsive — he responds to threat by exhibiting his genitals, the shock he hopes to create causing him to feel powerful and masculine. But compulsive behavior of any sort, given the cooperation of the patient (and what patient will not cooperate when the alternative may be jail?), can be reversed through individual and group therapy. The outcome is especially favorable when the group therapy includes similarly afflicted individuals.

The second group — the statutory rapist — is not necessarily, according to the Kinsey research, deviated sexually or psychiatrically. He is simply a fellow who is careless about the age of his coital partner, or one who wishes to satisfy his sexual urge in the simplest, most expedient manner. He typically "learns his lesson" once he is arrested and rarely is charged a second time on the same count. He obviously requires no cure for his sexual behavior, other than a warning to be a bit more careful in the future about birth dates.

The third group — the noncoital offender against minors — when studied in the light of the Kinsey statistics appear to effect a self-cure. Of the Kinsey offenders against children (under twelve years of age, according to their definition) 40% were first offenders, and only one-fourth had had as many as two convictions. (Alcohol was a major factor in many cases, and in only 6% was coitus attempted.) Of the Kinsey offenders against minors (girls between the ages of twelve and fifteen years), one-third experienced no coitus. Many of this group were boys very near the age of the girls involved, and others were merely careless about the age of their partner, as I said before. Relatively few, whether or not they had coitus with the girl, were ever convicted a second time. The Kinsey researchers regarded this near-peer group of offenders as a moral problem rather than a legal one, a group that should be dealt with through warnings and misdemeanor charges. "We shall always have with us our quota of well-intentioned extroverts who are not very bright, and we do no one a service by branding their errors of judgment as felonies."

The fourth group, the homosexual offender, presents quite a different emotional complexity from that of the other three. He is frequently not emotionally deviated, although most behavioral scientists would agree that he is sexually so. This group is particularly resistant to psychotherapeutic treatment, rarely seeking it unless forced to do so by relatives or legal pressures. The prognosis for a successful outcome — that is, conversion to a heterosexual way of life — is bleak. When the homosexual does voluntarily seek help to lead a "straight" sexual life, he is, in the opinion of many therapists, not a true homosexual, but a person who turns to homosexuality for reasons other than its sexual attractions. He may actually prefer women as sexual partners but be so afraid of them, or unsure of himself in heterosexual relationships, that he seeks out men to satisfy his sexual needs. In any event, more and more states and countries have decreed that homosexuality among discreet, consenting adults is not punishable as a crime.

Of the three hundred offenders in the New Jersey study, only 3% constituted that most fearsome group of sex offenders, the forcible rapist. Whether the rapist chooses a minor or an adult as his victim, his behavior is typically the outgrowth of his general asocial, aggressive character. His is a classic history of juvenile delinquency, and he emerges in adulthood as a criminally bent man who takes whatever he wants, sexual and otherwise, as he wants it — by force, if necessary. Rape, then, is simply an expression of his general criminality, and the treatment accorded him must therefore be the same as that given any other convict who is truly criminally minded.

But the great majority of offenders do not use force or threat; and as they are, in the main, inadequate, frightened, inept men, human compassion compels us to view them with pity rather than vengeance. As with the nonsexual offender against the law of the land, the sexual offender who is put on probation or shunted into prison — very likely possessing little, if any, insight into why he did what he did — and is left to serve his term without any form of counseling, becomes a prime candidate for repetition of his offense. Furthermore, his self-esteem has suffered the blow of being exposed to his community as a "sexual creep," and he now has the additional stigma of a jail or prison sentence, or probation. These humiliations add to the deterioration of his personality, thus rendering him more likely to repeat his transgression, or similar ones.

The man obviously needs help and support to understand why he feels compelled to exhibit himself, or to masturbate in public, or to spy on the sexual activities of others. He must be helped to recognize that such behavior damages him and his family, first and foremost. As alcohol is frequently a catalyst in unacceptable sexual behavior, this problem must be dealt with through psychotherapy and, perhaps, Alcoholics Anonymous.

The truly psychotic sexual aggressor, the social psychopath lacking in any sensitivity for the feelings and rights of others, and the consistent recidivist will all, no doubt, be better off in a full-fledged prison or institution for the criminally insane. Certainly the public is better off. However, it is clearly the duty of every citizen to recognize the difference between the few who are truly dangerous and the many whose behavior is merely inappropriate and self-defeating. It is our further duty to see that attitudes of compassion and reason are reflected in local legislation governing sexual behavior. The third step is the establishment of a program of psychological diagnosis or evaluation for each convicted offender. And, as Albert Ellis suggests, the most promising form of treatment in each case should be determined *before* sentence is passed. Whether the man is sent to prison or is placed on probation, facilities must be made available for his treatment; this is especially important in the case of first offenders.

FALLACY:

SEX OFFENSE OCCURS BECAUSE THE OFFENDER IS OVER-
SEXED.

FACT:

The phrase "sex offender" conjures up in many people's minds the figure of a "sex fiend" — a man of such unquenchable sexual craving that no outrage or crime is too heinous to commit in his search to satisfy it. Horrible sex crimes do, of course, occur; but the men committing them, and others using less violent means to achieve their illicit sexual ends, make up a scant 3% of all convicted sex offenders. Most important, even these severely disordered 3% were quite likely motivated not by a strong sex drive but by severe emotional problems that result from a sick mind. The reason that the public is so misled with respect to the "sex fiend" is simple: The reports of a demented man who stalks and grotesquely murders a series of five women are a seller of newspapers. The dreary procession of men constituting the bulk of sex offenders — the exhibitionist, the pedophile, the homosexual — is hardly so newsworthy.

An examination of the personality and sex drive of the "typical" sex offender — which implies, in this instance, the most commonly arrested one — reveals quite a different picture from what one would expect. His sexual maturity was probably arrested at the juvenile level. He is lacking in masculine aggressiveness and feels markedly inferior to other men. A man bedeviled by timidity, fearfulness, anxiety, and guilt, he is passive in his relationships with women. Measured in terms of frequency of intercourse, the age at which his sexual activity began, and the number of his sexual partners, he can only be judged as being undersexed, rather than oversexed.

The Kinsey study of sex offenders is the most comprehensive research into the subject ever made. Every category of offense, offender (or aggressor), and victim is meticulously detailed and analyzed, and the data indeed discredit the argument that most men who commit sexual offenses are oversexed, as examination of each group will show.

Consider, first of all, the pedophile — the man with a sexual interest in children — whose numbers constitute a large proportion of sex-offense arrests. (The sex offender uses no force, as opposed to the aggressor.) The pedophile is driven toward children because his associations with adult women are severely hampered by his feelings of inferiority and inadequacy. It is, then, sexual deprivation rather than an over-strong sex drive that motivates him. Mental defectives form the second largest group of offenders against children. While such a man is not bothered by feelings of inferiority or shyness, he usually does have a low sex drive and is probably driven by loneliness to seek out children. In both instances, the impelling force is not the man's being oversexed, but his feelings of inadequacy and loneliness.

The offenders against minors (girls aged twelve to fifteen years) are of two kinds, according to the Kinsey data: the careless man, whom I have already discussed, who regards as fair sexual game any female who approaches adult size; and the young man who chooses a sexual partner so near his own age that it is a psychologically appropriate choice, even though the girl is legally under age. Intellectually, offenders against minors are a very dull group and stand low on the socioeconomic ladder. The sight or thought of females arouses little response in them, which would hardly be the case if they were oversexed. Their arrest is probably just accidental; they are dull-witted and easygoing enough to be careless about the selection of a sexual partner. These men are obviously not driven by an insatiable craving for sex.

The arrested sex offenders against adults — implying adultery (in those states having laws against it), or sexual contact with a girl who is over sixteen years of age but under the legal age of consent — constitute the lowest socioeconomic grouping of all sex offenders. This offender characteristically is incapable of responding to psychological or abstract erotic stimuli, responding only to the simple stimulus of direct physical contact. He uses no force or threat. His partner is usually willing; or she alleges that he forced his attentions on her ("he made me do it"); or one or both partners are married to someone else, hence the charge of adultery. It is his free-wheeling, opportunist attitude toward sex, rather than an abnormal sex drive, that places him in the toils of the law.

Even an examination of the sexual aggressors in the Kinsey sampling — those men using force or threat in their sexual contacts — fails to reveal a man who is oversexed. The aggressor against children is typically plagued with alcoholism (two-thirds of them are drunk at the time of the attack), a dull intellect, and a restrained and puritanical attitude toward sex. His relationship with women remains poor all his life, despite multiple marriages. He makes some preliminary sexual overture, which the child resists; being in a drunken state, he then uses force to achieve compliance. The assault is typically unpremeditated; and, as there is such a strong taboo against (1) a child as a sexual partner and (2) the use of force, alcohol must be regarded as the precipitating force. His offense, then, is not the result of an overly strong sex drive, but of the combination of a disorganized and neurotic personality and an inability to restrain an impulse of the moment, his defenses having been weakened by alcohol. The aggressor against children is one of the most criminal (nonsexual as well as sexual crime) of all sex offenders, and one can therefore conclude that sexual assault reflects his general asocial attitude.

The aggressors against minors are another of the most criminal groups of sex offenders and have amassed the highest record of juvenile delinquency. The assault arises perhaps because a naive girl of twelve or fifteen is far more sexually provocative than she realizes, and the man so enticed is determined to make her fulfill her promises, "to teach her a lesson." Often the partner is willing in the beginning but attempts to back off as the sex activity progresses. This aggressor possesses a strong sex drive, to be sure, but he cannot be said to be oversexed. He is an amoral and asocial individual who often proceeds to accumulate a criminal record of other violence and serious nonsexual offense. His aggression against a sexual partner appears to be related to his general inability to defer gratification and to his aggressive nature, rather than to be the outgrowth of an abnormal sex drive.

Aggressors against adults (e.g., forcible rapists) are primarily motivated, not so much by hostility toward women, as by the promise that women are on earth merely to gratify man's sexual desires. These men, in company with the previously described aggressors, are amoral delinquents who take what they want - be it a woman, money, or a car — when and as they want it. A few, however, are motivated by a strong hostility toward women, a hostility that is tinged with strong sadistic tendencies. It is probably from this group that the terrifying sexual assailants and murderers of whom one reads come. Others of these aggressors are drunks who become hostile when their efforts at seduction are rebuffed, and who consequently force sexual intercourse. Still others are conventional, restrained men who have a personality defect or who come under a situational stress that erupts into a sexual assault.

Leaving the aggressors, we come to a quite different category of sex offenders: the incest offender. The offender against children (under twelve) is characterized by the Kinsey researchers as an ineffectual, often drunk, often unemployed man who is preoccupied with sex (which does not imply that he is oversexed — perhaps just deprived). Because he is often unemployed, he spends much of his time at home. He is therefore alone with the young children, since his wife and older children must work to support the family that he neglects.

Drink and being alone at home with a child are also a typical combination in cases of incest offenders against minors (girls twelve to fifteen years of age). Sex in itself is not very important to these men; but once having broken the incest taboo, they continue because of ease of access. Availability and ease of access: these are the motivating forces in this uneducated, sexually rather restrained group. They manage to break the incest taboo despite the fact that they are the most religious of all sex offenders, most being members of fundamentalist religions. In the cultural milieu to which they belong, furthermore, incest is regarded as an unfortunate, but understandable happenstance. People of more fortunate socioeconomic and educational background are far less tolerant of incestuous relationships.

The Peeping Tom or voyeur is typically a young man who is beset with strong feelings of inadequacy, is shy with women, and has an inadequate heterosexual life. He has much less heterosexual experience than other young men his age have, and, if anything, must be declared undersexed.

The exhibitionist — constituting one-third of all arrests for sex offenses (probably ten times that number never get into legal difficulites) — acts largely out of compulsion. It is exceedingly rare that he so much as touches one of his victims; his behavior, in fact, stems from some psychological stress, rather than from physiological need. He has been sexually rejected or ridiculed, or otherwise made to feel sexually inadequate. Through the shock that he causes the women to whom he exposes himself, he attempts to prove to himself that he is truly masculine, truly a male. Rather than being oversexed, the exhibitionist is quite conservative in his sexual activity, certainly having no more and probably having less premarital or extramarital associations than the other groups of offenders and aggressors do. Once again, the basic problem is not one of being oversexed; the exhibitionist's behavior represents an attempt to fend off feelings of masculine inferiority.

Sex offense and sex crime, then, are motivated by an entire spectrum of forces: inappropriate, self-defeating attempts to combat feelings of inadequacy; opportunism, carelessness, or drunkenness; a general criminality and a callous disregard for the rights of others; mental dullness or deficiency; and various degrees of mental illness and personality disorders. In practically no category does the offense occur because the offender is oversexed and cannot control an overpowering erotic urge.

―――――

FALLACY:

THE TYPICAL SEX OFFENDER, PARTICULARLY AGAINST CHILDREN, IS AGGRESSIVE AND POTENTIALLY HOMICIDAL.

FACT:

As pointed out in the foregoing section, the "sex maniac" of popular fiction rarely exists in fact. Misconceptions about the number of these maniacs stalking the streets no doubt arise from the enormous and usually lurid publicity accorded sex crimes of violence.

One cannot deny the horror of crimes committed by such murderers as the

Boston Strangler or Jack the Ripper. Homicides are particularly tragic when the victim is a child, whose innocence and trust inevitably make it even more defenseless. Nonetheless, grossly disordered minds in combination with sexual deviation and a predilection for violence are extremely rare. In the criminal events of this country, as a matter of fact, rape homicide has been variously estimated to occur one time per one to four million population, whereas the rate of all homicides is about fifty per million population. (Motor accidents, by contrast, account for about two hundred and ten deaths per million population.)

Let us consider specifically the typical behavior of molesters of little girls – pedophiles, as they are called – since they represent a sizable number of those persons arrested for sexual offense. The Kinsey investigators point out that the majority of these men only caress the girls and do not often make any attempt to touch their genitals. Force or threat is rarely involved. Moreover, most of these men are impotent, or nearly so. Wishing to protect himself against sexual failure, a pedophile approaches a child because she poses no threat to his male self-image. Typically the man is not a stranger to the child, and she is consequently only dimly aware of what has happened. She quite likely experiences very little upset at the time of the incident, and there is small likelihood that any lingering effects will emerge in later years – unless, of course, her parents or teachers react hysterically. (This latter point is an extremely important one for all parents to remember if their child ever becomes the victim of sexual molestation.)

Murder in aggressive cases against children is "extremely rare," say the Kinsey investigators. As a matter of fact, the New York Times carried accounts of only twelve such murders in the whole of a recent three-year period. Sex-linked child murders are usually not part of a sadistic sex act, but occur accidentally in the effort of the attacker to stop the child from attracting attention, or in a moment of guilt or panic after the event.

Another category of sexual offense against children is incest. These incest offenders are typically nonaggressive; they are ineffectual men, who drink heavily and are sex-preoccupied because of frustrations in other areas of their lives. They are opportunists, in that they take advantage of frequent periods of unemployment, during which they are left at home with the children while the mother is away working.

Since this section deals with the allegation that the "typical" sex offender is aggressive and homicidal, it is interesting to look once again at the group constituting one-third of all arrests for sex offense, the exhibitionist. He is an average citizen, characteristically leading a very conservative sexual life. The exhibition usually occurs in a public place before several people. No physical contact is intended or takes place, whether his victims are women or little girls. His purpose is to shock, thereby to convince himself that his erect penis is indeed an impressive, potent appendage. That he takes no great pains to prevent apprehension or to disguise himself suggests that he has an unconscious wish to be arrested and punished, so that his feelings of guilt over his behavior will be alleviated. It is almost unheard of that he go on to commit more serious sexual offense or criminal violence.

It is most significant that the six leading categories of sex crimes committed by the 1356 prison inmates in the Kinsey study were classified as *offenses*, not aggressive acts, since no force or threat was used. Furthermore, it is important to remember that the number of men *imprisoned* on sex-offense charges falls far short of the number who have been *arrested* on similar charges. It is to be assumed that only a certain percentage of those arrested for sex offenses are ultimately convicted and imprisoned; the minor nonaggressive offender, therefore, is less likely than the aggressive sex offender to end up in prison. Since the Kinsey subjects were imprisoned following their conviction on sex-offense charges, one would logically expect the sampling to be weighted toward aggressive rather than nonaggressive offenders. But this is not the case, as the Kinsey tabulations demonstrated.

"The vast majority of sex offenders are frightened, guilty, woefully inadequate, harmless people." This judgment of Dr. Ralph Slovenko, Professor of Law at the University of Kansas, sums up the opinion of behavioral scientists in the matter of the "typical" sex offender. Only one in five of them ever uses any form of force or threat against his victim, and homicide rarely occurs. In the matter of homicide, it is worth noting that nine out of every ten murders occur within the family group or circle of close friends. The likelihood of being done in by Uncle Charlie or by old Fred next door, whose lawnmower you have consistently neglected to return, is far greater than your being murdered by a wild-eyed, panting "sex fiend."

———————

FALLACY:
SEX OFFENDERS ARE TYPICALLY UNRELIGIOUS.

FACT:
The problem here, as it is with all generalities having to do with sex offenders, is mainly one of definition. Is one speaking of the relatively normal man who has come afoul of outdated local laws? Or of the man who really is a sexual deviate, but who is not deviated otherwise? Or of the man whose basically disordered personality breaks out in unacceptable sexual behavior?

The Kinsey researchers did, in fact, find that, on the whole, sex offenders were less devout than the general public is. In the following table are shown the Kinsey findings in this respect. The *control group* represents the 477 men in their sampling who had never been to prison on any charge, and the *prison group*, 888 men imprisoned for crimes other than sex offenses (the 1356 *sex offenders* being, of course, the primary subjects of the study):

Degree of Religious Devoutness

	Inactive	Moderate	Devout
Control group	36%	35%	28%
Prison group	59%	26%	15%
Sex offenders	[about the same percentages as those of the prison group, say the Kinsey researchers]		

When categories of sex offenders in the Kinsey survey are examined separately, however, wide variations of devoutness emerge, showing once more the danger of generalizations about that nebulous group. Among offenders against adults, for example, 64% were religiously inactive and only 12% were devout. On the other hand, incest offenders (as an example) against adult daughters were the "most religious" of all offenders. Only 36% of them were inactive, while 40% were devout. This incest group presents a strange picture, incidentally. Their attitudes in general were moralistic, intolerant, and sexually inhibited, yet their history was one of drunkenness, violence, and sexual activity that violated the tenets of their own religion (which, incidentally, was nearly always Pentecostal, "hardshell" Baptist, or Methodist). Of the homosexual offenders against children, 30% listed themselves as devout, but only 15% of the exhibitionists and 13% of the rapists considered themselves to be so. The heterosexuals who offended against children were also a moralistic, conservative lot — they were believers in the double standard, were guilt-ridden, exhibited strong religious convictions, assessed women as being either "good" or "bad," and tended to deny their guilt. This last factor, in the Kinsey view, made them highly unresponsive to psychotherapy.

In the Ellis-Brancale survey of three hundred consecutive cases of sex offense in New Jersey, 30% of the offenders claimed to attend church regularly. If attending church regularly is equated with the "devout" designation in the Kinsey sampling, then the number of New Jersey offenders claiming devotion to religion is almost double that of the Kinsey inmates. Perhaps the difference is that the subjects in the Ellis-Brancale survey were an unselected group of offenders who had committed anything from a relatively minor infraction of the law to a major sex crime (their punishments ranged from fines to prison sentences). One would therefore expect the New Jersey sampling to be more representative of the general population than the Kinsey subjects were, since the latter had all committed offenses serious enough to warrant prison sentences.

Whatever the reason for this disparity, the Kinsey researchers' comment is that, on the "other side of the wall," prisoners who are religiously inactive outnumber those who are devout, and that devotion to religion does appear to reduce unacceptable sexual behavior in the individual. Nevertheless, the number of prisoners convicted of sex crimes who profess a moderate or devout degree of religious fervor suggests that religion of itself cannot be considered a deterrent to unacceptable sexual behavior.

FALLACY:

SEXUAL MOLESTERS OF CHILDREN ARE TYPICALLY OVER SIXTY-FIVE YEARS OF AGE.

FACT:

On the subject of sex offense and the elderly man, one of the most compassionate statements ever made — and certainly an accurate one, as we shall see — came from Dr. Frederick E. Whiskin of the Harvard Medical School. He called an old man alleged to be a sex offender the most maligned person in our society — a "benign and impotent" creature, whose actions typically are not genital in origin but spring from tragic loneliness.

There is special pathos in the plight of the older man charged as a sex offender. So many old people, in their loneliness and emotional starvation, reach out to a child for warmth and affection. If an elderly woman caresses a child, the act is regarded as normal and natural. But if an elderly man does so, his simple gesture — which rarely bears any sexual overtones — may well meet with the hysterical cry of "molester!" from the child's parents.

The facts exonerating the man past sixty-five as the chief molester of children were firmly established by the Kinsey researchers in their study of the dynamics and circumstances involved in the various forms of sex offense. To repeat, the Kinsey group classified anyone under the age of twelve as a child and defined the child molester (or pedophile) as an adult having a sexual contact with a child without the use of force or threat.

The Kinsey data flatly disprove the popular image of the sex offender as a "dirty old man." The average age of child molesters is only thirty-five! Only one-sixth of all men arrested on charges of child molestation, as a matter of fact, are past the age of fifty. A comparison, according to age groups, of all paroled sex offenders in the state of Pennsylvania in the year 1960 heaps further discredit on this popular misconception. Only 4.58% of these offenders were past sixty; yet men in this age group constituted nearly 20% of the state's total male population. The largest number of sex offenders (23%) fell in the age range of twenty to twenty-four years, yet men in this age group comprised only 8% of the male population of Pennsylvania.

If not an elderly, lecherous man, then who is the "typical" sex offender against children? What is he like? The Kinsey researchers found that he is usually a man who approaches a child because of his inability to postpone sexual gratification until a suitable partner comes along. This lack of control in some cases is due to a basic character defect; in others, to varying degrees of mental deficiency; and in still others, to an inability or fear of sexual interaction with another adult. In 30% of the cases, a heavy intake of alcohol was also involved. A pedophile does not, by definition, typically use force or threat on his victims, even when the children are not particularly willing partners. And when pedophiles' brushes with the law involve nonsexual matters, their criminality is minor and unaggressive. If there is further sexual offense, it also is unaggressive, taking the form of exhibition and offenses against minors, rather than such sexual violence as rape.

In the Kinsey group's survey, the subject of the senile man as child molester, another popular and equally fallacious stereotype, was also examined. They concluded that senility in such offenses is a "quite uncommon" factor, involving perhaps only one in twenty offenders against children. In those rare instances in which the offender was in fact senile, one finds a man who had heretofore functioned quite adequately in the sexual, social, and intellectual aspects of his life, but whose mental deterioration had weakened his judgment and moral restraints to the extent that he could allow himself to approach a child. Statistically, furthermore, such behavior is generally brief, in all probability a one-time-only occurrence.

With respect to the homosexual molester of young boys, the public once again clings to the stereotyped picture of a morally loose, senile old man. The truth, however, is that these offenders are much younger fellows; the average age is 30.6 years. Mental deficiency or alcohol is more likely to figure in this behavior than senility is. These homosexuals would no doubt prefer older people as companions or sexual partners; but, as in the case of the molester of little girls, they feel more adequate and at greater ease with a child. Force is rarely used.

We have thus far considered only children under the age of twelve in this discussion, but it is also of interest to look at offenses against youngsters between the ages of twelve and fifteen. The Kinsey researchers categorize these youngsters as minors and regard them as having reached at least a degree of sexual maturity. Rather than being a deteriorated, senile old man, the typical offender against minors is just under twenty-five. These offenders are an intellectually dull group, irresponsible and unimaginative by nature, who happen to be careless about the age of their partners — most of whom, indeed, are willing partners, if not actually the provocateurs in the relationship. Such precipitating factors as senility, drunkenness, mental deficiency, or true pedophilia were involved in a scant 20% of the offenses tabulated by the Kinsey group.

Far more typically, the molester of minors is a man who gambled on the statistical probability that the girl was of legal age, and lost. He seems, in fact, not to deserve the label of sex offender. In their book *Sex Offenders*, the Kinsey group recounted a not untypical case history of a man snared in such a situation. The girl involved had appeared to him quite mature, even though somewhat heavily made up and provocatively dressed; she drank her liquor with ease and held her own in sexual banter. She proved to be an experienced and satisfactory sexual partner. Unfortunately, she was under legal age of consent and the man was taken to court. "I knew I was done for," he stated, "when I saw they had braided her hair in pigtails and had given her a rag doll to hold."

In homosexual offenses against minors we once again find no evidence that an older man is the chief offender. The average age of these homosexuals, as a matter of fact, is 32.6 years. The large majority of such offenders are exclusively homosexual men who purposely seek out youths because of a desire to dominate; or who, although they essentially prefer adult male partners, select an adolescent boy for some other reason (e.g., inferiority feelings with adults or lapse of control in face of temptation). It should also be mentioned that in 83% of the cases of homosexual offense against minors, the boy is a willing partner. The senile man, then, figures most insignificantly in the history of homosexual offense against adolescents.

It must be conceded, of course, that a person who yearns for the warmth of human contact may, under the stress of intoxication, senility, or emotional upset, lose control over his mental and moral restraints against such behavior and attempt to molest a child. What started out as a mere physical contact without any sexual overtones may thus become a sexual one. But the important thing to remember is that the senile old man in these circumstances is no more liable to undergo such a lapse than a young man or a middle-aged man.

FALLACY:

PORNOGRAPHY HAS A CORRUPTIVE EFFECT ON THE MINDS AND BEHAVIOR OF PEOPLE, ESPECIALLY CHILDREN.

FACT:

Derived from the Greek words meaning *harlot* and *writing*, assumed to mean advertisements made by prostitutes, pornography by current definition is written or pictorial material that is purposefully designed to cause sexual stimulation. Those possessed of a passion for expurgation and a determination to control the moral behavior of others typically cite two reasons why someone (usually themselves) should sit in judgment on what others may or may not read: (1) children's minds are corrupted by such material; and (2) it provokes sexual criminality. In this section we shall examine the first premise, and the linkage between pornography and sexual acting out will be considered in the next section.

The first question that immediately arises is just what constitutes pornography. No matter how many laws are passed, lechery, like beauty, is inevitably in the eye of the beholder. A massive Rubens nude will evoke admiration for its artistic merit in one person, some degree of sexual arousal in another, and moral indignation in a third. The same nude might evoke in a fourth only thoughts of the local reducing salon. Is the Bible pornographic? Shakespeare? Chaucer? St. Augustine? John Donne? Benjamin Franklin? All have, amazingly, been subjected to censorship, which is an indispensable tool in the business of purification. That prototype of the self-appointed guardian of public morals, Dr. Thomas Bowdler, was heard to say, "Shakespeare, Madam, is obscene, and thank God, *we* are sufficiently advanced to have found it out!" Lady Macbeth's famous cry "Out, damned spot" was therefore rendered "Out, crimson spot." The mention of Queequeg's underclothing in *Moby Dick* was carefully deleted. Huckleberry Finn's being "in a sweat" became "in such a hurry." Ridiculous? Of course it is. But based on false premises and administered by the unenlightened or overzealous, as it nearly always is, censorship almost inevitably comes to a ridiculous or dangerous end.

No sensitive person can deny that pornography exists; but, apart from its presenting sex often unrealistically, and sometimes as something ugly and unhuman, the chief objection to it must lie in its literary or pictorial worthlessness, rather than in its power to corrupt. I should imagine that even the most diligent and dedicated purchaser of pornography must grow weary of the atrociously written, tediously repetitious accounts of human sexual behavior, real and imagined. Even the most uncritical must begin after a while recognize that these books hardly "tell it like it is."

Even when pornography falls in the hands of children, the contention that its effects are degenerative is highly debatable. Certainly there is no research or clinical data to support the argument. As the most recent evidence, the President's Commission on Obscenity and Pornography — a nineteen-man team of experts conducting a two-year study — stated among its preliminary conclusions in August 1970: "There is no evidence to suggest that exposure of youngsters to pornography has a detrimental impact upon moral character, sexual orientation, or attitudes." The prominent sociologist and family-life educator Helen Branson has pointed out that almost all moralistic laws are passed in the name of "protecting our youth." But does not, she says, the responsibility of protecting the young from the demoralizing or dehumanizing effect of any force in society belong to the family? Inculcating in the young proper attitudes toward life in general and sex in particular will prevent pornography from having a detrimental effect on youngsters.

Mrs. Branson thinks that it is healthy to have pornography out in the open and advocates discussing it in the classroom — and, more important, in the home. Pornography will thus be stripped of its secrecy and will therefore lose much of its appeal. It can be turned into an excellent springboard for factual sex instruction. (Mrs. Branson questioned her students about where they had come upon the pornography they had read. The answer is intriguing: More than half claimed that they had found it among the personal effects of their fathers!)

Dr. John Money, Professor of Medical Psychiatry and Pediatrics at Johns Hopkins, also finds pornography a useful tool. Demonstrating, as it usually does, the positive and negative sides of sex, it can be used to instruct the young in the difference between the two. It does not cause the children to imitate, he says, any more than reading the Bible "sets them to playing Crucifixion games."

An experiment was recently reported by Dr. Clifford B. Reifler to the American Psychiatric Association wherein twenty-three young men "for the sake of science" were exposed to considerably more stag films and other pornography than the average person would encounter in a lifetime. At the beginning of the experiment, the subjects were all enthusiastic participants and admitted that they would be willing to pay for such an opportunity. By the end of it, however, their only reaction was boredom, and many reported that they had thereafter turned down private opportunities to view pornography. Dr. Reifler's study was possibly the first to measure experimentally the effect of extensive exposure to pornographic material, and the results indeed weaken the argument that pornography will send the reader or viewer into a frenzy of sexual acting out. As a matter of fact, research studies reported on at a September 1970 meeting of psychologists indicate that limited exposure to pornography can help bring about adult patterns of acceptable heterosexual interest.

No one denies that the young are more vulnerable to what they read than those who are older, more sophisticated, and more critical of what they see and read. However, by extrapolating from Mayor Jimmy Walker's observation that no girl was ever ruined by a book, one can safely say that pornography has a negative effect only on the mind that was disordered to begin with. (Examining the other side of the coin, one might wonder at the continued behavior of sexually loose and active girls who, in their frequent visits to hotel and motel rooms, typically find only the Gideon Bible to read.)

"If the purpose of pornography is to excite sexual desire," says Malcolm Muggeridge (formerly editor of *Punch*), "it is unnecessary for the young, inconvenient for the middle-aged, and unseemly for the old." No one admires or wishes to encourage pornography (except, of course, the writers or purveyors thereof). But the alternative to it is censorship — which would mean that the *Song of Solomon* is in as much danger of oblivion as the eastern rag called *Screw*.

―――――――

FALLACY:

> PORNOGRAPHY STIMULATES PEOPLE TO COMMIT CRIMINAL SEX ACTS.

FACT:

This is a favorite argument of law-enforcement officers who, when making an arrest for a sex offense, may find the back seat of the culprit's car sagging under a collection of dirty books and magazines. However, the question of the chicken and the egg immediately arises: which came first, interest in pornography or the sex crime?

As in the case of the harm that pornography is alleged to cause children, there is no scientific evidence supporting the linkage between pornography and sexual criminality. The preliminary report of the President's Commission on Obscenity and Pornography, mentioned in the last section, also contains this statement: "Research indicates that erotic materials do not contribute to the development of character defects, nor operate as a significant factor in antisocial behavior or in crime. In sum, there is no evidence that exposure to pornography operates as a cause of misconduct in either youths or adults." Rather, a careful examination of imprisoned sex offenders shows that they "have histories of sexual repression as youngsters growing up in strict families," suggesting that this repression, "not stimulation by pornography, is what leads them to sex crimes." The Kinsey group's twenty-five-year study of sex offense shows that pornography has quite a different effect from what it is commonly believed to have. Of their entire sample of 2721 men, of which fewer than half were imprisoned sex offenders, only fourteen had never been exposed to pornography. This almost universal exposure provides a valid basis for certain conclusions to be drawn about the effects of pornographic material.

For a man to respond strongly to pornography, two conditions are important: youthfulness and imagination, and the latter is characteristically lacking in sex offenders. As a group, they are not youthful; and, since they are poorly educated, their imaginativeness and ability to project, to "put themselves in somebody else's shoes," are limited. Their response to pornography is accordingly blunted. The Kinsey researchers suggest that a typical reaction of a sex offender might be: "Why get worked up about a picture? You can't do nothing with a picture."

Not only did the Kinsey group reject the premise that pornography is a spur to sexual criminality, but it also went further to suggest that a man's *inability* to gain vicarious sexual pleasure through some form of erotica may possibly cause him to break out into a display of unacceptable overt sexual behavior. While this view was once judged simply as being the thoughtful speculation of researchers who have spent a great many years studying sex offenders, it has recently received empirical support from research conducted in this country as well as from a recent and much-publicized experiment in Denmark.

Scientific investigations reported at the September 1970 Convention of the American Psychological Association showed that the childhoods of child molesters and other sexual deviates are marked by little permissiveness in the home with respect to any degree of nudity, little sex instruction from the parents, and *minimum* exposure to pornography as teen-agers.

In the belief that what is banned has extraordinary attraction, the Danes, in 1969, abolished all laws against the sale of pornography to anyone over sixteen. The results are intriguing. Sales of pornography — books and magazines, films, and still photographs — dropped significantly, even when price tags were drastically cut. For example, sex movies that previously sold for $40 a reel soon remained unsold at $8.50. The Danish Minister of Justice, Knud Thestrup, was led to comment that the public is interested in pornography simply through "curiosity about what is forbidden." The lifting of the ban also led one pornography vendor to comment ruefully that the legalization of pornography was throttling business.

The most significant consequence of the Danish experiment was a 31% drop during 1969, in comparison with 1968 figures, in the overall number of sex crimes committed in Denmark. Criminologists there point out, however, that the figures may be unduly misleading, since there was no similar drop in the incidence of aggressive sexual crimes, such as rape and sexual assault. Neither, however, was there a rise in them — which seems as important. Furthermore, Danish school officials state that the relaxation of the law has not increased children's contact with obscene material.

It may be argued that the present statistics on sex criminality in Denmark reflect a more relaxed attitude on the part of the public with respect to less serious sex crimes, or a growing disinclination on the part of the police to crack down on these offenders, rather than a dramatic decline in the incidence of these offenses. What *does* clearly emerge, however, is the initial evidence that making pornography freely available to the public has not caused a flourishing of sexual offense in the country of such experimentation, as those who would impose censorship warn will happen if vigilance against pornography is ever relaxed.

. Writing two or three years earlier, the Kinsey researchers possibly established an explanation for the results of the Danish experiment insofar as pornography's apparent lack of effect, one way or the other, on violent sex crimes is concerned. In the Kinsey assessment, rapists and other sexual aggressors are unlikely to be affected by sexually stimulating writings, as other factors are the primary motivating forces in their behavior. The sexual aggressor is essentially a psychopath, taking whatever he wants when and as he wants it, regardless of the harm to others or the consequences to himself. Rape or assault, then, is but part of his general criminality. His is a socially disordered mind, not a sexually deviated one upon which pornography might act as a trigger.

A challenge to the premise that pornography corrupts comes from still another quarter. A 1966 survey of New Jersey psychologists and psychiatrists revealed that practically none had ever seen a normal patient whose delinquent behavior had been prompted by pornography. Two-thirds of these professionals thought, as a matter of fact, that such "literature" would reduce delinquent acts by providing substitute outlets.

Some 3400 psychiatrists and psychologists were polled by the University of Chicago Department of Psychiatry as part of a research project to determine what relationship they had observed to exist between pornography and such asocial sexual behavior as rape. It is obviously difficult to measure, experimentally, long-term effects of pornography; this research was therefore concentrated on the clinical experience of professionals dealing with disordered human behavior. While a scant 7.4% reported cases in which they were "somewhat convinced" of the linkage between pornography and sexual acting out, 80% said that they had never encountered such a case. An even larger number — 83.7% — were convinced that the person exposed to pornography was no more likely than the unexposed person to commit an act of sexual aggression. Furthermore, 86.1% of these psychotherapists thought that people who were so intent on stamping out pornography were frequently bedeviled by their own unresolved sexual problems. Two-thirds of the clinicians, incidentally, opposed censorship because of the climate of oppression it creates, and because of the inhibition it imposes on human creativity.

Dr. Clifford Allen, an English psychiatrist and author of several books on sexual aberrations, has commented that he does not consider "girlie" magazines to be a corrupting force. They do not, he says, lead men to rape, which has an entirely different psychological cause. The danger he sees in pornography is that lonely young men, instead of seeking the reality of taking a "real, live girl" to the movies or to a dance, may instead seek the vicarious, distorted, daydream world created by these books or magazines. One might also argue, however, that pornography does add some spice to what would otherwise be the completely dull and lackluster sex life of these unfortunate men. It is highly doubtful that perusing pornographic material would psychologically hinder such a man when he eventually attempts to establish a normal social relationship with a girl.

In 1644, John Milton — a Puritan among Puritans — addressed Parliament in opposition to censorship, which he regarded as the handmaiden of tyranny. He argued that reading everything is the means of attaining knowledge of the good and evil and the ugly and beautiful that flourish indiscriminately in the world. Corrupting forces, he said, are everywhere present, and they can only be met by building up an inner discipline and *the ability of rational choice* [italics my own]. Censorship serves no such purpose, especially since its course, as history reveals, has led inevitably to the imposition on the masses of the prejudices, tyrannies, and, usually, the stupidity of the few.

FALLACY:

PORNOGRAPHY AND OBSCENITY LEAD TO SEXUAL EXCESS AND SEXUAL ACTING OUT.

FACT:

Laws concerning obscenity and pornography are ambiguous. They are subject to a variety of interpretations and frequently appear to be used in the course of legal prosecution to satisfy the unconscious needs and desires of the accuser rather than to protect society from the accused. The American culture regards sexual behavior with such intense emotionality (shame, guilt, and fear) that almost any literary or pictorial representation of sexual interaction is liable to be interpreted by *some*one as being obscene, hence unlawful.

Despite the fact that the United States Supreme Court has been called upon several times recently to settle questions of law regarding obscenity, there remains much ambiguity over what is and is not obscene and pornographic. Such ambiguity in the past, as a matter of fact, has led to the censorship or restriction of sale, at one time or another, of such classics as *Alice in Wonderland, Huckleberry Finn, Adventures of Sherlock Holmes, Robinson Crusoe, On the Origin of Species,* and *The Scarlet Letter.* An authority on censorship once declared that if the Holy Bible were to be written today, about the most the public could expect would be some sort of an expurgated edition — if, indeed, it would be allowed to be published and distributed under any circumstances. However, in light of some of the salacious films, books, and magazines currently bombarding the public, that commentator is clearly behind the times.

Two 1957 U.S. Supreme Court rulings indicate the difficulty of defining what is and is not obscene. The rulings held that, while the First and Fourteenth Amendments give no one the right to purvey obscene material, the Constitution does not restrict any matter "having even the slightest redeeming social importance . . . ," however unpopular the ideas therein contained. But what the Court did hold as obscene is any material "utterly without redeeming social importance . . . in which to the average person, applying contemporary community standards, the dominant theme of the material taken as a whole appeals to prurient interest." One can see the endless possibilities for divergent evaluation of the same piece of material, since it is the responsibility of each township, county, or state to pass on the purity of a particular work. What might not cause an eye to widen in Greenwich Village might well cause near apoplexy in some small mid-Western town.

A continual battle rages around the possible dangers of pornography. Admittedly, pornographic matter can stimulate sexually, but there is no significant empirical or clinical evidence to support the contention that pornography causes sexual deviation or violence. Only when perusal of such material is preferred to heterosexual activity should it be considered abnormal, as it is well known to psychotherapists that normal, sexually well-adjusted people often enjoy the erotic stimulation of certain written and pictorial matter.

In its preliminary report, the President's Commission on Obscenity and Pornography concludes from its investigation that during the twenty-four hours following the viewing of highly erotic material there may be some sexual arousal and, in some cases, increased sexual activity. But, the commission observes, basic attitudes and sexual patterns do not change because of such sexual stimulation. In several experiments reported by the group, a large number of men and women watched pornographic films. It was found that 90% of the couples aged twenty to twenty-five years, and from 30% to 60% of those between forty to fifty years of age, were aroused by what they saw (women as well as men, it should be pointed out). The commission's report contained the comment "that there are no recorded instances of sexual aggression, homosexuality, lesbianism, exhibitionism, or sexual abuse of children attributable to reading or receiving erotic stimuli among several hundred participants in the twelve experiments reviewed."

Young people, it is generally conceded, are particularly vulnerable to the arousal of strong sexual desires as a result of reading prurient material. But it is also possible that pornographic material serves as a harmless psychological release that might actually be an aid to those who are burdened with certain sexual repressions. Here again, there is no significant amount of empirical or clinical proof to support the contention.

To be sure, a paper was presented at the September 1970 meeting of the American Psychological Association by two psychologists who contended that if boys are exposed to heavy doses of erotic material before the age of fourteen, they may develop deviant sexual patterns as adults. These findings stand in stark contrast to the findings of other investigations concerning the effects of pornography. Close evaluation of this study must therefore be undertaken, as well as replication of it — meaning a duplication of the investigation with other subjects — before its conclusions can be accepted. Even if the findings of these two psychologists hold up under future investigation, there is nonetheless no scientific evidence on hand indicating that an adult's exposure to pornography will result in sexual problems for him, except, perhaps, in those cases in which definite emotional problems already existed.

It is known that strong response to pornography is related to imaginativeness, to an ability to make abstractions and to project, to sensitivity (all of which increase as education increases), and to youthfulness. Probably because sex offenders, as a group, are neither well educated nor young, they respond less to pornography than those who do not commit such offenses. The Kinsey group sums up the effects of pornography fairly well: "Pornography collections follow the pre-existing interest of the collector. Men make the collections, collections do not make the men."

It is interesting, by the way, to consider some of the factors that, in general, cause one written passage or picture to be evaluated as being more pornographic than another. Studies have shown that a picture printed on cheap pulp or heavy paper is considered more pornographic than one printed on expensive, slick paper. Similar differences emerge when the effects of color and black-and-white pictures are compared. A picture in black-and-white is usually judged as being more pornographic than if it is in good color. Men rate pictures of partially clad women as being more pornographic than pictures of women similarly posed, but completely nude. Pictures that "accidentally" show a glimpse of the thigh above stocking top (the sort of picture that appears daily in almost any newspaper) are seen as being more exciting than pictures that show considerably more thigh but in which the disclosure is purposeful, such as poses in bathing suits.

. . . and Other Fallacies

Although this is something of a wastebasket section, it nevertheless touches on some extremely important errors made by many Americans. Perhaps the two most important ones concern the oft-repeated allegation that today's youth are running amok and the fear that sex education is a Svengali leading inevitably to the country's downfall.

In view of the almost daily newspaper accounts of the outrages committed by certain groups of young radicals, I suppose it is easy to conclude that America's youth are destruction-bent — if one reads uncritically. But is this disruptive behavior of some young people typical of most of them? I am decidedly of the opinion that it is not.

The final part in this section, on sex education, is really what the whole book is about. Had we all received timely and appropriate sex instruction, most sexual mythology (to say nothing of many sexual hangups) would never have developed and flourished. It is much easier to guide a young person's mind from the outset into patterns of accurate thinking on sexual matters than it is to redirect his thinking once it has been caught in a morass of ignorance and bad information.

It is not too late for any of us to be reeducated in sexual subjects. But we need to do more than reeducate ourselves. It is our responsibility to see that others have the chance to receive an adequate, unbiased sex education, thus making the likelihood greater that the individual will achieve personal adjustment in his adulthood and that the mental health of the nation will improve.

FALLACY:

THE AVERAGE PHYSICIAN IS WELL TRAINED AND
EMOTIONALLY EQUIPPED TO DEAL WITH HIS PATIENTS'
SEXUAL PROBLEMS.

FACT:

Dr. Harold Lief (Professor of Psychiatry at the University of
Pennsylvania Medical School) once pointed out that as recently as 1964 only
one medical school in this country required its students to take a course in
sexology and marriage counseling, and only one other medical school
included such a course in its curriculum as an elective. Fortunately, these
circumstances have changed since 1964, although, sadly, not to a significant
degree. A major difficulty that medical schools encounter in attempting to
introduce courses in human sexuality is finding instructors who have
sufficient training to teach a well-structured, meaningful course, and who at
the same time are comfortable in discussing this traditionally taboo subject.

Within the past few years, several investigations have revealed just how
severely limited the sex education of medical students and practicing
physicians actually is. For example, a survey of physicians in North Carolina
showed that the only ones who felt that they had received an adequate
training in sexual matters were psychiatrists and obstetricians. However, even
these specialists did not consider that they had been exposed to really valid or
helpful instruction until their residency.

A canvass made of recently graduated medical students of the University
of Southern California revealed that the fledgling physicians were almost
unanimous in their opinion that the medical school had not provided them
with adequate instruction in sexual matters. The investigation further
revealed that 55% of these young doctors were currently experiencing some
form of anxiety or conflict concerning their own sexual potency; 40%
harbored fears of homosexual tendencies in themselves, fears that had
generated pronounced symptoms of anxiety; 40% expressed anxiety over
their own masturbation, while 47.5% stated that they would have difficulty
working with patients beset with conflicts over masturbation; 50% felt
anxious about the possibility of treating sexually provocative patients; and
many of the new physicians associated their masturbation with fear of latent
homosexuality (although the two, of course, have no cause-and-effect
relationship).

A survey made in June 1969 showed that fewer than 20% of a particular
group of senior medical students understood what was meant when a patient
said that she was a practicing lesbian. Yet another study revealed that medical

students were reluctant in their clinical work to probe into any sexual problems that their patients might have, even when these problems quite obviously had a significant bearing on the patient's disorder. The students conceded that their own sexual problems and anxieties stemmed from the lack of a proper sex education, and that their ignorance and sexual conflicts would adversely affect their dealings with their patients. Only in the past few months a psychiatrist writing in a medical magazine said that a man becoming impotent in his forties would just have to accept impotency as part of the general aging process!

A significant survey was recently made of a large group of students from several medical schools. One of the most startling revelations was that nearly half the students subscribed to the long-since-discredited belief that mental illness is frequently caused by masturbation. Even more distressing was that one-fifth of the faculty members polled in these medical schools held the same belief.

Apparently these distressing academic shortcomings are not limited to the medical schools of the United States. A study of newly licensed English physicians revealed that fewer than half of them had anything approaching an adequate sex education before they began their practice.

It is an unfortunate truth that, except for their knowledge of reproductive processes, too many physicians are grievously ignorant in matters of human sexuality, as well as being rather prudish in their attitudes toward sex. There is evidence, however, of a growing awareness among medical faculties and students alike of this void. Sensitive to the importance of treating the whole man and prodded into action by doctors like Harold Lief, an increasing number of medical schools are making the study of sex something more comprehensive than an efficient presentation of human "plumbing."

FALLACY:

THE VIRGINITY OF THE WOMAN IS AN IMPORTANT FACTOR IN THE SUCCESS OF A MARRIAGE.

FACT:

Most of the scientifically sound investigations into the effect of a woman's premarital sexual experiences on marital adjustment show that there is only a slight correlation between happiness in marriage and the lack of premarital sexual experience. However small the correlation is, the indications are nevertheless slightly in favor of premarital chastity.

The importance to either men or women of their prospective marriage partner's chastity at the time of marriage is apparently diminishing gradually. Studies were made at the University of Wisconsin in 1939 and 1956 to determine the components that students considered important in a happy marriage. In the intervening years between the two surveys, chastity dropped in importance from tenth to fourteenth place. Kinsey's studies indicate that over 40% of men wanted to marry virgins, while only 23% of women expected their prospective husbands to be without coital experience.

Studies have shown that mothers who have had premarital sexual intercourse usually have no regrets and state that they would do the same thing again. Paradoxically, however, they want their own daughters to remain virgins before marriage. Mothers are more rigid in their attitude toward premarital coitus than their daughters are. When both groups were asked, "How important do you think it is that a girl be a virgin when she marries?" 88% of the mothers replied "very important," and 12% said "somewhat important"; none indicated that it was "not important," despite the fact that studies show that 50% or more of these mothers themselves had premarital sexual intercourse. The percentage of the daughters replying in the same three categories was, respectively, 54%, 33%, and 13%.

During the early part of marriage, those women who have had premarital coitus seem to enjoy sexual intercourse more than those who have not had; but the differences in the level of satisfaction eventually diminish as the marriages grow older. Sexual compatibility in marriage is dependent upon compatibility at the many levels of a couple's day-by-day living together. Having premarital sexual intercourse, however satisfactory, is therefore no guarantee of a happy sex life after marriage. This truth stands in opposition to the arguments that many young men present to sexually reluctant girl friends, and to the threadbare cliché that "only a fool would purchase shoes without first trying them on."

Whether or not a woman has premarital coitus is not nearly so important to marital adjustment as are other factors, such as happiness of parents, adequate sex education, length of engagement, emotional stability, dependability, and economic security.

―――――――――――

FALLACY:

NATURE COMPENSATES FOR THE NUMBER OF MALES KILLED DURING TIME OF WAR.

FACT:

It is axiomatic that man depends upon the laws of nature to keep his physical life in balance. Particularly after the shattering experiences of war, he finds some comfort in the notion that nature compensates for the combatants killed during hostilities by increasing, in some mystical way, the ratio of male to female births. Indeed, at first sight it seems that just such a miracle occurred after World Wars I and II when there was, in fact, an increase in male births. Scientists, however, have fairly sound explanations for this phenomenon.

It is an established fact that many more males than females are conceived, whatever the reason may be. From conception onward, however, the rate of female survival is higher than that of the male: the conception ratio is about one hundred and sixty males to one hundred females; the zygote implantation ratio, about one hundred and twenty males to one hundred females; and the birth ratio, one hundred and five males to one hundred females.

The noted biologist and anthropologist Ashley Montagu has offered a convincing explanation for what happens with respect to male and female births in wartime. People marry during a war, he points out, at a younger age than during peacetime. The younger mothers, being strong and healthy, give *fertilized* eggs (of which the larger percentage is male) a greater chance for survival and implantation. These mothers therefore tend to give birth to a higher percentage of male babies than older mothers do. Furthermore, since these young mothers are usually separated for long periods from their husbands during wartime, the enforced spacing between births is longer than usual, leaving the wives in a stronger physical condition to carry the next child to term, and thereby increasing the likelihood of a male birth.

In sum, what happens during wartime, according to Dr. Montagu's reasoning, is that more male than female zygotes are implanted in the uterus, and fewer male embryos die. The resulting births therefore produce more boy babies than girls.

———————

FALLACY:

IF A WHITE WOMAN HAS A BLOOD TRANSFUSION FROM A NEGRO DONOR, THE CHILD SHE LATER CONCEIVES MAY BE BLACK.

FACT:

I have already discussed the precise mechanism through which the newly conceived individual's entire physical inheritance is determined. The twenty-three chromosomes of his father's sperm pair with the twenty-three nearly identical chromosomes of the mother's ovum; and, in what is truly a package deal, everything that the individual is to inherit is at that instant decided — color and texture of hair, color of skin, blood group, conformation of the body, shape of the fingernails, the tendency toward certain physical disorders (cystic fibrosis, hemophilia, and some forms of dwarfism, as examples), and, perhaps, temperament. Neither egg nor sperm contains any blood; furthermore, it is physiologically impossible for the blood, as such, of the parents or of any blood donor to have the remotest influence on either egg or sperm. The chromosomes, and the thousands of genes clustered on them, alone have this fantastic capacity. No one can affect this new human being's biological heritage other than his mother and father (and, indirectly, their forebears).

In the absence of factual information on the mechanism of inheritance, confusion about the true role of blood is understandable. Through the ages, much symbolism has attached to blood. Indeed, it has long been used as a symbol of life itself. "I am innocent of the blood of this just man," said Pontius Pilate; to which the crowd retorted, "Let his blood be upon us and upon our children." God accused Cain of taking Abel's life with the words, "The voice of thy brother's blood crieth unto me from the ground."

Blood has been used to symbolize the essence of an individual's character or of his inheritance. We hear that the renegade comes from "bad blood"; that the half-caste whose parents are of different races has "tainted blood"; that "blood will tell" when a child of a tempestuous parent acts tempestuously. We also hear of the aristocrat who is of "gentle blood"; and of "blue-blooded" nobility. The queen of England is the descendant of "royal bloodlines." Salt air is "in the blood" of an old sea captain.

It is certainly understandable that in the transference or transfusion from one person to another of something so critical to life as blood, the idea might arise that properties other than plasma are being transfused as well. And, indeed this attitude toward blood has existed through the centuries. It is said that Romans rushed into the arena to drink the blood of dying gladiators in order to rejuvenate themselves, and that ancient Egyptians took blood baths to hasten their recuperation from illness.

One of the earliest true blood transfusions on record (noted in the mid-17th-century *Diary* of Samuel Pepys) was, as a matter of fact, performed to cure not a physical ailment but a mental one. A gentleman healthy of body but afflicted with "mild insanity" was transfused with the blood of a lamb. (More symbolism, perhaps, in that the lamb suggests innocence and gentleness, his blood thus being capable of bringing ease to a troubled mind.) It was reported that, despite the known incompatibilities between the blood groups of different species, the man maintained his good health — as well as his mental affliction.

It has not been until the last one hundred years that scientists have understood the complexities of inheritance sufficiently to discount with scientific proof unrealistic claims regarding the "power" of blood. Through present-day knowledge of chromosomes and genes, it is now known that skin color is a matter of heredity. The only way that a baby can be born black is if at least one parent carries the genes for Negro skin pigmentation. If a white woman with no Negro ancestry giving birth to a child with true negroid features should claim that the father was white, and that the Negro features are a result of an earlier transfusion of Negro blood, one can only conclude that she is trying very hard to cover up an indiscretion.

———

FALLACY:

HEART PATIENTS NEED NOT WORRY THAT SEXUAL ACTIVITY WILL BE DETRIMENTAL TO THEIR HEALTH, AS LONG AS THEY REMAIN PHYSICALLY INACTIVE AND QUIET DURING COITUS.

FACT:

Heart patients who do not understand the marked changes that inevitably occur in heart rate and blood pressure during human sexual response may be endangering their lives or health by sexual arousal. During sexual excitement and climax, the heart rate may increase from 70 beats per minute to 150 or more, and blood pressure may rapidly increase from 120 mm Hg to 250 mm Hg or more (systolic). Both husband and wife should understand that, even if the heart patient plays a physically inactive role during the sexual act, the heart beat and blood pressure will unquestionably rise to very high peaks as the result of the sexual response alone.

This is not to say that the heart patient cannot draw considerable benefit from sensible sexual behavior. What he *is* warned against is prolonged coition, fatiguing sexual positions, and extended sex play. Control of these circumstances permits him the fulfillment and release of coitus with no undue threat to his health. Death can be caused, and indeed has been, by violent coronary response to sexual activity, and heightened blood pressure can lead to rupture of blood vessels, especially in older persons. Such severe reactions, however, are rare, and the admonition to observe total (or near total) sexual abstinence is not applicable to most patients suffering from heart disease; such advice, rather, is reserved for those with serious coronary involvement.

It is quite possible under proper circumstances for heart patients to lead active sex lives. But in this regard, as in other medical questions, a physician should be consulted and his prescriptions (or proscriptions) followed carefully. In addition to controlling the physical activity in sex play and coition, the heart patient would do well to remember that control of anxiety, whatever its source, is of utmost importance in the management of cardiac conditions. Tensions can frequently be alleviated by the patient's discussing whatever is disturbing him with his wife (or wife with husband, as the case may be) and with the physician. In severe or persistent cases of tension, a psychotherapist may be of significant help.

The essence of the problem of whether or not the heart patient should have sex is fairly well expressed by the story of the recovering coronary patient who questioned his physician in his own behalf on this issue.

> "By all means, have sexual intercourse," replied the doctor, "but only with your wife. I don't want you to become excited."

There may be too much truth in that joke for it to be humorous. In a recent study of men with heart disease who died as a result of coitus, twenty-seven of the thirty-four deaths occurred during or after extramarital intercourse.

FALLACY:
     TODAY'S YOUNG ADULTS ARE "GOING WILD" SEXUALLY.

FACT:
     Since the beginning of recorded history, older generations have been
in a state of shock and horror at the suspected immorality and other
unacceptable behavior of younger generations.

     About 2400 years ago Socrates wrote:

>   Children now love luxury. They have bad manners, contempt for
>   authority. They show disrespect for elders, and love chatter in place
>   of exercise. Children are now tyrants, not the servants of their
>   household.

It is not surprising, then, that newspaper and magazine articles, organized
groups, and individuals are crying out that America is on the brink of ruin
because of the sexual misconduct of its young people. There are, to be sure,
those incidents that incite public outrage and that are offered as evidence of
general moral degeneration among the young. But there have always been
such occurrences, and there are no more now — if as many — than in the past.
The evidence is overwhelming that the young people of today are as
emotionally well-adjusted, as mentally capable, as mature in their responsibil-
ities, and as decent a group of citizens as America has ever known.

     Sociological and psychological investigations indicate that very few
changes are occurring in the sexual mores of today's boys and girls, although,
as one expects of members of any new generation, young people are working
out new standards of thinking, believing, and behaving. Americans are not
having sexual relations at an earlier age than before, promiscuity is not
rampant among college students, and there has been no great leap forward in
sexual permissiveness since about 1920.

     Any present-day professional worker in the field of human sexual behavior
would be naive if he did not recognize that there has been a certain increase
in very recent years in the incidence of premarital sexual intercourse. During
the early 1960's, research studies consistently showed that while there had
been a distinct change toward liberalism in sexual attitudes among young
people — especially college students, who were the subjects of most of the
studies — there had not at that time been an increase in the incidence of
premarital sexual intercourse (although the incidence of heavy petting had
increased).

     Attitudes and behavior are not necessarily the same, however. Generally
speaking, it is thought that, in sexual matters at least, behavioral changes lag
behind attitudinal changes by about ten years, and recent research findings

seem to support this belief. Scientific studies in the late 1960's and early 1970's show conclusively that the incidence of premarital coitus has increased especially among college girls (at least on certain campuses), although the majority of these girls still remain virgins. In addition, research findings show that there has been a distinct drop in recent years in the guilt feelings experienced by both males and females as a result of premarital intercourse.

These changes in attitude and behavior tend to lead some of the public to believe that there is a general moral decay among today's young adults. However, there is considerable evidence that young people are behaving responsibly, demonstrating moral strength in their active concern for the welfare and rights of others. Young men of today do not lie, cheat, or otherwise trick girls into bed as their fathers might have done; and girls entering into sexual relationships with young men before marriage do so because they want to, and because they expect to enjoy the experience — an experience, it might be added, that women today are more likely to enjoy than ever before, because of the gradual dissipation of the Victorian and puritanical inhibitions that have traditionally hampered women's sexual enjoyment.

When the youths of today do rebel against the rules and regulations of authority that the older segment of the population hold as sensible and worthy of recognition, we have to ask ourselves: "What has happened — and why?" It strikes me that we have to look to our own behavior for the answer. As long as we who are older continue in some of our own neurotic and self-defeating behavior patterns, we are not likely to get very far in persuading young people to listen to what we have to say.

Why should a youngster believe an adult about the dangers of, say, smoking marijuana, when that same adult smokes cigarettes from a package clearly labeled: "Warning: The Surgeon General Has Determined that Cigarette Smoking Is Dangerous to Your Health." The additional admonition that smoking marijuana is illegal, while smoking tobacco is not, will likely be ignored. Youth is simply not thoroughly convinced of the value of laws, because of the parents' defiance of them — for instance, when they drive fifty miles an hour in a forty-mile-per-hour zone. The fact that there is little traffic does not change the existence of the law any more than does the fact that many authorities question the actual danger or hazard to health of marijuana. These same principles, of course, apply to the sexual behavior of parents and their children.

There will always be rebellious youth whose behavior outrages certain segments of the citizenry, and such outrage has a tendency to radiate in the public mind to include all youth. But every new generation has contained a core of rebellion, and, given the present-day climate of unrest, the only surprise is that there are not more acts of rebellion. As a matter of fact, group rebellion has often forced some of our most needed social reforms, although when such insurgence begins, it is interpreted by many simply as further evidence of the failure of adults to maintain proper control of their charges.

FALLACY:

SEX EDUCATION HAS NO PLACE IN OUR SCHOOLS, BECAUSE IT IS A COMMUNIST PLOT TO DESTROY THE COUNTRY FROM WITHIN, AND BECAUSE IT LEADS TO:
1. SEXUAL ACTING-OUT BEHAVIOR;
2. A RISE IN PROMISCUITY;
3. AN INCREASE IN PREMARITAL PREGNANCY;
4. ETC., ETC., ETC.

FACT:

Whether sex education should be taught in our schools is a question that has become the center of heated controversy in recent months. The question, as such, is meaningless, however, since sex education has always been taught in the schools, one way or another, and undoubtedly always will be. Surveys have shown that roughly 80% of students claim to have received their sex information from their peer group. The only question to be answered, then, is whether we want sex to be taught in the schoolyard or the schoolroom.

A recent survey of high-school honor students revealed that the shortcoming for which they were the most critical of their parents was the latter's failure to discuss with them the subject of human sexuality. About 70% of the women questioned in another investigation reported that they had been led to believe (chiefly by their mothers) that sex was dirty. Study after study appearing in educational and scientific journals point clearly to the fact that proper sex education is *not* being provided in the home. First of all, parents are so filled with shame and guilt about sex that they cannot force themselves to discuss the subject freely and in sufficient detail with their children. Second, parents are often woefully ignorant about sexual matters. They are so misinformed, in fact, that the sex information that they pass on to their children is liable to cause more harm than good.

Conducted by Dr. Marguerite Barfield, a scientific investigation on my own university campus into the sex-education background of a group of 1100 college students revealed some curious relationships between the primary source of sex information and its accuracy. When physicians and ministers were the source of such information, there was no relationship, either negative or positive, between source and accuracy. What is more important, there was a highly significant *negative* relationship between the main source and its accuracy when the source was either the peer group or the student's parents. The only significant positive relationship that emerged involved those students who had received their sex education in the formal atmosphere of a classroom or who had read sex-information books of authenticated accuracy.

These findings suggest two things. *First:* although no thoughtful educator would disagree with the argument that the home is the ideal setting for a child's sex education, ideal and actuality have, unfortunately, proved to be poles apart. Parents are not, generally speaking, discharging their obligation to provide their children with the accurate, timely instruction essential to the youngsters' future good mental health. Until parents themselves acquire a proper sex education and manage to resolve their own sexual conflicts, the child's sex instruction must take place in a classroom atmosphere, like it or not. *Second:* since the most common source of sex information today is the peer group, those peers should be properly educated, so that the information that they pass on to the younger and more impressionable members of the group will at least have the ring of accuracy.

Why the vociferous minority opposing sex education in the schools do so is baffling. I should like now to examine some of their allegations.

Sex education leads to sexual acting out. There is *no* scientific evidence supporting the claim that sex education in the schools generates an increase in unacceptable sexual behavior. What is ignored in this argument is that sex education is typically first taught in the schools during the student's high-school years. This is also the time at which the student has reached adolescence, when sexual interests and drives first reach a peak. There would, therefore, have been an acceleration in sexually oriented interest and activity of some form or another, in any case, whether or not sex education was being taught in the school — or at home or church, for that matter.

Sex education inevitably leads to an increased incidence of premarital pregnancy. Although sex education in the schools does not, according to surveys made, appear to reduce the incidence of first premarital pregnancy, neither has its incidence increased in the schools having such courses — an important observation in view of the critics' contention that all manner of sexual misbehavior will break out among youngsters exposed to the depravity of sex education.

The circumstances leading to premarital intercourse have little relationship to sex education, as a matter of fact. Typically, a boy and girl — especially the girl — have no intention of engaging in actual sexual intercourse as they start to neck or pet. Unfortunately, however, they get caught up in the emotionality of the moment and "go further" than they had originally intended. Their decision to have sexual intercourse, then, is based on emotional needs of the moment, and not on what they have been taught in the home or school. Curiously, many of these acts of premarital intercourse (some of which lead to pregnancy, of course) occur among the religiously devout who, despite their determination to "refrain from sin," somehow lose control of their emotions and get swept into the act of sexual intercourse.

Of considerable interest in a discussion of sex education and illegitimacy is a recently completed survey covering a 20-year period. The data revealed that the smallest increase (108%) in illegitimate births during the 20 years was among girls between 15 and 19 years of age; the largest increase (453%) was among women aged 25 to 29 years (the second greatest increase, 444%, was among women between 30 and 34 years). It is unlikely that the illegitimate births among these older woman were a result of sex education in the schools!

The experience of the Anaheim (Orange County, California) school district vividly illustrates how the public can be misled to believe that there is a linkage between sex education and a burgeoning illegitimacy rate. For years the Anaheim high-school curriculum had included a thoughtful, well-structured, and widely publicized sex-education program, until the recent efforts of the area's strident, extremist-Right opponents of sex education succeeded in having the program removed. One of these extremists' arguments was that 50% of the girls of that school district were pregnant at the time of their graduation. There is, of course, no way of determining the actual incidence of pregnancy among the girl students of any school, since many such pregnancies are terminated or are carefully hidden. Statistics from the Anaheim school district and from the state of California itself, however, paint an entirely different picture from that suggested by the extremists. Since Anaheim graduates approximately 3000 girls each year, it appears highly unlikely that 1500 of them are pregnant at graduation, or ever have been pregnant in their school careers. The Anaheim school authorities do know that far less than 1% of the girls in their district are pregnant at any one time, based on the number enrolled throughout the year to receive home teaching. Moreover, at the last survey Anaheim's illegitimacy rate was 3.1 per 1000 women of child-bearing age, whereas the figure for the entire state was 9.3 per 1000. The allegation that a wildly spiraling incidence of premarital pregnancy is the inevitable consequence of sex education in the schools is a classic example of "the big lie" techniques used by extremist groups to scare parents.

While sex education does not appear to reduce the incidence of first premarital pregnancies, it apparently does act to reduce the number of subsequent premarital pregnancies. Yale University Hospital recently studied the effect of sex education in the control of illegitimate pregnancies. Young unmarried patients at the hospital, who were pregnant for the first time and whose average age was seventeen, were separated into matched groups of equal numbers. One group was given instruction in the human reproductive systems and in birth control methods; the second group received no such instruction. Within a year, 57% of the girls in the group receiving no sex education reappeared at the hospital, pregnant a second time. By contrast, a scant 7% of the group that had been given sex instruction had a second pregnancy before they married.

A recent survey of unwed mothers in Chicago revealed that 50% did not even know how they got pregnant. As examples, some of them believed that kissing caused the pregnancy; others thought that the responsibility lay with breast fondling. How can one honestly argue that sex education would have been other than a benefit to these girls and society?

Venereal disease will soar to epidemic proportions among students exposed to sex education in the schools. Very little scientific investigation has been made into the relationship between venereal disease and sex education (or the lack of it). It is well known, nonetheless, that young people in an impoverished educational and cultural milieu are the most likely ones to contract and spread venereal diseases. In what is undoubtedly the best known of the few studies made of this problem, the American Social Health Association carefully investigated the background of six hundred teen-age VD patients. The primary conclusion made by these investigators was that the crucial need of these young people was for "better education about sex and venereal disease."

Teaching about sex in the comparatively sterile setting of a classroom strips the subject of its moral and ethical connotations. The child learns about morality and immorality in whatever setting that he finds himself — in the school no less than in the home and church. Civics and social-science courses, as well as literature and history, are daily exercises in morality. Through the first two subjects the student learns of man's obligations to his society; the last two are historical and fictional demonstrations of the varying results of man's acceptance or denial of those obligations.

Particularly insidious in all these arguments against sex education is the implied suggestion that the school teacher giving sex instruction is (or might be) an unethical, perhaps morally depraved creature intent upon seducing the innocent into paths of immorality. I am convinced, however, that few among us are so deluded that we cannot recognize American school teachers for what they are: intelligent, dedicated, and responsible men and women, whose ethical values are beyond reproach and will inevitably radiate into any subject that they teach.

* * *

Robert Welch, founder of the John Birch Society — probably the most powerful of the anti-sex-education groups — calls sex instruction a "filthy communist plot." (This proclamation is particularly curious in light of the accusation, made by the official Russian communist newspaper *Pravda*, that sex education is part of "the western imperialistic, capitalist plot"!) A recent Gallup poll showed that more than seven of ten parents favor sex education as part of school curricula, and I find it hard to believe that 71% of the U.S. population has communist leanings. Some of the most prestigious organizations in the country, as a matter of fact, have publicly endorsed sex education in the schools — as examples, the Interfaith Commission on Marriage and Family Life (consisting of the Synagogue Council of America, the U.S. Catholic Conference, and the National Council of Churches), The National Congress of Parents and Teachers, The American Medical Association, the YMCA and YWCA, and the U.S. Department of Health, Education and Welfare. About the most charitable comment that one can make of Mr. Welch's views on sex education is that they are distorted.

One cannot, however, ignore the genuine concern of certain parents that sex education might be presented in too dry and dehumanized a fashion in the classroom, or that there is "too much too soon," most particularly among the primary-school children. Indeed, not all teachers giving sex instruction are ideally equipped to teach the subject — a criticism equally applicable, of course, to teachers of any subject. Perhaps a course taught to the very young student in this school or that does go overboard in explicitness. But how can a well-thought-out, effective sex-education course be constructed in a community in which the well-intentioned school administrators and teachers are being outrageously harassed, if not maligned, by members of the public (not necessarily parents, mind you) who are variously concerned, confused, scared, ignorant, and cynically opportunistic.

In connection with opportunism, I am reminded of the observations of Mary Breasted in her recent book, *Oh! Sex Education!*

> The national movement against sex education was positively glutted with [leaders on the Right] . . . . All you had to do to become a leader was to speak out against sex education with some passion. It helped a little if you could throw in a few false statistics from Sweden or a shocking story from some distant school district . . .

Miss Breasted reflects my own indignation when she writes that, although

92% of the adults of Anaheim's citizenry were in favor of sex education in their schools,

> ...its opponents had, for the present, triumphed. Social science would tell me why, when 71 per cent of the American public said *they* supported sex education (according to George Gallup, June, 1969), cowardly foundations had stopped giving SIECUS money, the Birchers were saying that sex education "could be the greatest boost to recruiting" that they had ever had, and anti-sex education legislation was finding its way into nineteen state legislatures.

No thoughtful person can deny the great need for appropriate sex education and the lamentably ineffective way in which that need has been met to date. It is therefore distressing that objections to sex education in the schools should be based on the tenuous grounds that such a course of study would do the students more harm than good. The students themselves would be the last to agree to such a conclusion, I suspect.

The findings of the noted sociologist Clifford Kirkpatrick, as a case in point, clearly demonstrate the need for an appropriate sex education as a prerequisite to successful marriage. He found that among important ingredients to a happy marriage, an *adequate sex education* ranked third, preceding which in importance came only *happiness of parents' marriage* and *adequate length of courtship and engagement*.

I am also reminded of a group of one hundred teen-age boys and one hundred teen-age girls who, when surveyed, ranked sex first on a list of thirty subjects as being the most difficult ones to discuss with their parents. Surely this indicates that, since sex is so difficult to discuss in the home, the discussion must take place in another, less supercharged atmosphere — an atmosphere in which objectivity and honesty exist, and in which the subject can be discussed openly and with accurate information. Where can this be done better than in the school?

———————

BIBLIOGRAPHY

Beach, F. A. (Ed.), *Sex and Behavior*. New York: John Wiley and Sons, 1965.
A collection of scholarly papers on animal and human sexual behavior. Each of the articles is written by an expert in the field, and each presentation is followed by a discussion and analysis.

Beigel, H. G. (Ed.), *Advances in Sex Research*. New York: Harper & Row, 1963.
Surveys of recent findings in the theoretical and clinical aspects of sexual problems. The primary foci of interest are sexual behavior and attitudes, sex and the aging process, artificial insemination, and sexual deviations.

Brecher, Ruth, and E. Brecher (Eds.), *An Analysis of Human Sexual Response*. New York: New American Library, 1966.
A series of analyses of the Masters and Johnson book *Human Sexual Response*, made by a group of experts from the point of view of their own special fields of interest.

Broderick, C. B., and Jessie Bernard, *The Individual, Sex, and Society*. Baltimore: The Johns Hopkins Press, 1969.
A SIECUS handbook for teachers and counselors. This text contains papers dealing with sex education and the cultural and social aspects of human sexuality. Sexual abnormalities are also discussed in comprehensive detail.

Cuber, J. F., with Peggy B. Harroff, *The Significant Americans*. New York: Appleton-Century, 1966.
A summary of a detailed investigation into the sexual attitudes, sexual behavior, and marriage patterns among successful middle-aged, middle-class Americans. The research data and excerpts from the case histories contained in this book combine to present a clear picture of human sexuality as it exists in many contemporary American marriages.

DeMartino, M. F. (Ed.), *Sexual Behavior and Personality Characteristics*. New York: Grove Press, 1966.
A collection of related articles by twenty-four authorities in the fields of psychology, sexology, and sociology. The papers are designed to show primarily the relationships existing between particular forms of normal sexual behavior and the individual's self-esteem.

Eastman, N. J., and L. M. Hellman, *Williams Obstetrics* (12th Ed.). New York: Appleton-Century-Crofts, 1961.
A medical textbook of exceptional accuracy and detail, which deals with gynecological and obstetrical problems. Although the book is highly technical in content and prose, many laymen will find it a valuable source of information on the two subjects.

Ellis, A., and A. Abarbanel, *Encyclopedia of Sexual Behavior* (2nd Ed.). New York: Hawthorn Books, 1967.
> One of the most definitive texts in the field of sex-related behavior, attitudes, physiology, psychology, anthropology, history, and law. Extensive bibliographies are included after each section, which make the two volumes invaluable sourcebooks on the subject of human sexuality.

Ellis, A., *Sex Without Guilt.* New York: Hillman Periodicals, 1959.
> A popular and easy-to-read book containing selected essays reflective of a permissive attitude toward sex. Largely through the success of this book, the author has taken a leading role in directing the American public toward a more liberal and relaxed view of sexual behavior.

Flanagan, Geraldine Lux, *Nine Months of Life.* New York: Simon & Schuster, 1962.
> A well-written description, liberally supplemented with photographs, of what happens to the human organism during the nine months between fertilization and birth.

Ford, C. S., and F. A. Beach, *Patterns of Sexual Behavior.* New York: Harper, 1951.
> A classic in the field of sexual behavior. This book is an impressive compendium of anthropological, cross-cultural, and biological influences that have a unique bearing on particular patterns of sexual behavior.

Gebhard, P. H., J. H. Gagnon, W. B. Pomeroy, and C. V. Christenson, *Sex Offenders.* New York: Harper & Row, and Paul B. Hoeber, Inc., 1965.
> An epic 25-year study made by the staff of the Institute for Sex Research (the Kinsey group). This book presents in exhaustive detail the sexual attitudes and behavior, as well as the emotional, educational, economic, and familial backgrounds, of male prisoners convicted of various sex offenses. These patterns are then compared with those of a group of males who were imprisoned on convictions for other than sex offense and with those of a second group who had never been convicted of any crime.

Green, R., and J. Money, (Eds.), *Transsexualism and Sex Reassignment.* Baltimore: The Johns Hopkins Press, 1969.
> An encyclopedic text containing a series of papers authored by thirty recognized international specialists in the field of sex reassignment.

Hoffman, M., *The Gay World.* New York: Basic Books, 1968.
> A detailed investigation, made by a social psychiatrist, of the homosexual as he goes about his everyday life in his usual surroundings. This realistic study of homosexuality is a marked departure from most such studies, which tend to assess the homosexual as he appears in the psychotherapist's office or in the courtroom.

Kinsey, A. C., W. B. Pomeroy, and C. E. Martin, *Sexual Behavior in the Human Male.* Philadelphia: W. B. Saunders, 1948.
> The first of the famous Kinsey reports and a pioneering study of human sexual behavior. This is one of the most significant books ever published on the subject of human sexuality. Its data pointed clearly to the vast difference existing in American society between officially sanctioned sexual behavior and that which is actually practiced.

Kinsey, A C., W. B. Pomeroy, C. E. Martin, and P. H. Gebhard, *Sexual Behavior in the Human Female.* Philadelphia; W. B. Saunders, 1953
    The companion volume to the epic study of male sexual behavior published five years earlier by the Kinsey group. This survey contains not only findings on female sexual behavior, but also comparative data on female and male sexual behavior.

Masters, W. H., and Virginia E. Johnson, *Human Sexual Response.* Boston: Little, Brown, 1966.
    A documentation of the physiological reactions of men and women during the excitement, plateau, orgasmic, and resolution phases of the sexual response cycle. The book is based on the authors' meticulous laboratory and clinical findings and is a landmark in sex research.

Masters, W. H., and Virginia E. Johnson, *Human Sexual Inadequacy.* Boston: Little, Brown, 1970.
    An extremely important resource book for professionals and others who are seriously interested in causes and treatment of such sexual disorders as impotency, ejaculatory problems, and vaginismus. The book is based on careful, intensive, and extensive clinical research conducted by two of America's leading sexologists, and it describes the methods of treatment.

Mazur, R. M., *Commonsense Sex.* Boston: Beacon Press, 1968.
    Written primarily for the unmarried, this book covers such topics as masturbation, petting, mutual masturbation, contraception, premarital intercourse, and homosexuality.

McCary, J. L., *Human Sexuality.* New York: Van Nostrand Reinhold, 1967.
    A comprehensive volume that includes material on the anatomy, physiology, psychology, and sociology of human reproduction and sexual behavior. It is the most widely used college textbook in its field today, and it doubles as a well-received marriage manual.

Medical Aspects of Human Sexuality. 18 East 48th Street, New York, N.Y. 10017.
    A monthly publication to which the contributors are predominantly physicians and psychologists. The journal is designed to provide authoritative information on sexual problems that will enable the professional person to deal more effectively with his patients.

Money, J., *Sex Research: New Developments.* New York: Holt, Rinehart, and Winston, 1965.
    This book contains a series of essays that present some of the most meaningful and significant research in the field of sexual behavior that has been done in recent years.

Money, J., *Sex Errors of the Body.* Baltimore: The Johns Hopkins Press, 1968.
    Written by a renowned authority in the field of sex-development abnormalities. Sexual disorders are examined in terms of cause and psychosexual effects. Most important, the author suggests methods of supportive counseling of the individual, as well as guidance for individuals or parents of an affected child by which they may achieve the understanding and attitudes necessary for an eventual psychological adjustment to the physical problem.

Neubardt, S., *A Concept of Contraception*. New York: Trident Press, 1967.
   A careful examination of present-day techniques of contraception, with emphasis not so much on the mechanics as on the crucial role that contraception plays in the sex life of a couple.

Reiss, I. L., *The Social Context of Premarital Sexual Permissiveness*. New York: Holt, Rinehart, and Winston, 1967.
   Analyses of the results of investigations into the sexual attitudes and behavior among black and white high-school youths, college students, and adults. The author, a sociologist, also formulates a theory concerning the nature of premarital sexual permissiveness.

Rubin, I., *Sexual Life After Sixty*. New York: Basic Books, 1965.
   A book of particular value to those older men and women who are concerned about their sexual capacity and expression. Research data on the sexual needs, attitudes, and behavior of the aging man and woman are presented in such a way as to aid them in coping with their problems.

Sex Information and Education Council of the U.S. (SIECUS) (All publications.) 1855 Broadway, New York, N.Y. 10023.
   SIECUS study guides, newsletters, books, booklets, films, and reprints of great value to laymen and professionals alike. Publications by the SIECUS organization cover all aspects of sex education and human sexuality in a professionally authoritative yet readable manner.

Sex News. 7140 Oak, Kansas City, Mo. 64114.
   A monthly digest of news, views, events, publications, and resources related to human sexuality.

Sexology. 200 Park Ave. South, New York, N.Y. 10003.
   An easy-to-read magazine that is published monthly in both English and Spanish editions. Devoted to frank and authoritative sex guidance, the publication has for years led the field of similar publications in the presentation of useful information to the layman.

Sexual Behavior. 299 Park Ave., New York, N.Y. 10017.
   A new publication designed to be a serious and informative resource for the well-educated layman.

The Journal of Sex Research. Suite 1104, 12 East 41st St., New York, N.Y. 10017.
   Published quarterly, a journal serving "the interdisciplinary exchange of knowledge in the field of sex." Its aim is "to represent all arts and sciences, the scope of which includes the exploration of factors contributing to and determining sexual behavior."

Vincent, C. E., *Human Sexuality in Medical Education and Practice*. Springfield, Ill.: Charles C. Thomas, 1968.
   Arranged in encyclopedia fashion, this volume contains a wide range of chapters dealing with problems of sex education, attitudes, and behavior. This comprehensive volume is especially directed toward medical schools and professional health personnel.

DICTIONARY OF

SEX-RELATED TERMINOLOGY

abortifacient. A drug or other agent that causes abortion.

abortion. Premature expulsion from the uterus of the product of conception—a fertilized ovum, embryo, or nonviable fetus.

abstinence. A refraining from the use of or indulgence in certain foods, stimulants, or sexual intercourse.

adolescence. The period of life between puberty (appearance of secondary sex characteristics) and adulthood (cessation of major body growth).

adultery. Sexual intercourse between a married person and an individual other than his or her legal spouse.

afterbirth. The placenta and fetal membranes expelled from the uterus following the birth of a child.

amenorrhea. Absence of the menses (menstruation).

amnion. A thin membrane forming the closed sac or "bag of waters" that surrounds the unborn child within the uterus and contains amniotic fluid in which the fetus is immersed.

ampulla. A flasklike widening at the end of a tubular structure or canal.

anal eroticism. Pleasurable sensations in the region of the anus.

anaphrodisiac. A drug or medicine that allays sexual desire.

androgen. A steroid hormone producing masculine sex characteristics and having an influence on body and bone growth and on the sex drive.

anomaly. An irregularity or defect.

aphrodisiac. Anything, such as a drug or a perfume, that stimulates sexual desire.

areola. The ring of darkened tissue surrounding the nipple of the breast.

artificial insemination. Introduction of male semen into the vagina or womb of a woman by artificial means.

autoerotic. Pertaining to self-stimulation or erotic behavior directed toward one's self; frequently equated with masturbation.

Bartholin's glands. Two tiny glands in a female, located at either side of the entrance to the vagina.

bestiality. A sexual deviation in which a person engages in sexual relations with an animal. Cf. ZOOPHILIA.

birth control. Deliberate limitation of the number of children born—through such means as contraceptives, abstinence, the rhythm method, *coitus interruptus,* and the like.

bisexual. Literally, having sex organs of both sexes, as in hermaphrodites; having a sexual interest in both sexes.

blastocyst. The fertilized egg in the early stage of cell division when the cells form a hollow sphere.

breech presentation. A birth position in which the baby is presented and delivered buttocks first.

Caesarean birth (also **Caesarean section**). Delivery of a child through a surgical incision in the abdominal and uterine walls.

carpopedal spasm. A spastic contraction of the hands and feet.

castration. Removal of the gonads (sex glands)—the testicles in men, the ovaries in women.

castration complex. In psychoanalytic theory, unconscious fears centering around injury or loss of the genitals as punishment for forbidden sexual desires; a male's anxiety about his manhood.

celibacy. The state of being unmarried; abstention from sexual activity.

cervix. Neck; in the female, the narrow portion of the uterus or womb that forms its lower end and opens into the vagina.

chancre. The sore or ulcer that is the first symptom of syphilis.

change of life. See CLIMACTERIC, MENOPAUSE.

chorion. The outermost envelope of the growing zygote (fertilized ovum), which later contributes to the formation of the placenta.

chromosome. One of several small rod-shaped bodies found in the nucleus of all body cells, which contain the genes, or hereditary factors.

circumcision. Surgical removal of the foreskin or prepuce of the male penis.

climacteric. The syndrome of physical and psychologic changes that occur at the termination of menstrual function (*i.e.,* reproductive capability) in the woman and reduction in sex-steroid production in both sexes; menopause; change of life.

climax. See ORGASM.

clitoris (adj. **clitoral**). A small, highly sensitive nipple of flesh in the female, located just above the urethral opening in the upper triangle of the vulva.

coitus. Sexual intercourse between male and female, in which the male penis is inserted into the female vagina.

coitus interruptus (also **premature withdrawal**). The practice of withdrawing the penis from the vagina just before ejaculation.

coitus reservatus. Prolonged coitus in which ejaculation is intentionally suppressed.

colostrum. A thin, milky fluid secreted by the female breast just before and after childbirth.

conception. The beginning of a new life, when an ovum (egg) is penetrated by a sperm, resulting in the development of an embryo; impregnation.

condom. A contraceptive used by males consisting of a rubber or gut sheath that is drawn over the erect penis before coitus.

congenital. Existing at birth, but not necessarily inherited.

continence. A state of exercising self-restraint, especially in regard to the sex drive.

contraception. The use of devices or drugs to prevent conception in sexual intercourse.

coprophilia. A sexual deviation in which sexual gratification is associated with the act of defecation; a morbid interest in feces.

copulation. Sexual intercourse; coitus.

corona glandis. The rim surrounding the base of the glans penis in the male.

corpus luteum. A yellow mass in the ovary, formed from a ruptured graafian follicle, that secretes the hormone progesterone.

Cowper's glands. Two glands in the male, one on each side of the urethra near the prostate, which secrete a mucoid material as part of the seminal fluid.

cremaster (adj. **cremasteric**). The muscles that elevate the male testes.

criminal abortion. Illegal termination of a human pregnancy by any type of medical, surgical, or other means of interference, as distinguished from *therapeutic abortion,* which is done to protect the health or life of the mother.

cryptorchidism. See UNDESCENDED TESTICLE.

cul-de-sac. The "blind alley" ending of the female vagina just beyond the opening into the womb (cervix).

cunnilingus. The act of using the tongue or mouth in erotic play with the external female genitalia (vulva).

curettage (also **curettement**). Scraping the lining of the uterus with a *curette,* a spoon-shaped medical instrument.

cystocele. Hernial protrusion of the female bladder through the vaginal wall.

cytogenic. Forming or producing cells.

defloration. The rupture of the hymen in a virgin's first experience of coitus or through vaginal examination.

detumescence. Subsidence of swelling; subsidence of erection in the genitals following orgasm.

diaphragm. A rubber contraceptive, used by women, that is hemispherical in shape and fits like a cap over the neck of the uterus (cervix).

Doderlein's bacilli. The bacteria (germs) normally present in the female vagina.

dorsal. Pertaining to the back (as the back of the hand, of the whole body, or of the upper surface of the penis), as opposed to the *ventral* (front) side.

douche. A stream of water or other liquid solution directed into the female vagina for sanitary, medical, or contraceptive reasons.

dry orgasm. Sexual climax in a male without any apparent ejaculation of semen; usually an instance of retrograde ejaculation, caused by some anomaly within the prostate, in which the semen is ejaculated backwards into the posterior urethra and bladder, rather than out through the penis. Removal of the prostate prevents production and ejaculation of semen, although capability for orgasm remains.

dysmenorrhea. Painful menstruation.

dyspareunia. Coitus that is difficult or painful, especially for a woman.

eclampsia. A condition of convulsions and coma that can occur in a woman during pregnancy or immediately following childbirth.

ectoderm. The outermost of the three primitive or primary germ layers of the embryo, from which the nervous system, sense organs, mouth cavity, and skin eventually develop.

ectopic. In an abnormal place, *e.g.*, an *ectopic pregnancy,* in which the unborn child develops outside the uterus, either in an ovary, the abdominal cavity, or in a Fallopian tube.

ejaculatio praecox. Premature ejaculation.

ejaculation. The expulsion of male semen, usually at the climax (orgasm) of the sexual act.

Electra complex. Excessive emotional attachment of a daughter to her father

emasculate. To castrate; to deprive of manliness or masculine

embryo. The unborn young in its early stage of development   ne week following conception to the end of the second month.

emission. Discharge of semen from the male penis, especially when involuntary, as during sleep (nocturnal emission).

endemic. Pertaining to or prevalent in a particular district or region; pertaining to a disease that has a low incidence but is constantly present in a given community.

endocrine gland. A gland that secretes its product (hormone) directly into the bloodstream.

endoderm. The innermost of the three primitive or primary germ layers of the embryo, from which the digestive and respiratory systems of the body develop.

endometriosis. The aberrant presence of endometrial tissue (uterus lining) in other parts of the female pelvic cavity, such as in the Fallopian tubes or on the ovaries, bladder, or intestines.

endometrium. The mucous membrane that lines the cavity of the uterus in the female.

epididymis. The network of tiny tubes in the male that connects the testicles with the sperm duct.

episiotomy. Incision in a woman's perineum to facilitate the birth of a child.

epispadia. A congenital defect in males in which the opening (meatus) of the urethra is on the upper surface of the penis instead of at its tip. *Cf.* HYPOSPADIA.

epithelium (adj. epithelial). The outer layer of cells covering the internal and external surfaces of the body.

erection. The stiffening and enlargement of the penis (or clitoris), usually as a result of sexual excitement.

erogenous zone. A sexually sensitive area of the body, such as the mouth, lips, breasts, nipples, buttocks, genitals, or anus.

erotic. Pertaining to sexual love or sensation; sexually stimulating.

estrogen. A steroid hormone producing female sex characteristics and affecting the functioning of the menstrual cycle.

estrus. A recurrent period of sexual receptivity in female animals, marked by intense sexual urge.

eugenics. A science that seeks to improve future generations through the control of hereditary factors.

eunuch. A castrated male.

eunuchoid. Having the physical characteristics of a eunuch without actually being castrated.

excitement phase. The initial stage in the human sexual response cycle that follows effective sexual stimulation.

exhibitionism. A sexual deviation in which the individual—usually male—suffers from a compulsion to expose his genitals publicly.

extragenital. Originating or lying outside the genital organs.

extramarital. Literally, outside of marriage; usually used in reference to adulterous sexual intercourse.

Fallopian tube. The oviduct or egg-conducting tube that extends from each ovary to the uterus in the female.

fecundity. The ability to produce offspring, especially in a rapid manner and in large numbers.

fellatio. The act of taking the penis into the mouth and sucking it for erotic purposes.

fertility. The state of being capable of producing young; the opposite of *sterility*.

fertilization. The union of egg (ovum) and sperm (spermatozoon), which results in conception.

fetishism. A sexual deviation in which sexual gratification is achieved by means of an object, such as an article of clothing, that bears sexual symbolism for the individual.

fetus. In humans, the unborn child from the third month after conception until birth.

fibrillation. Spontaneous contraction of individual muscle fibers no longer under control of a motor nerve.

follicle. The small sac or vesicle near the surface of the ovary in the female that contains a developing egg cell (ovum).

follicle-stimulating hormone (FSH). A hormone secreted by the pituitary gland that stimulates, in the female, the growth and development of the ovarian follicles and, in the male, the production of sperm by the seminiferous tubules.

foreplay. The preliminary stages of sexual intercourse, in which the partners usually stimulate each other by kissing, touching, and caressing.

foreskin. The skin covering the tip of the male penis or female clitoris; prepuce.

fornication. Sexual intercourse between two unmarried persons (as distinguished from *adultery*, which involves a person who is married to someone other than his coital partner).

fourchette. The fold of mucous membrane at the posterior junction of the labia majora in the female.

fraternal twins. Two offspring developed from two separate ova (eggs) usually fertilized at the same time.

frenulum. A delicate, tissue-thin fold of skin that connects the foreskin with the under surface of the glans penis; frenum.

frenulum clitoridis. The clitoral prepuce.

frenum. See FRENULUM.

frigidity. Coldness, indifference, or insensitivity on the part of a woman to sexual intercourse or sexual stimulation; inability to experience sexual pleasure or gratification.

frottage. A sexual deviation in which orgasm is induced by rubbing against an individual of the opposite sex, usually a stranger.

fundus. The base or part of a hollow organ farthest from its mouth.

gamate. The mature reproductive cell of either sex—sperm (male) or ovum (female).

gene. The basic carrier of hereditary traits, contained in the chromosomes.

genital organs (or genitals or genitalia). The sex or reproductive organs.

germ cell. The sperm (spermatozoon) or egg (ovum).

gerontosexuality. A sexual disorder in which a young person chooses an elderly person as the subject of his sexual interest.

gestation. Pregnancy; the period from conception to birth.

glans clitoridis. The head of the female clitoris.

glans penis. The head of the male penis.

gonad. A sex gland; a testicle (male) or ovary (female).

gonadotropin. A substance having a stimulating effect on the gonads (sex glands).

gonorrhea. A venereal disease, transmitted chiefly through coitus, that is a contagious catarrhal inflammation of the genital mucous membrane.

graafian follicle. A small sac or pocket in the female ovary in which the egg (ovum) matures and from which it is discharged at ovulation.

gynecologist. A physician specializing in the treatment of the problems of the female sexual and reproductive organs.

gynecomastia. Female-like development of the male breasts.

heredity. The transmission of bodily traits and characteristcs or of diseases from parents to offspring.

hermaphrodite. An individual possessing both male and female sex glands (ovary and testicle) or sex gland tissue of both sexes. *Cf*. PSEUDOHERMAPHRODITE.

heterogeneous. Consisting of dissimilar elements; the opposite of *homogeneous*.

heterosexuality. Sexual attraction to, or sexual activity with, members of the opposite sex; the opposite of *homosexuality*.

hirsutism. Abnormal hairiness, especially in women.

homologous. Corresponding in position, structure, or origin to another anatomical entity.

homosexuality. Sexual attraction to, or sexual activity with, members of one's own sex; the opposite of *heterosexuality*.

hormone. A chemical substance produced by an endocrine gland that has a specific effect on the activities of other organs in the body.

human chorionic gonadotropin (HCD). A hormone secreted early in pregnancy by the chorionic villi (and later by the placenta); because of its excretion in the urine, it makes possible the biological tests for pregnancy.

hydrocele. An accumulation of fluid in the male scrotum.

hymen. The membranous fold that partly covers the external opening of the vagina in most virgin females; the maidenhead.

hyperplasia. The abnormal multiplication or increase in the number of cells in a tissue. *Cf.* HYPERPLASIA.

hypertrophy. The abnormal multiplication or increase in the number of cells in a tissue. *Cf.* HYPERTROPHY.

hypospadia. A congenital defect in males in which the opening (meatus) of the urethra is on the underside of the penis instead of at its tip. *Cf.* EPISPADIA.

hypothalamus. A small portion of the brain that controls such vital bodily processes as visceral activities, temperature, and sleep.

hysterectomy. Surgical removal of the female uterus, either through the abdominal wall or through the vagina.

hysterotomy. Incision into the uterus.

identical twins. Two offspring developed from one fertilized ovum (egg).

implantation. Embedding of the blastocyst (fertilized egg) in the mucous membrane, or endometrium, lining the uterus.

impotence. Disturbance of sexual function in the male that precludes satisfactory coitus; more specifically, inability to achieve or maintain an erection sufficient for purposes of sexual intercourse.

impregnation. The act of fertilization or fecundation; making pregnant.

incest. Sexual relations between close relatives, such as father and daughter, mother and son, or brother and sister.

infanticide. The murder or murderer of an infant.

inguinal canal. The passageway from the abdominal cavity to the scrotum in the male through which the testicles descend shortly before birth or just after.

insemination. The deposit of semen within the vagina.

intercourse, anal. A form of sexual intercourse in which the penis is inserted into the partner's anus; sometimes termed *sodomy*.

intercourse, sexual. Sexual union of a male and a female, in which the penis is inserted into the vagina; coitus.

interstitial cells. Specialized cells in the testicles that produce the male sex hormones.

interstitial cell-stimulating hormone (ICSH). A hormone secreted by the pituitary gland that stimulates, in the male, the maturation of the sperm cells.

intrauterine contraceptive device (IUCD). A small plastic or metal device which, when fitted into the uterus, prevents pregnancy. Also termed *intrauterine device (IUD)*.

intromission. The insertion of the male penis into the female vagina.

invert. A homosexual; one who is sexually attracted to persons of his own sex.

involution. An inward curvature; a shrinking or return to a former size, as of the uterus after childbirth; the regressive alterations in the body or its parts characteristic of the aging process.

jel, contraceptive. A nongreasy substance containing an ingredient toxic to sperm that is introduced into the vagina before sexual intercourse to prevent conception.

kleptomania. An irresistible compulsion to steal, usually without any use for the article stolen.

Klinefelter's syndrome (XXY). An abnormality afflicting males, in which the sex-determining chromosomes are XXY, instead of the normal XY, the ovum having somehow contributed an extra X at the time of fertilization. Symptoms of the condition include small testicles, sterility, and often a distinctly feminine physical appearance.

labia majora (sing. **labium majus**). The outer and larger pair of lips of the female external genitals (vulva).

labia minora (sing. **labium minus**). The inner and smaller pair of lips of the female vulva.

lactation. The manufacture and secretion of milk by the mammary glands in a mother's breasts.

lesbian. A female homosexual.

libido. Sexual drive or urge.

lochia. The discharge from the uterus and vagina that takes place during the first few weeks after childbirth.

luteinizing hormone (LH). A hormone secreted by the pituitary gland that stimulates, in the female, the formation of the corpus luteum.

maculopapular. Spotted and raised or elevated.

maidenhead. The hymen.

masochism. A sexual deviation in which an individual derives sexual gratification from having pain inflicted on him.

masturbation. Self-stimulation of the genitals through manipulation; autoeroticism.

meatus. An opening, such as at the end of the urethral passage in the male penis.

menarche. The onset of menstruation in girls, occurring in late puberty and ushering in the period of adolescence.

menopause. The period of cessation of menstruation in the human female, occurring usually between the ages of 45 and 55; climacteric; change of life.

menstruation. The discharge of blood from the uterus through the vagina that normally recurs at approximately four-week intervals in women between the ages of puberty and menopause.

mesoderm. The middle layer of the three primitive or primary germ layers of the embryo, from which the muscular, skeletal, excretory, circulatory, and reproductive systems of the body develop.

miscarriage. Spontaneous expulsion of a fetus from the onset of the fourth to end of the sixth month of pregnancy.

Monilia. A yeast-like infective organism (fungus) causing itching and inflammation of the female vagina.

monogamy. Marriage between one man and one woman.

mons veneris (or **mons pubis**). A triangular mound of fat at the symphysis pubis of a woman, just above the vulval area.

mucoid. Resembling mucus.

mucosa. A mucous membrane; a thin tissue that has a moist surface from the secreting of mucus.

mucus (adj. **mucous**). The thick, slippery fluid secreted by mucous membranes.

multipara (adj. **multiparous**). A woman who has given birth to two or more children.

myoma (pl. **myomas** or **myomata**). A tumor consisting of muscle tissue that grows in the wall of the uterus; also called *fibroid*.

myotonia. Increased muscular tension.

narcissism. Excessive self-love; sexual excitement through admiration of one's own body.

necrophilia. A sexual deviation in which an individual has a morbid sexual attraction to corpses.

neural tube. The epithelial tube that develops from the neural plate to form the embryo's central nervous system and from which the brain and spinal column develop.

nidation. The implantation of the blastocyst (fertilized ovum) in the lining of the uterus in pregnancy.

nocturnal emission. An involuntary male orgasm and ejaculation of semen during sleep; a "wet dream."

nullipara (adj. **nulliparous**). A woman who has never borne a viable child.

nymphomania. Excessive sexual desire in a woman.

obscene. Disgusting, repulsive, filthy, shocking—that which is abhorrent according to accepted standards of morality.

obsession. A neurosis characterized by the persistent recurrence of some irrational thought or idea, or by an attachment to or fixation on a particular individual or object.

obstetrician. A physician specializing in the care of women during pregnancy, labor, and the period immediately following delivery.

Oedipus complex. Excessive emotional attachment, involving conscious or unconscious incestuous desires, of a son in relation to his mother.

onanism. Withdrawal of the male penis from the female vagina before ejeculation; *coitus interruptus.*

oophorectomy. The surgical removal of an ovary or ovaries.

oral eroticism. Pleasurable sensations centered in the lips and mouth.

orgasm. The peak or climax of sexual excitement in sexual activity.

orgasmic phase. The third stage in the human sexual response cycle during which the orgasm occurs.

orgasmic platform. The area comprising the outer third of the vagina and the labia minora, which displays marked vasocongestion in the plateau phase of the female sexual response cycle (term used by Masters and Johnson).

os. A mouth or orifice, as the external os of the cervix (*os externum uteri*).

ovary. The female sex gland, in which the ova are formed.

oviduct. The Fallopian or uterine tube through which the egg (ovum) descends from the ovary to the uterus.

ovulation. The release of a mature, unimpregnated ovum from one of the graafian follicles of an ovary.

ovum (pl. ova). An egg; the female reproductive cell, corresponding to the male spermatozoon, that after fertilization develops into a new member of the same species.

oxytocin. A hormone secreted by the pituitary gland that stimulates the muscles of the uterus to contract during childbirth.

paraphilia. Sexual deviations; aberrant sexual activity.

paresis. A chronic syphilitic inflammation of the brain and its enveloping membranes, characterized by progressive mental deterioration and a generalized paralysis that is sometimes fatal.

parthenogenesis. Reproduction by the development of an egg without its being fertilized by a spermatozoon.

parturition. Labor; the process of giving birth.

pathogenic. Causing disease.

pathological. Pertaining to a diseased or abnormal physical or mental condition.

pederasty. Male sexual relations with a boy; also sexual intercourse via the anus.

pedophilia. A sexual deviation in which an adult engages in or desires sexual activity with a child.

penile agenesis. Abnormal smallness of the penis; microphallus.

penis. The male organ of copulation and urination.

penis captivus. A condition in humans in which it is alleged that the shaft of the fully introduced penis is tightly encircled by the vagina during coitus and cannot be withdrawn. Most authorities say this condition occurs only in animals, notably the dog.

perineum (adj. perineal). The area between the thighs, extending from the posterior wall of the vagina to the anus in the female and from the scrotum to the anus in the male.

peritoneum (adj. peritoneal). The strong, transparent membrane lining the abdominal cavity.

perversion. Sexual deviation from normal; paraphilia.

petting. Sexual contact that excludes coitus.

Peyronie's disease. A condition, usually in men of middle age or older, in which the penis develops a fibrous ridge along its top or sides, causing curvature.

phallus. The male penis, usually the erect penis.

phimosis. Tightness of the foreskin of the male penis, so that it cannot be drawn back from over the glans.

pituitary. Known as the "master gland" and located in the head, it is responsible for the proper functioning of all the other glands, especially the sex glands, the thyroid, and the adrenals.

pituitary gonadotropins. Hormones produced by the pituitary gland that stimulate the gonads (sex glands).

placenta. The cake-like organ that connects the fetus to the uterus by means of the umbilical cord, and through which the fetus is fed and waste products are eliminated; the afterbirth.

plateau phase. The fully stimulated stage in the human sexual response cycle that immediately precedes orgasm.

polyandry. The form of marriage in which one woman has more than one husband at one time.

polygamy. The form of marriage in which a spouse of either sex may possess a plurality of mates at the same time.

polygyny. The form of marriage in which one man has more than one wife at the same time.

pornography. The presentation of sexually arousing material in literature, art, motion pictures, or other means of communication and expression.

postpartum. Occurring after childbirth or after delivery.

potent. Having the male capability to perform sexual intercourse; capable of erection.

precocious sexuality. Awakening of sexual desire at a prematurely early age.

pregnancy. The condition of having a developing embryo or fetus in the body; the period from conception to birth or abortion.

premature ejaculation. Ejaculation prior to, just at, or immediately after intromission; *ejaculatio praecox.*

prenatal. Existing or occurring before birth.

prepuce. Foreskin.

priapism. Persistent abnormal erection of the penis in males, usually without sexual desire.

procreation. The producing of offspring.

progesterone. The female hormone (known as the pregnancy hormone) that is produced in the yellow body or corpus luteum, and whose function is to prepare the uterus for the reception and development of a fertilized ovum.

prolactin. A hormone secreted by the pituitary gland that stimulates the production of milk by the mammary glands in the breasts (lactation).

promiscuous. Engaging in sexual intercourse with many persons; engaging in casual sexual relations.

prophylactic. A drug or device used for the prevention of disease, often specifically veneral disease.

prostate. The gland in the male that surrounds the urethra and the neck of the bladder.

prostatic fluid. A highly alkaline, thin, milky fluid produced by the prostate gland that constitutes a major portion of the male's semen or ejaculatory fluid.

prostitute. A person who engages in sexual relationships for payment.

prudish. Extremely or falsely modest.

pseudocyesis. False pregnancy.

pseudohermaphrodite. An individual who has both male and female external sex organs, usually in rudimentary form, but who has the sex glands (ovary or testicle) of only one sex, and is thus fundamentally male or female. *Cf.* HERMAPHRODITE.

psychogenic. Of psychic or emotional origin; functional.

puberty (or pubescence). The stage of life at which a child turns into a young man or young woman: *i.e.,* the reproductive organs become functionally operative and secondary sex characteristics develop.

pudendum (pl. pudenda). The external genitalia, especially of the female (the mons pubis, labia majora, labia minora, and the vestibule of the vagina).

pyromania. A compulsion, usually sexually oriented, to start fires.

rape. Forcible sexual intercourse with a person who does not give consent or who offers resistance.

rectocele. A hernia in females in which part of the rectum protrudes into the vagina.

rectum. The lower part of the large intestine, terminating at the anus.

refractory period. A temporary state of psychophysiologic resistance to sexual stimulation immediately following an orgasmic experience (term used by Masters and Johnson).

resolution phase. The last stage in the human sexual response cycle during which the sexual system retrogresses to its normal nonexcited state.

retrograde ejaculation. Backward ejaculation in males into the posterior urethra and bladder, instead of into the anterior urethra and out through the meatus of the penis.

retroversion. The tipping of an entire organ backward.

rhythm method. A method of birth control that relies on the so-called "safe period" or infertile days in a woman's menstrual cycle.

sadism. The achievement of sexual gratification by inflicting physical or psychological pain upon the sexual partner.

"safe period." The interval of the menstrual cycle when the female is presumably not ovulating.

saliromania. A sexual deviation, found primarily in men, that is characterized by the desire to damage or soil the body or clothes of a woman or a representation of a woman.

salpingectomy. Surgical removal of a Fallopian tube from a woman.

satyriasis. Excessive sexual desire in a man.

scoptophilia (or scotophilia). A sexual deviation in which a person achieves sexual gratification by observing sexual acts or the genitals of others. *Cf.* VOYEURISM.

scrotum. The pouch suspended from the groin that contains the male testicles and their accessory organs.

secondary sex characteristics. The physical characteristics—other than the external sex organs—that distinguish male from female.

seduction. Luring a female (sometimes a male) into sexual intercourse without the use of force.

semen. The secretion of the male reproductive organs that is ejaculated from the penis at orgasm and contains, in the fertile male, sperm cells.

seminal emission. A fluid composed of sperm and secretions from the epididymis, seminal vesicles, prostate gland, and Cowper's glands that is ejaculated by the male through the penis upon his reaching orgasm.

seminal vesicles. Two pouches in the male, one on each side of the prostate, behind the bladder, that are attached to and open into the sperm ducts.

seminiferous tubules. The tiny tubes or canals in each male testicle that produce the sperm.

serology. The study of antigen and antibody reactions in blood serum tests.

sex drive. Desire for sexual expression.

sex flush. The superficial vasocongestive skin response to increasing sexual tensions that begins in the plateau phase (term used by Masters and Johnson).

sex gland. A gonad; the testicle in the male and the ovary in the female.

sex hormone. A substance secreted by the sex glands directly into the bloodstream, *e.g.*, androgens (male) and estrogens (female).

sex organ. The genital or reproductive organs, usually the male penis or the female vulva or vagina.

sex skin. The skin of the labia minora in the female, which shows a discoloration response in the plateau phase of the sexual response cycle.

sexual inadequacy. Any degree of sexual response that is not sufficient for the isolated demand of the moment or for a protracted period of time; frequent or total inability to experience orgasm.

sexual intercourse. See INTERCOURSE, SEXUAL.

sexual outlet. Any of the various ways by which sexual tension is released through orgasm.

shaft, penile. The body of the male penis, composed of three cylindrical bodies and a network of blood vessels, which are encircled by a band of fibrous tissue and covered by skin.

smegma. A thick, cheesy, ill-smelling accumulation of secretions under the foreskin of the penis or around the clitoris.

sodomy. A form of paraphilia, variously defined by law to include sexual intercourse with animals and mouth-genital or anal contact between humans.

somatic. Pertaining to the body, as distinct from the psyche or mind; organic, as distinguished from functional or psychosomatic.

sperm (or spermatozoon). The mature reproductive cell (or cells) capable of fertilizing the female egg and causing impregnation.

sperm duct. The tube or duct in males that conveys the sperm from the epididymis to the seminal vesicles and urethra; the vas deferens.

spermatic cord. The structure in males, by which the testicle is suspended, containing the sperm ducts, nerves, and veins.

spermatogenesis. The process of sperm formation.

spermatozoon (pl. spermatozoa). A mature male germ cell.

spermicide. An agent that destroys sperm.

sphincter. A ring-like muscle that closes a natural orifice.

sterility. The inability to produce offspring.

sterilization. Any procedure (usually surgical) by which an individual is made incapable of reproduction.

stricture. The abnormal narrowing of a canal, duct, or passage.

"sweating" phenomenon. The appearance of little droplets of fluid on the walls of the vagina early in the excitement phase of the female sexual response cycle.

symphysis pubis. The articulation between the pubic bones in the lower abdomen.

syphilis. Probably the most serious venereal disease, it is usually acquired by sexual intercourse with a person in the infectious stage of the disease and is caused by invasion of the spirochete Treponema pallidum.

systemic. Spread throughout the body; affecting all body systems and organs.

taboo. An absolute prohibition based on religion, tradition, social usage, or superstition.

telegony. The alleged appearance in the offspring of one sire of characteristics derived from a previous sire or mate of the female.

testicle. The testis; the male sex gland.

testis (pl. testes). The male sex gland or gonad, which produces spermatozoa.

testosterone. The male testicular hormone that induces and maintains the male secondary sex characteristics.

thrombosis. The clogging of a blood vessel as the result of the formation of a blood clot within the vessel itself.

transsexualism. A compulsion or obsession to become a member of the opposite sex through surgical changes.

transvestism. A sexual deviation characterized by a compulsive desire to wear the garments of the opposite sex; cross dressing.

trichomoniasis. An infection of the female vagina caused by infestation of the microorganism Trichomonas and characterized by inflammation, usually resulting in a vaginal discharge and itching and burning.

trimester. A period of three months; one of the three time divisions of a pregnancy.

troilism (or triolism). A sexual deviation in which, ordinarily, three people (two men and a woman or two women and a man) participate in a series of sexual practices.

tubal ligature. A surgical procedure for sterilizing a female in which the Fallopian tubes are cut and tied.

tumescence. The process of swelling or the condition of being swollen.

Turner's syndrome (XO). An abnormality afflicting females, in which one of the sex-determining pair (XX) of chromosomes is missing, leaving a total of 45 rather than the normal 46 chromosomes. Symptoms of the condition include incomplete development of the ovaries, short stature, and often webbing of the neck.

umbilical cord. The flexible structure connecting the fetus and the placenta; navel cord.

undescended testicle. A developmental defect in males in which the testicles fail to descend into the scrotum; cryptorchidism.

urethra. The duct through which the urine passes from the bladder and is excreted outside the body.

urethrocele. Protrusion of the female urethra through the vaginal wall; a hernia.

urologist. A physician specializing in the treatment of the diseases and disorders of the urinary tract of both sexes, as well as of the genital tract of the male.

uterine tube. The Fallopian tube, which extends from each ovary to the uterus in the female.

uterus. The hollow, pear-shaped organ in females within which the fetus develops; the womb.

vagina. The canal in the female, extending from the vulva to the cervix, that receives the penis during coitus and through which an infant passes at birth.

vaginal barrel. The vaginal cavity in women.

vaginal lubrication. A clear fluid (like sweat) that appears on the walls of the vaginal barrel within a few seconds after the onset of sexual stimulation.

vaginal orgasm. A term of ambiguous meaning, apparently referring to an orgasm that a woman allegedly can achieve vaginally without any clitoral stimulation.

vaginismus. Strong muscular contractions within the vagina, preventing intromission of the penis when intercourse is attempted.

vaginitis. Inflammation of the female vagina, usually as a result of infection.

varicocele. A swelling or enlargement of the veins in the male spermatic cord.

vas deferens (or ductus deferens.) The sperm duct(s) in males, leading from the epididymis to the seminal vesicles and the urethra.

vasectomy. A surgical procedure for sterilizing the male involving removal of the vas deferens, or a portion of it.

vasocongestion. Congestion of the blood vessels, especially the veins in the genital area.

venereal disease. A contagious disease communicated mainly by sexual intercourse, such as syphilis or gonorrhea.

verumontanum. A small mound in the portion of the male urethra passing through the prostate, which contains the openings of the ejaculatory ducts.

vestibule. The area surrounding and including the opening of the vagina in the female.

virginity. The physical condition of a girl or woman before first intercourse.

voyeurism. A sexual deviation in which a person achieves sexual gratification by observing others in the nude. *Cf.* SCOPTOPHILIA.

vulva. The external sex organs of the female, including the mons veneris, the labia majora, the labia minora, the clitoris, and the vestibule.

Wassermann test. A blood test used to determine whether or not a person has syphilis.

wet dream. See NOCTURNAL EMISSION.

withdrawal. See COITUS INTERRUPTUS.

womb. The uterus in the female.

X chromosome. A sex-determining chromosome present in all of a female's ova and in one-half of a male's sperm; the fertilization of an ovum by a sperm having an X chromosome will result in the conception of a female (XX).

Y chromosome. A sex-determining chromosome present in one-half of a male's sperm; the fertilization of an ovum by a sperm having a Y chromosome will result in the conception of a male (XY).

zoophilia. A sexual deviation that involves an abnormal degree of affection for animals. *Cf.* BESTIALITY.

zygote. The single cell resulting from the union of two germ cells (sperm and egg) at conception; the fertilized egg (ovum).

INDEX

201